LANDLORDS AND PROPERTY
CAMBRIDGE HUMAN GEOGRAPHY

Edited by

BRIAN ROBSON
Professor of Geography, University of Manchester

DAVID LEY
Professor of Geography, University of British Columbia

DEREK GREGORY
*Lecturer in Geography, University of Cambridge, and Fellow of
Sidney Sussex College*

Cambridge Human Geography will provide an important new framework for the publication both of the fresh ideas and initiatives often embodied in postgraduate work and of the more substantive research and wider reflective output of established scholars. Given the flux of debate within the social sciences as a whole, the series will seek to attract authors concerned to address general issues of the conflicting philosophies within and between the 'political science' and 'liberal' approaches. Much of this interdisciplinary debate will be developed through specific studies: of production and economic restructuring; of the provision and management of public goods and services; of state investment and collective consumption; of human agency and of the human-environment interface. The central aim of the series will be to publish quite simply the best of new scholarship within the field of human geography.

Landlords and property

Social relations
in the private rented sector

JOHN ALLEN and LINDA MCDOWELL

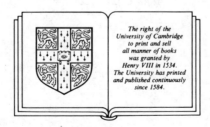

The right of the
University of Cambridge
to print and sell
all manner of books
was granted by
Henry VIII in 1534.
The University has printed
and published continuously
since 1584.

CAMBRIDGE UNIVERSITY PRESS

CAMBRIDGE

NEW YORK   PORT CHESTER   MELBOURNE   SYDNEY

Published by the Press Syndicate of the University of Cambridge
The Pitt Building, Trumpington Street, Cambridge CB2 1RP
40 West 20th Street, New York, NY 10011, USA
10 Stamford Road, Oakleigh, Melbourne 3166, Australia

First published 1989

Printed in Great Britain at the University Press, Cambridge

British Library cataloguing in publication data

Allen, John, *1951–*
Landlords and property: social relations in
the private rented sector. – (Cambridge
human geography),
1. England. Privately rented residences.
Landlords
I. Title II. McDowell, Linda
333.5

Library of Congress cataloguing in publication data

Allen, John, 1951–
Landlords and property: social relations in the private rented
sector / John Allen and Linda McDowell.
p.   cm. – (Cambridge human geography)
Bibliography.
Includes index.
ISBN 0-521-36028-5
1. Rental housing – Great Britain. 2. Landlord and tenant – Great
Britain. I. McDowell, Linda. II. Title. III. Series.
HD7288.85.G7A45   1989
33.5′4′0941 – dc19   88-31882

ISBN 0 521 36028 5

Contents

Figures and tables

FIGURES

TABLES

vii

Preface

The private rented sector of the housing market, for all its overall decline, has remained an object of interest and fascination to researchers in a wide range of disciplines. Each, from their own perspective, have attempted to describe and explain the key attributes of this decline. What we hope we have done here is to provide a new perspective, a different way of looking at the changes that have taken place in this sector of the market since 1945. The arguments in this book cross established disciplinary boundaries. We draw upon evidence from many areas but if we are to be classified at all we fall into what may be termed the 'new geography' with its concern to link the particular to the general; that is to preserve both aspects of social change in one explanation. We attempt to explain the general decline of the private rented market in Britain, the wider processes of investment and disinvestment which lie behind the decline, without losing sight of particular form that the processes have taken in different local housing markets.

This book is the end product of an enjoyable research collaboration between the two authors over a six year period at the Open University. The collaboration was made possible by grants, at various times, from the Social Science Research Council, The Nuffield Foundation and the Research Committee of the Social Science Faculty at the Open University. We are grateful to all these bodies for their financial support. We should also like to thank our colleagues at the Open University, especially those involved in writing the geography course D205: *Changing Britain, Changing World*. Arguments and debates in that course team helped us clarify many of the issues raised in this book.

We derived our information from a wide range of sources. In particular we had help in selecting the samples from the Housing Departments of the London Boroughs of Hackney and Islington. We are very grateful to them for opening their records to us. We also received information from a wide range of organisations and individuals, too numerous to list, involved in private renting in one way or another. Thanks to them but in particular to the households and tenants who so patiently answered our questions. We hope they find what follows interesting.

I

Introduction

The background to the research reported here is located in two General Elections in Britain, 1964 and 1979. In the 1964 election, housing assumed a central political role, which indirectly can be traced to the activities of one west London private landlord named Rachman. Interest in Rachman was the by-product of the Profumo Affair, a ministerial sex scandal, which rocked the Conservative Government and led to its downfall in 1964 (see Green, 1979). Rachman and his rent collectors provided the key issue over which the 1964 election was fought: the poor physical condition of the housing stock, the absolute need for housing and the necessity for the state to intervene in housing to remove the worst excesses of the private provision of housing. In the early 1960s, private rented housing comprised approximately one-third of the housing stock in England and Wales, and in urban areas such as Greater London the majority of households were private tenants. At that time, private rented housing provision was a significant political issue.

It was not until 1979 that housing reappeared as a crucial election issue, but in the context of a radically new debate and a new set of policy issues. The focus of the debate over housing was no longer the problem of supply, the condition of the housing stock, but rather one of demand, the problem of tenure. Throughout the 1960s and 1970s, slum clearance, improvements to the housing stock and new building reduced the number of households living in poor conditions. Against this background of improved housing conditions, the traditional problems of housing shortages and substandard housing was displaced by the new problem of tenure; in essence, the dissatisfaction with council housing and the frustrated ability of households to secure their 'natural' desire for home ownership.

The 'other' tenure, private rented housing, had virtually disappeared from the political debate. The Conservative Party's commitment to a policy of council house sales and their encouragement of private activity to promote owner-occupation set the terms of the debate and found the Labour Party wanting in their response. Dispossessed by the Conservative Party donning the mantle of freedom of choice in the sphere of housing, the Labour Party vacillated over what response to offer in order to protect their electoral base.

It would appear that the two and a half million households dependent upon the private rented sector for accommodation at that time were marginal to this consideration.

Though the debate over housing in the late 1970s and early 1980s has centred on tenure, the tenure of private rented housing has, for all the major political parties in Britain, occupied a residual political status. Paradoxically, it has remained an acutely sensitive political issue. The legacy of Rachmanism, the negative ideas associated with private landlordism in the 1960s, act as an ideological reservoir which is tapped whenever the issue of the future of private rented housing reaches the formal political agenda. Despite its marginal political significance, there remains a deep-seated political divide over the future of private landlordism and the rented housing market. The issue may not be central politically, but it still touches a raw political nerve.

In one sense, this book is an attempt to agitate that political nerve, to raise the political status of the issue of private rented housing and place it firmly on the political agenda. Since the early 1960s, private renting has declined from just under a third of the housing stock in England and Wales to less than a tenth and it has done so in an unplanned, geographically uneven manner, leaving much of the sector to operate outside the legal regulation designed to safeguard tenants' rights. Moreover, private tenants continue to suffer arbitrary eviction from their accommodation and private rented dwellings still comprise much of the worst housing stock in the country. If the politics of tenure is to remain an integral aspect of the politics of housing, then the future of private renting should become, once again, a crucial issue in housing debates.

One of the fundamental obstacles to this inclusion is a lack of knowledge about the nature and character of private landlordism and tenants' housing needs. The heterogeneous nature of the rented housing market, the diversity of interests of those who provide and of those who live in private rented accommodation is recognised descriptively in academic literature and government publications, but rarely explained in theoretical terms. Surveys of how different types of landlords and groups of tenants act in the market are of interest as they reveal something of the diversity of these groups and may cast light on their reasons for adopting certain courses of action. The focus of this book is primarily upon the nature of private landlordism in Britain in the early 1980s, the form and scope of landlords activities, in order that we may be able to understand more clearly what types of policy interventions can and cannot exert leverage on the rental market. More significantly, the analysis of landlordism presented here provides the basis to assess what current role and future place, if any, private rented housing provision has in relation to the two major housing tenures, privately owned and state owned housing.

The aim of the book, however, is, first and foremost, to provide an explanation of how the private rented housing market in urban areas presently operates, and how it has changed over time in different ways in different places. In the last chapter we return to the question of policy and offer a series of policy initiatives that arise from the preceding analysis of the current state and direction of the private rented housing sector.

Explanation and housing change

Explanation is a beguiling term. When it is invoked it tends to convey a sense of rigour, of coherence and the security of completeness. It is invariably considered to be better than commonsense, more penetrating than description, and in advance of mere generalisations cast about a particular subject matter. To attach the accolade 'explanation' to an account appears to endow the account with a certain value – it deserves to be taken seriously. On close scrutiny, however, the term in abstract is fairly meaningless. There are different types of explanation, including that of commonsense explanation, and each type may possess its uses and its limitations with respect to particular objects of study. If we are to judge whether a particular type of explanation is adequate or not we need to ascertain what the investigator wishes to know about a particular object or event. In the analysis of the same object, different sets of questions that imply different modes of explanation and methods of investigation may be asked.

If the objects and the questions asked of them are different, then the modes of explanation employed may not be directly comparable. A concern, for example, to understand the constructed reality, the taken for granted assumptions which inform and make sense of the practices by which rent officers determine the level of a fair rent, is likely to require a different type of explanation from a study which addresses the possible relations between fair rent levels, domestic house prices, and the decline of the rented housing market. The former is likely to involve an interpretative mode of explanation, whereas the latter is likely to employ a more formal, extensive mode of explanation. There may, of course, be some overlap or compatibility in the results expressed through the different types of explanation, but it is not valid to suggest that one type of explanation is better than the other.

In the second instance, where the objects or events to be explained are common to two or more types of explanation *and* the questions asked of them are of a similar kind, the terrain is eminently contestable. In our case, the object of investigation is the structure of private landlordism and what we wish to explain are the quantitative and qualitative changes that have shaped both the past and the present structure of the private rented housing market. Needless to say that this is not a new topic of investigation; there is no shortage of studies which attempt to make sense of how the market has changed over time. There is considerable difference, however, over the type and scope of explanation employed to account for changes in the rented market. In brief, our argument is directed at the incompleteness of many of the explanations advanced. In one sense, any explanation is incomplete, for the obvious reasons that existing knowledge is always revisable and that the object under investigation is subject to change, episodic or otherwise. Our concern, however, is with more significant forms of incompleteness; ostensibly what has been left out or neglected in an explanation, given the questions asked of a particular object.

Drawing upon developments in the exposition of a realist philosophy of science,[1] we would argue that to adequately explain why the private rented market has changed in certain ways requires an understanding of what it is about the market, that is, those who constitute it, that enables particular processes of change, such as residential disinvestment or investment, to occur. The focus of this type of enquiry is directed, in the first instance, at the object to be explained – the changing structure of the private rented market – rather than beyond it to, say, developments in the two main related tenures which have affected private renting, for example, the inflated sales price of owner-occupied dwellings, or changes in the demand for home ownership or public housing.

The rationale for initially adopting a restricted focus rests upon the need to critically examine the nature of the object under investigation rather than simply taking its known character for granted and looking elsewhere to seek the causes of change. Working within a realist framework is not without its problems, which we will note shortly, but one of its strengths, in our view, is the emphasis it places upon problematising the very object which is to be explained. At root, the market is *about* the different types of relations between landlords and tenants, their economic character, their political

---

[1] Realism has taken a number of different forms in the history of philosophy. In the social sciences, largely through the works of Bhaskar (1975, 1979), one version, transcendental realism, has gained considerable influence. In this book we have drawn upon the explanatory form and methodological approach of transcendental realism set out by Sayer (1984). Indeed, we have also followed his constructive account of research designs which flow from a realist philosophical standpoint (1984, chapter 9). The modes of conceptualisation advocated in the text are set out in Allen (1983b).

form, and their ideological complexion. It is within this set of social relations that particular causal powers may be located which have enabled the sector to change in the ways that it has done in recent years.

Implicit in this view of explanation, then, are assumptions about methodological procedure and about the nature of causality. With respect to method, an emphasis is placed upon the meticulous conceptualisation of the basic relationships that make up the object of enquiry, the agents that are involved here and the social forces to which they are subjected. Too often, explanations of the structure of private renting are incomplete because they fail to interrogate who is in the market and why, and under what conditions they tend to act. To draw up a category of, say, 'small' landlords and then rather hastily attempt to show through quantitative analysis how such a group generally responds to changes in the financial rate of return on their property or to changes in the legislation governing the sector, tells us little about why 'small' landlords tend to act in certain ways. Is there some explanatory value attached to the notion of 'smallness'? Is the ownership of a few properties a determining characteristic of response to change, or is it simply the most obvious characteristic, which, once frozen as an abstraction, is placed on one side to allow the research process to continue?

Now it may be the case that the ownership of a few properties is a significant characteristic for some private landlords, but to pass over other characteristics that they may possess, for example, the capital funds available to them, or the meaning they attach to the ownership of property or their role as landlords, is to dismiss by fiat these characteristics from the explanation. Such an explanation is incomplete because it limits other possible avenues of enquiry which may lead to a richer form of explanation. Moreover, the conceptualisation is inadequate because the causal significance of the characteristic 'small' is not specified. Landlords who own a few properties may have nothing else in common except that characteristic. Invariably, we are left, for example, with an empirical association between an unexamined generalisation such as 'small landlords' and a set of events, the sale of their properties, under a set of social conditions, a rise in domestic house prices. This is an interesting empirical pattern, but it is not a causal explanation.

From a realist standpoint, causal explanations are specified not by an association between separate phenomenon and events, but by reference to particular causal characteristics, in this instance of a group of landlords, which tend to make them act in certain ways by virtue of the characteristics they possess. In this view, causes are separate from the empirical events they produce. Explanation is concerned with the discovery of what kind of relations obtain for particular landlords which give them the power to act in certain ways and under what social conditions such power may be activated. The specification of what it is about particular landlords that enables them to operate in certain ways can be identified separately from what landlords actually do in the market place. The residential property of, say, a large charitable trust may enjoy a symbolic significance for the trust which tends to prohibit the sale of the properties, but whether a strategy of retention is pursued will depend upon the actual set of circumstances that make up the housing market at any one point in time.

From this brief review of the type of explanation we have employed, it should be apparent that conceptualisation is central. The identification and specification of the kinds of basic relations that obtain in the rented housing market are essential to an understanding of the different trends that we observe in the market. To arrive at a full account of what has actually taken place in the market, however, requires a further methodological step.

The identification of groups of landlords in possession of certain causal attributes, in itself an exercise open to revision and fraught with analytical uncertainty, is only, as we have indicated, one aspect of the type of explanation employed. To ascertain why the market is in decline, or is relatively stable, or is growing, perhaps in different ways in different parts of the country, cannot be known on the basis of a simple checklist of the basic relations of private landlordism. We cannot 'read off' from the knowledge that different types of landlords are constituted in particular ways, their specific response to different circumstances. We know only that each type will have a propensity to act in certain ways. What actually happens in different housing markets, whether it be the sale of the rented stock, or a growth in furnished lettings, or an increase in unregulated lettings, will vary over time and in accordance with the particular social conditions of the different markets.

Put another way, there are a possible range of outcomes to the causal powers inscribed in different types of landlords. What landlords actually do in the different housing markets is contingent upon the peculiar array of circumstances – the type of tenant demand, mix of tenures, local government policy, type of housing stock and so forth – that combine to make each housing market in one sense, unique. It follows from this observation that we can explain how, when and why the rented housing market of a particular area changed in the ways that it did, but we are restrained in our ability to predict a similar pattern of change for other areas, even if those areas possess similar types of private landlord.

These are empirical questions, as indeed is the process of conceptualisation advocated earlier. Conceptualisation as an activity does not take place in an autonomous realm separate from or prior to submersion in empirical investigation. There is a constant interplay between the observation of events and the identification and specification of the types of relations that make it possible for the events to be of a certain sort. To reason towards a possible set of causal relations from which the events are explicable as a matter of course is part and parcel of the research process and an integral aspect of explanation. Equally integral to the type of explanation adopted in this book, however, is the recognition that the contingent nature of local housing conditions may modify, alter or affect the potential ways of acting inscribed in the character of different types of landlords over time. The two aspects of explanation, the meticulous conceptualisation of the basic, causal relations that constitute different types of landlords, and the detailed investigation of how such relations manifest themselves in different ways at different times in different places are the strengths we have drawn from a realist approach which are often neglected or unacknowledged in alternative explanations of the operation of the private rented housing market. These aspects are not of merely academic interest, they also raise a different set of questions which policy initiatives have to address if they are to exert any leverage upon how the market operates in general and in specific ways.

Processes and places

One of the attractions of working within a realist framework in investigating the changing structure of the private rented market is that this framework allows for, indeed is based on the assumption, that general processes of change will take particular forms in different places. The general process of, say, disinvestment from the rented housing market is likely to have a different impact in different housing markets because of the diverse structure of the different markets. Moreover, the process of disinvestment itself is likely to be the product of a range of factors which contribute towards different types of landlords acting in a similar manner. An adequate explanation should be able to capture both the diverse impact of wider processes and be sensitive to the variety of factors that produce a seemingly unified response by some landlords.

The ability to explain the particular outcomes of broader processes of change is particularly pertinent to geographical studies which are, to a large degree, concerned to account for the differences between places – the uneven processes of social change. In line with recent developments within the discipline of geography we would go further and argue that one of the important tasks of geography is precisely to demonstrate how wider social processes of change are modified by the social characteristics of places in which they operate to effect a unique outcome (Massey and Allen, 1984). In this sense, the uniqueness of places is produced and reproduced by the reciprocal relationship between processes and places. Too often within geographical studies the unique characters of places has either been the subject of rich, descriptive accounts with little or no reference to the effects of broader social processes, or the differences between places has taken the form of a methodological nuisance, a deviation, as it were, from the normal pattern of events and something to be explained away.

It is now necessary to assert the explicability of the particular, without losing sight of the wider processes of change that structure the pattern of unevenness. This is an ambitious aim that requires considerable effort on the one hand, to avoid simply 'tacking on' empirical outcomes to an elaborate abstract explanation, and, on the other hand, to avoid an over-zealous concern to preserve the uniqueness of events in particular places which then remain unconnected to the more abstract, expansive processes of change. The aim is to provide a synthetic kind of explanation which combines both abstract and concrete research findings; a synthesis which demonstrates how the specific characters of places modify and in turn are modified by the general process of change that operates across space.

There are a number of risks attached to this approach. The first risk is that of over-ambition; the inability to restrict the focus of the enquiry solely to an examination of the social relations within an area that are considered relevant to the wider process selected for study. Any place is an amalgam of economic, political and cultural relations, but not all of the relations present will have an incisive bearing upon the questions asked of a particular process of change. It is important to be selective rather than exhaustive in choosing which social relations to focus upon if the synthesis is to be both plausible and manageable. So, for example, in a consideration of the structure of private renting certain characteristics of places such as the tenure structure, socio-demographic profile, local state policies and employment structure are likely to be among the main characteristics which will affect processes of disinvestment from and investment in rented housing. There will, of course, be other considerations thrown up in the research process, but each aspect should be assessed for its degree of relevance to the questions asked of the sector.

A second concern is related to the practice of synthesis. Faced with the task of putting together a rather complex mosaic of social relations, it is essential that they are not simply added together but considered as a combination of relations in which each qualitatively modifies the other. This is obviously easier to state, than to achieve; it requires a recognition, for example, that the interrelation between housing and labour market change may take different forms in different places. It is not a question of simply adding together the geography of housing and the geography of employment.

Thirdly, it is also important to note that in this type of explanation there may be several causal powers emanating from the different characteristics of places which affect the shape of the local rented housing market. Causality is not located at any one spatial level; explanation does not proceed from the level of broad processes of change and work down to specific local housing markets. Places are the crucible, as it were, of causal change; the point of interaction between the general and the particular which determines the direction and shape of housing change.

The approach adopted here is to recognise the spatial variations in the changing structure of private renting, the different roles the market performs across the country and simultaneously to keep a grip upon the fundamental processes that are affecting the market in general. Both the particular and general aspects of housing change are important, both to explanation and policy formulation.

The structure of the book

The thrust of the book is both substantive and conceptual. Initially, we look at the well-established decline of the private rented housing market and argue that the reasons for the decline have been largely misrepresented. Concentrating on the period since 1945 and, in particular, on changes within the sector over the last decade we identify in Chapter 2 three processes that have been operating in the sector in various combinations at different times and in different places. Together, the three processes – disinvestment, investment and informalisation – are shown to produce a market that is structured unevenly rather than simply declining in a linear, uniform fashion.

Each of these three processes is, itself, composed of a set of alternative actions. Disinvestment may take place through sale, either to owner-occupation or to the local housing authority, by holding the property empty temporarily or permanently or by outright abandonment. In addition, the compulsory purchase of properties under slum clearance schemes might be labelled involuntary disinvestment. Investment may occur through new purchase or by intensification of the use of existing stock, possibly although not necessarily associated with improvement and conversion and the shift from the unfurnished to the furnished sub-sector of the rental market. Informalisation, our third category, is a less self-explanatory concept. We have used it to refer to a marked trend in parts of the private rented sector towards small-scale landlordism, often associated with resident landlords, entering the market on a temporary, informal basis. Their motives are not necessarily explicable solely in formal economic terms.

These three processes are associated with particular sets of national and local circumstances ranging from the overall state of the economy, through changing interest rates down to the policies of local councils and the socio-demographic structure of the population in particular areas. In the next chapter, Chapter 3, to understand why these processes have been operated by private landlords, we step back from the processes themselves to analyse what it is about certain landlords that enables them to adopt such strategies and why they tend to act in certain ways and not in other ways.

A classification of types of landlords is presented based upon the role that residential property rent fulfils for different types of landlords by virtue of the economic and social characteristics that constitute them as distinct groups. The form of analysis focusses upon two dimensions of landlordism. First, the basic historical and ideological relations that landlords have exhibited in the development of the rented housing market, in particular the constitutive meaning they attach to the ownership of residential property. This is important if the contemporary activities of landlords are to be understood. The second dimension focusses upon the basic economic characteristics that shape landlords' activities: their size of capital, their source of funding, their economic liabilities and the type of capital involved. Within this framework, particular relations of landlordism are identified which bestow a degree of coherence upon certain groupings, that is, a structure which enables them to act, or potentially act in certain ways depending upon the spatial and temporal circumstances. This causal classification of landlords then acts as a basis for an explanation of the structured unevenness of the private rented market in terms of the three social processes identified in the previous chapter. The geographical varia-tion in the structure of the lettings market in Britain is explained as a diverse effect of the relations between local social conditions and the specific combination of the types of landlordism to be found in a particular housing market.

In Chapter 4 we outline the combination of intensive and extensive research designs we adopted to explain the structure of private rented housing provision in two local housing markets in inner London, and the nature of our sample. To convey a richer understanding of the relations that distinguish one type of landlord from another and some of the variations within types, we present, in Chapter 5, a series of case studies which look in depth at the combination of characteristics that comprise certain landlords, with particular reference to their practical ideologies. How landlords interpret and 'make sense' of their role and activities in the market is an oft neglected feature of the largely economic studies of private landlordism. Here we argue that such practical ideologies are not peripheral to economic factors; that the two factors influence and mould one another, and that together they have real consequences for how landlords operate in the market place.

Chapter 6 pulls together the analytical threads drawn in the previous chapters and represents them in the context of an extensive survey of the changing structure of private renting in the inner London boroughs of Islington and Hackney. It is in this chapter that the methodological issues outlined earlier, concerning an attempt to synthesise wider processes of housing change with the specific characteristics of local housing markets, are put into effect. We make no claims that the substantive findings of this research can be extended to other housing markets, for their validity is, by the nature of the explanation adopted, specific to the areas investigated. As we have indicated, this limitation is not considered as a shortcoming of the study, but a recognition that if an explanation is to be deemed adequate it should be able to deliver a knowledge of the general direction of change and of the particular circumstances of local change. The explanatory approach adopted has implications for further investigations of the structural unevenness of the rented housing market, but the findings are place specific.

Finally, in Chapter 7 we turn to a consideration of the implications of the study for policy initiatives at both central and local government level. Here it is argued that the current range of proposals for altering the structure of private rented housing provision have largely been shaped at the political level by the ideological confrontation between the advocates of a free market provision and the advocates of a social ownership solution, the abolition of private landlordism and the transfer of the rented housing stock to public agencies. The effect of this polarisation at the level of ideas has been to restrict the formulation of alternative initiatives which recognise the diversity of tenant demand for rented accommodation and the spatial variation of that demand.

In conclusion, we suggest a set of policy initiatives which stem from and reflect the explanation of rented housing change outlined in the preceding chapters, policies that are sensitive to the differences between local housing markets and that can exert leverage upon the operation of the market to meet the diverse housing needs of tenants. The suggestions may not satisfy radical exponents of either a free market or of a state based solution, but they do offer a way out of the current impasse which has successfully blocked radical change at the expense of those who depend upon the sector to meet their housing needs.

2

Private landlords:
the anatomy of uneven decline

The declining share of domestic property owned by private landlords has been a well-established feature of the British housing market for many years. Numerous general studies, conventionally relying on analysis by tenure, have documented, in more or less detail, this decline since 1914 (Cullingworth, 1963; Eversley, 1975; Greve, 1965; Nevitt, 1966). A figure of 90 per cent of all households living in privately rented property in 1914 is generally accepted as the basis from which the decline started, dwindling to a minority provision at whatever date the various studies terminate. However, private landlords still, in 1981, housed two million households, or 4.8 million people, a sizeable minority in itself and, in addition held vacant a proportion (2 per cent of all dwellings but 40 per cent of all vacancies in England and Wales in 1977 (Bone and Mason, 1980)) of the housing stock of this country, in anticipation either of reletting or selling. As well as being a sizeable, and highly contentious phenomenon – arguments about the pros and cons of residential letting, size of returns, concentration of housing problems in this sector are legion (Cullingworth, 1972, 1979; Murie *et al.*, 1976; Short, 1982). We argued in the introduction that the dimensions of the decline of private landlords have not yet been adequately revealed, nor have the practices of landlords themselves been fully understood. Perhaps, most surprisingly, very little is known about the geography of decline. In this and the following chapter we attempt to partially remedy these inadequacies.

The decline of the private rented sector is not a process that has been even in either time or space, nor has it had an undifferentiated impact on the types of landlords and types of properties remaining in the lettings market. Despite the long-term trend of decline, at certain times and in certain places there has been an increase in the provision of particular categories of lettings and new entrants to the residential lettings market have been recruited. Concomitantly, the search for universal explanations of decline, whether they are located in differential rates of profitability in particular categories of investment (Greve, 1965; Kemp, 1980), in internal changes in the tenure structure of the housing market (Murie *et al.*, 1976), in the relative profits from renting or sale (Hamnett, 1979), in the legislation relating to tenant security and rent levels (B.P.E., 1975) or in some addition of these factors

(House of Commons, 1982), is bound to be a fruitless one. These factors must all play a part in the overall anatomy of decline, acting in particular combinations in certain localities at different periods of time and affecting different categories of landlords in particular ways.

The process of decline has been neither uniform nor random, but rather one of structured unevenness, depending upon the interaction of a particular set of national changes and local circumstances within different areas at one point in time. This conclusion follows not only from the theoretical and methodological position we have adopted drawn from realism and from recent advances in the study of localities (Massey, 1983; Urry, 1982) but also inevitably follows from the current nature of the private rented sector. Private renting is now a residential tenure which is extremely heterogeneous. As the authors of an overview and review of the sector, published by the Department of the Environment (Todd *et al.*, 1982) emphasised: 'there is marked heterogeneity in the landlords, the accommodation, the households, the demand for and access to tenancies' (ibid., p. 1). However, the methodological implications drawn from this statement were rather different from ours. Whereas Todd *et al.* concluded that 'Generally of course the heterogeneity requires a cautious approach to using and interpreting averages because of the problems about the meanings of these when considerable variation exists' (ibid., p. 1), we believe that in order to make inferences about causality, this heterogeneity must itself be the object of analysis. Aggregate analysis at the best obscures, and at the worst distorts, explanation. A description of national rates of decline, however, is appropriate to establish the context within which structured variations take place.

Post-1945 decline of private landlords: a numerical overview

The proportion of the housing stock available for renting from private landlords declined from 90 per cent in 1914 to 13 per cent in 1977:[1] an overall decline of 5.7 million dwellings. The decline in the sector's proportionate share is, of course, accentuated by the overall increase in the total number of houses in the country. In fact, virtually all the net decline in private lettings has taken place since the end of the Second World War. In the inter-war period, some 800,000 new houses and flats came on to the private lettings market. During the 1930s there was an increase in building for renting when both interest rates and returns on industrial shares were low (see Marshall, 1968). Some of the new rentals, however, were the

---

[1] There is no figure for dwellings in the 1981 census, only households – 13.2 per cent were private renters.

consequence of a miscalculation of the longevity of the late 1920s and 1930s boom in house building for owner-occupation. Houses intended for sale were, in the event, offered for rent. Despite these increases, in total, some half million dwellings were lost to the private rented sector in the inter-war period. Part of the losses may be attributed to this same boom in owner-occupation as a proportion of landlords sold to individual owner-occupiers. Other losses occurred in slum clearance programmes and by conversion to non-residential use. The proportions however are incalculable as accurate records are not available. In 1938, though, 6.2 million lettings were still on offer by private landlords, only half a million less than in 1914.

At some time in the early post-war period, the nature of decline in the private rented sector changed and significant losses began to be apparent. The exact date is difficult to establish with any degree of accuracy as there was no national census between 1931 and 1951 because of the war. However of the 200,000 losses from the sector between 1938 and 1951, when the first post-war census was taken, it seems likely that bombing raids on Britain's major towns and cities accounted for a sizeable number of the losses. After the end of the war, deliberate and planned withdrawal by landlords from residential letting distinguished this period from the unplanned or more 'casual' losses of the pre-war period. Between 1951 and 1961, the sector declined by 1.7 million, followed by a further 1.3 million lettings between 1961 and 1971.

Also 1945 marked a significant change in government policies and attitudes towards economic management and social service provision which influenced the position of private landlords. From this date, there was widespread acceptance by politicians of all political persuasions of the essential nature of public housing provision (Duclaud-Williams, 1978; Short, 1982). The recommendations of the minority report of the 1st Ridley Committee (1937), for example, gained widespread currency after the war: 'We cannot agree that housing is a fit subject of commodity economics, but rather hold the view that so long as it is left to private enterprise, its management should be subject to public utility principle ... a social service of such extreme importance ought to be controlled' (Ridley, 1937, p. 55). Acceptance of such arguments became part of the widespread post-war acceptance of the ideals behind the creation of the welfare state and of the principles of demand-management of the economy. Linked to the creation of an integrated credit system and the growth of alternative investment opportunities, these factors altered the operating environment for private landlords and decreased their 'legitimacy' in the ideological shift of the post-war period. Landlords' uncertainty also was increased by changes in the legislation affecting their terms and conditions of letting – a factor made

Table 2.1 *Major post-war housing legislation affecting the private rented sector*

Government in power	Date of Act	Title	Content
1945–51 Labour	1946	Housing Act ⎫	Stimulated local authority building and decreased tenants reliance on the private sector
	1949	Housing Act ⎭	
1951–64 Conservative	1954	Housing Repairs and Rents Act	Permitted rent increases in the private rented sector after improvements
	1957	Rent Act	Attempt at rent decontrol
1964–70 Labour	1965	Rent Act	Security of tenure for some unjustified tenants; fair rents scheme introduced
	1968	Rent Act	Extended security of tenure and rent regulation provisions of the 1965 Act
	1969	Housing Act	Increased level of improvement grants, introduced GIAs
1970–4 Conservative	1972	Housing Finance Act	Extended the 'fair rent' system from private tenants to the public sector
1974–9 Labour	1974	Housing Act	Increased improvement grants, introduced HAAs, repealed Housing Finance Act, security of tenure extended to furnished tenants of non-resident landlords
1979–83 Conservative	1980	Housing Act	Increased rents and introduced shorthold and assured tenancies in the private rented sector

much of by the landlords' lobby. Rent control remained in force throughout the war until the early 1950s, when the then Conservative Government attempted to 'revive' the sector by lifting controls. In 1965 the Labour Government reintroduced some measure of control and also increased the security of tenure of unfurnished private tenants, extending these measures in 1968, and including furnished tenanats of non-resident landlords in 1974 (see Table 2.1 for a summary of the relevant legislation). However, these acts had little impact on the overall rate of decline (see Figure 2.1) as the acts themselves were based on a misunderstanding of the reasons for the decline.

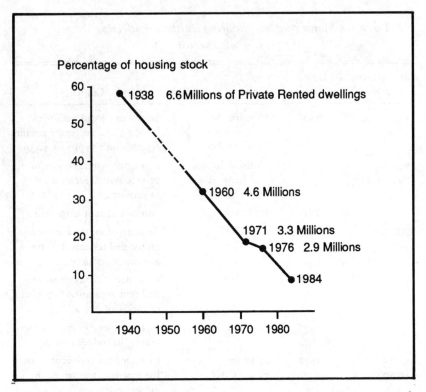

Figure 2.1 The rate of decline of the private rented sector in the post-war period
Source: Housing Policy Technical Volume 1977

Rather than being solely a response to legislative controls, landlords were taking advantage of opportunities to sell to owner-occupiers, particularly in the early post-war decades, and increasingly to local authorities and to housing associations in the later years. In addition, demolition of unfit properties in the accelerating slum clearance programmes between the early 1950s and mid 1970s accounted for a proportion of the losses. The figure also reveals an acceleration in the rate of losses from the sector in the later years of the period. Between 1971 and 1977, for example, 800,000 private lettings, a quarter of the total stock in the sector at the outbreak of the Second World War, ceased to be rented.

Overall, by 1977 there were four million fewer dwellings in the private rented sector than in 1938; 2.2 million in total, compared with 6.2 million in 1938 and 6.7 million in 1914. In Table 2.2 evidence from a number of sources is drawn together to produce estimates of the numbers of properties lost from the lettings market for different reasons in the post-war period.

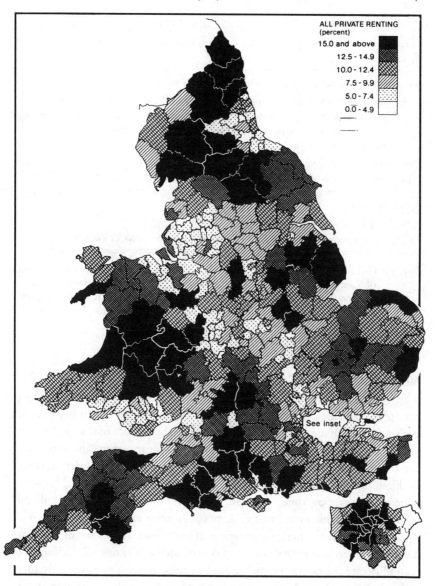

Figure 2.2 The percentage of households who in 1981 were renting privately in each of the 403 districts of England and Wales

Source: Kleinman and Whitehead, 1985

Table 2.2 *Decline of the private rented sector, 1938–77*

Tenure shifts	
3.1	million dwellings were transferred to other tenures	
22.7	million sold to owner-occupiers of which ≃ 65,000 private lettings per year were sold between 1938 and 1960 (1.4m in total) and ≃ 75,000 per year between 1961 and 1977 (1.3m in total)	4,000,000 sold to local authorities or housing associations

Demolished or change of use
1.5 million dwellings were demolished or withdrawn from residential use of which just over 700,000 were lost between 1938 and 1960 and almost 800,000 between 1961 and 1977

Added to the private rented sector
600,000 new lettings between 1938 and 1977 by new building or conversion

Sources: DoE, 1977, *Housing Policy*, Technical Volume, Part III, Cmnd 6851; House of Commons, 1982, 1st Report from the Environment Committee, *The Private Rented Housing Sector, Vol. 1 Report;* Merrett, S., 1979, *State Housing in Britain*, Routledge, London.

Three processes and landlords' strategies

The overall trends illustrated in the preceding section show that the predominant feature of the private rented sector since the end of the war has been its decline. However, for the individuals and companies holding residential lettings in a particular place at a certain point in this period, the decisions to be made and the strategies adopted in the face of this decline are not necessarily straightforward. A range of factors, from the type and condition of holdings, through to the demand for housing of different types in different tenure categories, to the nature of local and national housing policies at any one time, to changes in the national economy, will all influence their behaviour. In an attempt to illustrate variations through time and over space in its changing structure of the private rented sector, we first distinguish three main processes that contributed to the overall decline. We then illustrate the operation and impact of these processes on the structure of landlordism through an examination of some of the most important studies of private landlords that have been undertaken since 1945. A small number of these studies focus on national level changes (Greve, 1965; Paley, 1978), but the majority focus on landlords operating within the confines of a geographically specific local housing market (Cameron, 1978; Crook and Bryant, 1982; Cullingworth, 1963; Elliott and McCrone, 1975; Forrest and Murie, 1978; Francis, 1971; Gray and Todd, 1965; Harloe *et al.*, 1974; Housing Monitoring Team, 1980; Short, 1979; Stuart, 1982).

Disinvestment, investment and informalisation

As we argued in Chapter 1, the overall decline of the private rented sector is composed of three processes that we label here disinvestment, investment and informalisation. Different types of landlords are engaged in each process in different ways in particular localities depending upon the combination of factors that influence the demand for and supply of lettings in that area. These three processes are themselves composed of a number of sub-processes.

Disinvestment

As Table 2.2 indicates, disinvestment comprises sale to owner-occupiers, either before or after conversion and improvement and the sale of properties to local housing authorities or housing associations, almost without exception in an unimproved state. There are two further sub-categories, which we have designated temporary and involuntary disinvestment. The latter consists of compulsory purchases and of demolition in slum clearance programmes or after the issue of closing notices. The former consists of a temporary withdrawal of accommodation from the lettings market and its being held empty in anticipation of increased capital gains by a later sale or reentry to the lettings market under different terms and conditions or to a different sector of demand to that previously housed.

The overall scale of sales to owner-occupiers and its acceleration during the post-war period has been indicated in Table 2.2. The increased rate partially may be accounted for by the overall rise in the rate of owner-occupation nationally, encouraged by a number of financial incentives to purchase properties, especially older ones, and by subsidies to assist in their improvement. At a more general level, too, the overall ideological and material support for home ownership, from the lack of investment in council housing to composite tax arrangements and tax relief on home loans, has encouraged the transfer of dwellings from the private rented sector into owner-occupation (see Merrett, 1982, Chapter 9). This transfer has resulted in a diffusion of home ownership down the income scale and within ethnic minority groups. Older properties consistently have been less expensive to purchase than new property (DoE, 1982, p. 123) and so they have been sold disproportionately to lower income groups. Increased demand has encouraged landlords to place their properties, which typically are pre-1914 dwellings, on the market. An unintended by-product, however, has been an enormous acceleration in the problem of properties in poor condition owned by households who lack the financial resources to bring their properties into an adequate state of repair, (DoE, 1982).

From the late sixties, societies began to alter their criteria for lending on older properties in the inner city and so a greater number of prospective buyers were able to contemplate the purchase of a previously private rented dwelling. Until the mid 1970s, increased mortgage funds from local authorities, specifically earmarked for older properties and lower income first time purchasers, also increased landlords' opportunities to sell in favourable and profitable circumstances. The Leasehold Reform Act (1967) too accelerated the transfer of properties to owner-occupation. Further, it has been argued (Hamnett, 1973; Hamnett and Williams, 1980) that the short-lived but marked increase in the allocation of improvement grants in the early 1970s both encouraged landlords to sell and individual owners to purchase converted and improved properties – a phenomenon inelegantly dubbed gentrification as it typically was associated with changes in the social class of the occupants of the dwelling transferred from renting to owning. The number of grants awarded to private owners (as opposed to local authorities) rose from 80,000 in 1969 to a peak of 260,000 in 1973 but had fallen back to 80,000 again by 1976. However, there is evidence that speculative improvement for sale using, or rather abusing, the grants system still continued in many areas (Sunday Times, 16 March, 1983 and 3 March, 1983).

The opportunities for landlords to sell, however, and their likely capital gains, are dependent upon local circumstances as well as national policies. Certain types of lettings are more easily marketable than others, for example sales are both quicker and more profitable if the dwelling is an entire house or self-contained flat with vacant possession. The capital value of a house with vacant possession is approximately one and a half times that of one with a sitting tenant (Doling and Davies, 1982). In certain circumstances, though, sale to the sitting tenant or to a final remaining tenant of a previously multi-occupied property may be an attractive alternative to a landlord as it may be quickly achieved, usually without necessitating major expenditure on improvements in order to convert the dwelling into a marketable commodity. Between 1938 and 1964, three-quarters of a million owners bought their accommodation as sitting tenants and over the post-war period as a whole, one in four of the sales by landlords were to this category of purchaser (House of Commons, 1982).

The remaining three-quarters of sales (just over two million dwellings in total) were to first time purchasers or to individuals and households moving within owner-occupation. Here, the potential profits to be made by disinvestment vary between local housing markets, depending upon the socio-economic structure of the local population, the nature of the housing stock and the availability of property in other tenure categories. Figures from the

Table 2.3 *Regional variations in the selling price of second-hand dwellings and average incomes of mortgage borrowers during the 1970s*

| | 1971 | | 1975 | | 1979 | |
| | Dwelling price | Average income of borrower | Dwelling price | Average income | Dwelling price | Average income |
Region	£	£	£	£	£	£
North	4220	1894	9397	3802	14934	6045
Yorkshire and Humberside	3875	1826	8842	3540	14301	5897
East Midlands	4244	1820	9888	3606	15335	5877
East Anglia	4979	2010	11592	3881	18333	6361
Greater London	7842	2794	14735	4801	25710	8083
South East (including Greater London)	7298	2579	14511	4535	24437	7382
South West	5575	2127	12162	3891	20492	6398
West Midlands	4820	2003	10715	3738	18037	6209
North West	4362	1921	9550	3672	16435	6297
Wales	4717	2139	9977	3714	16760	6112

Note: The selling price of previously rented dwellings is likely to be somewhat below the average for all second-hand dwellings given the age and condition of most rented property.

Source: DoE (1982) *Housing and Construction Statistics 1971–1981*, pp. 124–7, Table 110.

joint Department of the Environment and Building Societies Association Survey of Mortgages (DoE, 1982) show the regional variations in the average prices paid and incomes of purchasers of 'second-hand' dwellings during the 1970s (Table 2.3). The actual rates of return to particular landlords, however, will depend on the date at which the properties originally were purchased and the flow of rental income over time.

Disinvestment through sales, given the inner-area location of a large proportion of previously private rented stock, is most likely in two different types of area, both within Britain's larger towns and cities. The first area is where there is little new building either by the local authority or for sale, high house prices and a relatively high proportion of the population in the higher socio-economic groups, and/or at the pre-child stage of their life cycle – the classic conditions for gentrification and for flat 'break ups'. Secondly,

Table 2.4 *Improvement grants for housing associations in England and Wales 1967–77*

Year	1967	1968	1969	1970	1971	1972	1973	1974	1975	1976	1977
No. approved	1712	2059	3185	4064	6168	6756	5051	5295	5279	13868	19000

Note: It is reasonable to assume that the majority of these grants were for properties purchased from private landlords, although a small proportion were used to renovate properties already in housing association ownership such as nineteenth-century tenement blocks and at the end of the period a very small number of properties within HAAs may have been purchased from individual owner-ocupiers rather than landlords.

Source: DoE, Housing and Construction Statistics, various dates.

sales are likely in other parts of the same large towns and cities with a concentration of members of ethnic minority groups excluded from other tenures. Sales are also probable, although less profitable, under a different set of conditions – in smaller towns with a relatively high proportion of low paid workers, or of students, unable to afford new private housing but who are prepared to purchase inexpensive, unconverted terraced properties, either to improve themselves, in the case of the first group, or to inhabit temporarily while studying. In certain north-eastern university towns, for example, there is some transfer of properties to individual students, and also sales by individual landlords to property companies, established specifically to cater for the students sub-market (Morgan and McDowell, 1979). This latter form of transfer, however, is not in fact disinvestment, but rather a changing ownership pattern within the private rented sector.

A second avenue for disinvestment is through sales into the public sector rather than to owner-occupiers. Almost half a million private lettings were transferred either to local authority or to housing association ownership between the end of the Second World War and 1977. The scale and timing of purchase by housing associations is difficult to account for with any degree of accuracy as national census definitions conflated private renting and housing association lettings in one category before 1981. However, the majority of sales both to housing associations and to local authorities took place towards the end of the period in question as national policy moved away from slum clearance and redevelopment towards rehabilitation and improvement. Some idea of the scale of purchases and improvement by housing associations of previously rented properties can be estimated from figures for improvement grants. Before 1967, the scale of improvement was minimal and, as Table 2.4 indicates, it gradually accelerated until 1975, after which date there was a marked leap in activity. This reflected the belief of the Conservative Government that 'a municipal monopoly of rented accommodation is unhealthy in itself' (DoE, 1973, p. 9), and the encouragement of housing association purchase, particularly in the small areas of 'housing stress', designated as housing action areas (HAA) under the 1974 Housing Act. The selective use of HAA legislation inevitably influenced landlords' opportunities for disinvestment through this channel. Similarly the opportunity for sale to local housing authorities varied temporally and spatially depending upon the commitment of different authorities to programmes of municipalisation.

In the earlier part of the post-war period, local authorities' impact on private landlords was not through transfers of the stock but through slum clearance programmes, resulting in what we have labelled here *involuntary disinvestment* and the absolute loss of previous lettings from local housing markets. Slum clearance accelerated during the 1960s so that, by 1975, over one-sixth of the total stock of privately rented dwellings in 1960 had been demolished or closed. In England and Wales, 1.45 million units in total were demolished between 1945 and 1977 – the vast majority of which were previously let privately. Local variations in involuntary disinvestment were less marked than in the opportunities for sale presented to landlords as the concentration of lettings in the older housing stock largely coincided with the distribution of unfit housing. In absolute terms, large urban authorities, with their heritage of Victorian buildings, undertook the largest clearance programmes. In inner Manchester, for example, 80,000 properties were demolished in the 1960s.

A final type of disinvestment is *temporary disinvestment* where landlords hold their property empty, either in anticipation of future capital gains or through virtual abandonment of unsaleable property. Until the Office of Population Censuses and Surveys published the results of the 1977 Vacant Property Survey carried out for the Department of the Environment (Bone and Mason, 1980) there were no national estimates available of the tenure distribution of vacancies nor any evidence about the reasons for holding such vacancies. The empty property survey revealed that 220,000 out of the total 550,000 vacant dwellings in Spring 1977 previously had been rented privately (115,000 were local authority owned, and 175,000 previously owner-occupied, the remaining 40,000 unknown). The investigation of why the properties were vacant supports our contention that the decline of the private rented sector cannot be attributed to a single cause or process. Less than 4 per cent of the previously private rented properties were empty solely because their owners objected to the Rent Acts, whereas a further 55,000 owners (25 per cent) partially attributed their withholding action to such legislation. Other factors, such as the poor condition of the dwellings, were also important. Ten per cent of the properties were vacant because they were to be demolished and so more accurately fall into our category of involuntary disinvestment. Thirty-two per cent were affected by building work or redecoration, whereas a further 14 per cent, although in poor condition, were neither to be demolished nor improved. It seems likely that this group will remain permanently empty, whereas the former 32 per cent eventually will either be sold or relet. In the case of dwellings where the condition of the property was not a sole or partial explanation of their vacancy, the authors of the survey were forced to conclude that 'no clear simple explanation dominates the picture. On the contrary a multiplicity of reasons ... emerges. Nor is it easy to discern any underlying pattern which might suggest that some relatively simple administrative active or legislation would remove most of the causes of vacancy not to do with the condition of the property.' Indeed, by the conclusion of the survey, no reason could be established why one in five (19 per cent) of the identified vacancies that previously had been privately rented remained empty.

Investment and reinvestment

While disinvestment has been the most noticeable feature of the private rented sector since the end of the Second World War, the overall losses of four million tenancies have not taken place without some internal changes and reorganisation of the structure of the private rented sector. This is a consequence of the variation in rates of disinvestment between particular categories of landlords and also because of new entrants to the private rented sector. New investment has tended to be relatively limited – approximately 600,000 new lettings, provided by new building or by conversion of existing properties, came on to the market between 1945 and 1977. The majority of these entered at the 'top end' in larger conurbations to cater for the transient or temporary needs of people such as overseas visitors, foreign embassy staff, weekly commuters needing a 'pied à terre' in town and, in the lower rent category, for groups of students and young workers. A high proportion were offered to let as furnished tenancies. Indeed, between 1961 and 1971, there appears to have been an *absolute* increase in the number of furnished private lettings, as well as their continued relative growth because of faster disinvestment from the unfurnished sub-sector. According to national census figures the number of furnished tenancies increased by almost 31,000 during the 1960s, although a change in the definition of a dwelling may partially account for the increase. It is, however, also extremely difficult to establish what proportion of these were new lettings and what proportion were the result of landlords shifting from unfurnished to furnished lets in particular areas in response to changes in demand and to legislative amendments. The investigation of the operation of the 1965 and 1968 Rent Acts (Francis, 1971) noted an increase in the furnished sub-sector in Greater London and in parts of the West Midlands conurbation which was attributed to internal shifts within the private rented sector rather than new investment *per se*. It was argued that the increase mainly resulted from the exclusion of furnished tenants from the security of tenure legislation introduced in these acts. However, other studies have shown that the switch was also demand-led as growing numbers of young, single workers and students left their parental homes during the 1960s and 1970s for a period of independent living, either alone or in groups (Chippendale, 1976; CDP, 1976; Morgan and McDowell, 1979; Raper, 1974). Even when security of tenure legislation was extended to furnished tenants in the 1974 Rent Act, landlords in several areas continued to concentrate on furnished lettings for mobile groups in the population (Henney, 1975; McDowell, 1976). The actual rates of movement into, within and out of this sub-sector of the lettings market are, however, impossible to establish from aggregate statistical sources.

There has also been another type of investment in private lettings in the period under consideration, which perhaps might most appropriately be labelled *temporary investment*. This consisted of investment by property companies, such as those of Berger and Freshwater, who, in the years before the 1974 property crash, purchased blocks of flats in relatively prestigious locations for 'break-up' (Hamnett, 1979). The aim of such investors was not long-term rental income but the prospect of high profits from the rapid disposal of vacant dwellings to owner-occupiers. Until the 1960s when building societies increasingly became willing to lend on the security of long leasehold flats, the prospects of break-up was limited but from the mid 1960s until the mid 1970s Hamnett has estimated that several thousand previously rented units were transferred into owner-occupation, either directly by the institutional owners of blocks of flats or through the aegis of companies specialising in break-up, such as Slater's Strongmead or Hagenbach's Westgrove Securities. Temporary investment, for the purpose of almost immediate disinvestment, has tended to be a spatially, as well as a temporally specific process, tending to be limited to a particular type of built stock in areas with a bouyant demand for middle-to-upper price bracket house ownership. However, Cameron (1978) also found such temporary investment by large-scale operators within housing action areas in Newcastle upon Tyne. Here too the motive of investment was for eventual sale to owner-occupation, but the type of property purchased was very different from the blocks of flats that typified Hamnett's sample. Finally, an additional type of temporary investment or transfer of ownership occurred as property and insurance companies switched their assets into holding of offices and other commercial premises in the early 1970s following the 1971 Barber budget. In many cases, portfolios of primarily commercial property included residential lettings and these institutional investors became reluctant landlords. It seems likely that in all cases except those of prestigious accommodation and/or high site values, the residential lettings were disposed of as expeditely as possible.

Informalisation

We have labelled the third of the three processes that together account for the uneven decline of the private rented sector *informalisation*. This process is both a result of the changes in the structure of landlordism as a consequence of the other two processes of disinvestment and investment and also in itself reflects the entry of new landlords. By informalisation we mean the continuance, and indeed expansion, of that section of landlords who trade as individuals, either living in and renting part of their own dwelling as a resident landlord or deriving all or a major part of their income from the rental receipts from a small number of tenancies. Paley's (1978) study of landlords in one hundred densely privately rented areas in England and Wales revealed, for example, the continued bouyancy of residential landlordism; a sub-category of the informalisation process.

In general, resident landlords consider their lettings first and foremost as part of their own homes and financial returns are a secondary factor. The relationship between landlord and tenant thus tends to be a personal one rather than a business arrangement. Resident landlords are themselves a diverse category, including long-established elderly landlords, members of ethnic minority groups catering primarily for kith and kin on their arrival during their stay in Britain (Davies and Taylor, 1970; Rex, 1968), and, increasingly in the later years of the period under consideration, the addition of what Kemeny (1981) has dubbed 'Owner-occupier landlordism' (ibid., p. 79). These landlords are small-scale, amateur and part-time operators, forced into letting because of their position in the owner-occupier sector. As owner-occupation has increased nationally and has been extended down the income scale, a growing proportion of poorer owner-occupiers find themselves having to let part of their homes to meet their mortgage repayments. In her survey, Paley (1978) found that the numbers of resident landlords were maintained at a constant level by a relatively high rate of turnover. Resident landlords who did not intend to relet were balanced numerically by owner-occupiers deciding to take in a boarder or a tenant.

As well as newly established owner-occupiers who tend to be young, Kemeny also identified households at the other end of the life cycle as potential members of this new owner-occupier landlord group. The motives of such owners stem from one or a combination of factors, such as the desire to utilise surplus space, to supplement current incomes or to make financial provision for old age. Whereas the younger owners are by necessity resident landlords, this latter group of middle-aged to elderly owners may either be resident landlords or non-resident landlords of one or of a small number of dwellings, in addition to their own home. For more affluent householders, a decline in relative, and often real, housing costs over their life time opens up the possibility of investing surplus funds in a second house, or of selling the family home when children grow up and purchasing a smaller property for occupation and a second house to rent out. When regarded as an investment to avoid poverty in old age, residential property has the advantage of security, a high degree of inflation-proofing and the prospect of at least a respectable capital return on sale, in addition to generating a small income flow from the rental. The previously quoted evidence from Paley's study, and the earlier quoted findings of the tenacity of the furnished rented sector, support our contention that private landlordism is a changing and dynamic phenomenon whose overall decline consists of a number of quite different trends. It is also quite clear that the actual extent of the growth of owner-occupied landlordism is impossible to establish. As Todd *et al.*, authors of a DoE survey of private renters (1982) argued 'there is greater uncertainty about its (the private rented sector) size and composition than in the information about other sectors' (ibid., p. 3). In the specific case of owner-occupier landlords, however, Todd *et al.* were quite clear that 'a dwelling obviously is owner-occupied where occupied by one such household and one or more private renting households' (ibid., p. 3). We would argue that this allocation to tenure is not in fact so obvious, and results in 'hidden landlords' in housing statistics based on dwellings; landlords who, incidently, are often desirous of remaining hidden because of letting restrictions imposed under the terms of their mortgage and/or because of taxation obligations. Underestimates also seem likely in household-based figures as there are enormous problems in defining 'self-containedness' because sharing facilities and living expenses is common. Thus the allocation of tenants of owner-occupier residential landlords to a particular tenure category is extremely problematical. It is clear, however, that owner-occupier landlordism is a growing phenomenon, particularly in areas of high house prices. In a sample survey of resident landlords in the London Borough of Islington, for example, a staggeringly high incidence of such landlordism was found. By 1981, one owner-occupier in three in that borough was a resident landlord, rising to double this incidence in housing action areas (Stuart, 1982).

The remaining part of the informal private rented sector consists of landlords of a small number of properties who continue to relet from a mixture of motives. Many of these 'individual' landlords are elderly and a high proportion of their properties are likely to be poorly maintained or unfit, and consequently difficult to sell even if their owners so desired. Further, a large number of the dwellings in the informal sector are multi-occupied making it virtually impossible to secure vacant possession. Finally, although such lettings typically are occupied by the poorest sections of the population, low maintenance inputs combined with tenants who stay only for brief periods and/or who may be uncertain of their legal rights, may give a sufficiently high rate of return to ensure reletting. In general, the rents charged by resident and individual landlords are privately agreed, and so, in the main, higher than rents which are registered under Rent Act legislation (Paley, 1978).

The net result of the operation of the three processes of disinvestment, investment and informalisation has been a qualitative change in the nature of private landlordism between 1945 and the end of the 1970s, as well as the quantitative decline of the sector. Large-scale investor landlords not only have left the sector at an accelerating rate but those that have continued to invest or entered the market in the post-war period tend to be interested in the appreciating capital values of residential property rather than long-term rental income. The trend has been paralleled by the relative increase in importance of small-scale or resident landlordism. Indeed, although it is difficult to cite detailed quantitative proof, this sub-sector probably has also increased absolutely in size. In England, the breakdown of Bone *et al.*'s sample of private landlords drawn from the National Dwelling and Household Survey (1977) was as follows: 64 per cent were individual landlords (of whom 6 per cent were resident), 22 per cent were employer landlords, 10 per cent property companies and 4 per cent unknown (ibid., p. 19). This compares with Paley's (1978) figures, based on 100 wards in England and Wales, of 47 per cent by individuals (of whom 12 per cent were resident), 25 per cent companies, 6 per cent by non-charitable trusts and housing associations and 6 per cent by public bodies. The discrepancies between the sets of figures lend support to arguments about the degree of heterogeneity in the private rented sector and the difficulty in using and interpreting average figures. They also support our arguments in the next chapter about the practical and conceptual inadequacies of such descriptive classifications of ownership.

Changes in the structure of landlordism have enormous significance for the future of private rented housing and for the success of policy measures designed to 'revive' or abolish private landlordism. This latter theme is taken up in the final chapter of the book. Those observers who have taken the increasing representation of small-scale operators in the sector as proof of its irreversible decline and eventual disappearance may be misinterpreting the evidence. If recruitment to landlordism is a structural consequence of rising rates of owner-occupation then its continuance may be ensured. In addition, the continued buoyancy of the sub-category of lettings catering for the young and childless, who are neither able to obtain nor generally desire council housing or home ownership, supports observations that the private rented sector is not about to disappear. It may be on the margins of the housing system, both in terms of people and of accommodation, and be a low yield investment, but its imminent collapse, so long predicted, is not yet in sight.

Structured unevenness: the spatial and temporal dimension

In the last section of this chapter, we sketch in the general outlines of the spatial patterns of the post-war decline of private landlordism in England and Wales, filling in the details where possible with evidence on the fortunes of landlords in particular parts of the country culled from the small number of existing studies. In the previous section, in several places we qualified statements about the set of opportunities facing landlords with provisos and suggestions about local circumstances. There are a whole range of different local circumstances under which disinvestment, investment and informalisation can take place. In some areas there is even an expansion of the private rented sector but yet in the country as a whole there is an overall loss of private lettings. We are not suggesting that the changing composition or decline of private landlords within local housing markets is a unique event, but rather that the actions open to them are structured by a particular combination of national changes and local circumstances within a particular locality at a certain time. These circumstances include, at the local level, the nature of the existing housing stock, both its physical condition and its tenurial divisions, the demographic and socio-economic structure of the local population and the outcomes of the policies of local councils: in other words the particular set of local circumstances that result from the interaction of regional and local differences with the structure of national economic, social and political processes to produce a particular environment. As the House of Commons Environment Committee recognised in their first report on the private rented sector published in 1982 'a more detailed examination of the current position of this sector reveals its diversity. Evidence highlighted the wide range of circumstances of landlords

and of tenants, the varied nature of the stock, its varying availability in
different parts of the country, and the wide range of rents charged' (p. xvi).

Here, we attempt to describe this diversity, based on a review of existing
empirical studies of the decline of the private rented sector. Although this
review enables us to delineate certain features of the uneven decline and to
draw out the variety in local circumstances, we shall argue in the succeeding
chapter that conceptual inadequacies in these studies mask rather than
reveal certain dimensions of the decline. Consequently, the rest of the book
is devoted to our own reconceptualisation of landlords and their activities
(Chapters 3 and 5) and an illustration of our methods (Chapter 4) in a study
of the changing structure of landlordism in a particular part of inner London
(Chapter 6).

Regional and local diversity

One of the main results of the decline of the private rented sector during this
century, and the concurrent expansion of council housing and owner-
occupation, has been the increasing spatial concentration of private lettings
in inner urban locations, and, although to a lesser extent, in certain regions
within the country. In the DoE survey (Paley, 1978), it was found possible to
include almost one-third of all privately renting households in England and
Wales by selecting only those 100 wards in the country where in 1971 private
renters outnumbered owner-occupiers. The wards typically were densely
populated city or central town areas. In all, 40 per cent of all households
recorded as private renters in the 1971 Census lived within the boundaries of
just six cities: Greater London, Manchester, Birmingham, Leeds, Liverpool
and Newcastle-upon-Tyne. Indeed, a quarter of all private lettings, and 37
per cent of furnished lettings, in England and Wales in 1971 were to be found
in Greater London, compared with only 16 per cent of households in all
tenures.

Throughout the decade, the pattern remained reasonably similar, with a
market concentration of lettings in the large conurbations. There were also
noticeable differences in the number and type of private tenancies between
the standard regions of the country as Table 2.5 demonstrates. This is based
on Todd *et al.*'s (1982) figures and a word of caution is necessary. It seems
likely that their sample was biased towards regulated and registered
tenancies, partly because of the inevitable difficulties involved in identifying
and tracing unregistered lettings. The authors themselves noted that their
study probably underestimated the number of resident landlords (p. 12).

Given this warning, the first set of figures shows how different types of
private lettings are distributed *between* the standard regions (a and b)

whereas the second set (c) shows the variation *within* each region. The national estimates (a) clearly reveal the London bias, whereas (b) and (c) show the regional differences in types of letting, for example it can be seen that resident landlordism appears to be a southern phenomenon and that controlled lettings were most likely in the Yorkshire and Humberside region.

As well as the variation within and between standard regions, there are also marked differences between small areas within towns and cities. In Greater London, for example, the *National Dwelling and Household Survey* (1977) revealed a range from Kensington and Chelsea at one end where half of all households were private tenants, to Sutton and Tower Hamlets at the other, where less than a tenth of households lived in private lettings. More recently, Kleinman and Whitehead (1985) have analysed the spatial variations in private renting using figures from the 1981 census (see Figure 2.3). Their analysis is interesting as they have disaggregated the sector into three constituent parts that, they argue, have different roles in the housing market and meet different needs. If the sector is mapped using aggregate figures, important spatial differences between these three sub-sectors are disguised or 'smoothed out'. The three sub-sectors distinguished were (i) a predominantly unfurnished 'traditional' sub-sector, housing mainly elderly people who remain from the time when private renting was the majority tenure; (ii) a 'modern' or 'pressure' sub-sector of furnished lettings meeting the demands of single, young and mobile people who are unable to or do not wish to become owners or council renters and finally (iii) a business and employment sub-sector. Whereas the first sub-sector is relatively geographically even, the second two are spatially concentrated. Furnished lettings are extremely highly concentrated in a handful of ports, coastal resorts and university towns mainly in the south of England and particularly in central, northern and western London. As we have already shown, the Greater London concentration is particularly marked. One third of all tenants in furnished accommodation live in Greater London. The employment subsector is clearly related to the occupational distribution of the two main groups who still live in tied accommodation: farm workers in East Anglia, Lincolnshire, the north and the Welsh border, and the Armed Services in Suffolk, Hampshire and Wiltshire. It is debatable whether the armed services accommodation should be classified as private rented. We have excluded it as we are not investigating the behaviour of public sector landlords. Although farm workers' housing is obviously not part of the inner London private rented sector, there are employment-related tenancies. These include accommodation for workers in the hotel and retail trades, and also for domestic workers such as nannies within their employers' own homes.

Table 2.5 *Region and privately renting sub-sectors*

	Privately renting sub-sectors							
	Regulated			Resident	Rent free	Business	Other and	All lettings
Region	Controlled	Registered	Unregistered	landlord		etc.	not known	
(a)	Thousands							
North	10	31	61	2	24	13	2	143
Yorkshire/Humberside	36	·58	96	4	25	16	2	236
East Midlands	21	44	69	4	23	13	1	176
East Anglia	9	15	47	2	15	7	1	95
South East								
Greater London	33	132	269	58	36	19	10	557
Rest of south east	16	82	232	36	75	22	4	468
South West	10	33	107	16	36	14	2	218
West Midlands	15	49	78	6	23	18	4	193
North West	26	84	119	11	17	15	4	278
England	176	529	1078	140	274	136	31	2364
(b)	Column percentages							
	%	%	%	%	%	%	%	%
North	6	6	6	2	9	10	7	6
Yorkshire/Humberside	21	11	9	3	9	12	7	10
East Midlands	12	8	6	3	9	10	3	7
East Anglia	5	3	4	1	5	5	3	4
South East								
Greater London	19	25	25	41	13	14	33	24
Rest of South East	9	16	21	26	27	16	13	20
South West	6	6	10	11	13	10	7	9

West Midlands	8	9	7	4	8	13	13	8
North West	15	16	11	8	6	11	13	12
England	100	100	100	100	100	100	100	100
Weighted sample size	243	730	1489	193	379	188	42	3264

(c) Row percentages

									England	Weighted Sample size
North	%	7	22	43	1	17	9	1	100	198
Yorkshire/Humberside	%	15	25	41	2	11	7	1	100	326
East Midlands	%	12	25	41	2	11	7	1	100	243
East Anglia	%	9	16	49	2	16	7	1	100	131
South East										
Greater London	%	6	24	48	10	6	3	2	100	769
Rest of South East	%	3	18	50	8	16	5	1	100	646
South West	%	5	15	49	7	17	6	1	100	302
West Midlands	%	8	25	40	3	12	9	2	100	266
North West	%	9	30	43	4	6	5	1	100	383
England	%	7	22	46	6	12	6	1	100	3264

Source: Todd et al. (1982).

Kleinman and Whitehead's study is an interesting attempt to begin to unravel the heterogeneity of the private rented sector and to illustrate the spatial diversity in its current distribution. In this sense, their approach is similar to our own arguments that the nature and pattern of decline cannot be understood without a more adequate classification of sub-sectors within the tenure. However, as we shall argue in Chapter 3, a conceptually more satisfactory classification must be based on the constituent characteristics of different types of landlord rather than on the basis of a description of different tenants. However, as we show later (in Chapter 6) the differences between the 'traditional' sub-sector and the 'modern' sub-sector are very important in interpreting landlords' reinvestment strategies in inner London.

Local studies

The number of British local area studies of the motivations and intentions of private landlords that have been undertaken in the post-war period are surprisingly few. However, landlords are a notoriously difficult group both to identify and to persuade to participate in survey investigations. The books by Cullingworth (1963) and Greve (1965) are the most frequently quoted sources, although both are now dated. In addition, the latter, strictly speaking, is not a local study as Greve's sample included 500 landlords or agents in 104 towns in England, with an admitted bias towards the north and south west. However, as local and regional breakdowns of his results were omitted from the book, his study has been excluded here.

As well as Cullingworth and Greve's work, there are a range of more recent studies of landlords' behaviour, either undertaken for official inquiries or by individual researchers and published in the somewhat ephemeral form of working papers, occasional series and articles in journals. Details of a range of local surveys in different parts of the country are summarised in Table 2.6.

The single overwhelming feature that emerges from our review of these local studies is diversity – in landlords' motivations and intentions, in their calculations of acceptable rates of return, in the time they had been in the market and in the property which they own. No simple even trend towards disinvestment and so decline was apparent. Different types of property were being sold or relet in different areas and consequently the implications for individuals and households attempting to gain access to the private lettings market also varied.

Three sets of local factors may be distinguished that influence the diverse reactions of landlords. These are, first, the level of demand for housing,

Table 2.6 *Local studies of the motives and intentions of private landlords in the post-war period*

Author(s)	Location	Date of survey	Size of sample
Cullingworth (1963)	Lancaster	1960	853 landlords of 2,385 dwellings
Gray and Todd (1965)	Great London	1963	978 rateable units
Francis (1971)	Greater London: the West Midlands	1970	278 landlords or agents 68 landlords or agents
Harloe *et al.* (1974)	London Boroughs of Lambeth and Sutton	1970	5 estate agents managing several hundred lettings for 'small' landlords; 3 property companies with approx. 25,000 dwellings in total in Greater London; 2 specialised agencies (Duchy of Cornwall and the Crown Commissioners)
Elliott and McCrone (1975)	Edinburgh	1973–5	Details of 7,654 landlords extracted from valuation rolls, sample survey of 200
Cameron (1978)	Newcastle-upon-Tyne	1976–7	Unspecified number of estate agents and non-resident landlords in housing action areas
Forrest and Murie (1978)	Cheltenham	1975	240 landlords or agents
Short (1979)	Bristol	1977–8	385 landlords
Housing Monitoring Team (1980)	Dudley	1978	171 landlords or agents
Crook and Bryant (1982)	Sheffield	1980	328 landlords or agents
Stuart (1982)	London Borough of Islington	1980–1	35 resident landlords in housing action areas

secondly, the type of landlords and properties in the areas and thirdly, the impact of local authority policies. In the area studies reviewed there was a clear dichotomy between those towns and inner areas of cities where the demand for private lettings was high, particularly from young and single individuals, whether working or studying, and those where demand was low. In the former, in inner areas of Greater London, Bristol and Sheffield, for example, and to a lesser extent in Cheltenham, there was clear evidence of a shift by landlords towards furnished lettings to cater for this group and also of some new investment. Advantages were seen in terms of the higher rent paying capacity of a group of unrelated individuals compared with a family household. The former group may all be earners. They also tend to move more frequently than families, permitting rent revisions. What we have described as 'informalisation' was also apparent in these high demand areas, particularly in inner areas with relatively large ethnic minority populations. As well as a buoyant demand for private lettings, landlords in the high demand areas were also able to disinvest relatively easily and relatively profitably as there also often was high demand for owner-occupation, from white-collar and professional groups and from members of ethnic minorities. However, the greater propensity for lettings to be in dwellings in multiple occupation in such areas acted as a restraining factor on rapid disinvestment.

In low demand areas, young single households were a far less significant element in the local population. In Dudley, and in Lancaster, at the time of Cullingworth's survey, for example, the dominant trend was of decline as predominantly 'small-scale' landlords, who had inherited a single or a small number of properties, reacted to the low rent paying capacity of their mainly elderly households by reducing maintenance expenditure to a minimum and/or by selling. The position in Lancaster, of course, may have altered since the establishment of a new university there in 1964, introducing several hundred students into the housing markets of the surrounding areas. Paradoxically it is in the 'low demand' areas where private landlords increasingly are housing elderly households with low rent paying capacities that rates of return on the capital value of their properties seem to be highest (Doling and Davies, 1982). This seemingly contradictory relationship arises because of the low level of demand for previously rented properties by owner-occupiers in low demand areas. Thus tenants in the Midlands and in the North of England pay higher rents in relation to the capital value of the properties they occupy than in the South and South East of England, although in absolute terms, weekly rents in the former areas generally are lower. Figure 2.3 shows the regional variations in rates of return based on an average of three hypothetical properties: a mid terrace two storey 1870s

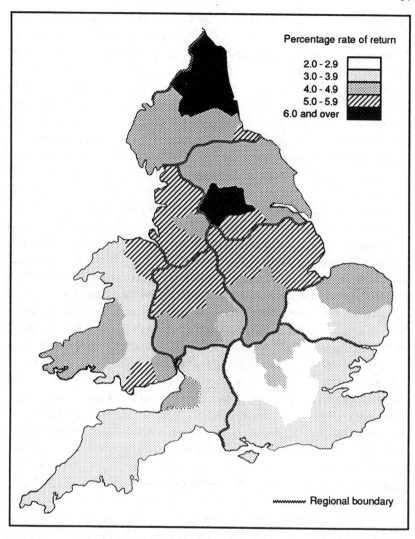

Figure 2.3 Regional rates of return in the private rented sector, 1981
Source: Doling and Davies, 1982

unimproved house, a mid terrace two storey 1880s improved house and a two storey semi-detached house built in the 1930s.

There also are marked variations between areas in the concentration of ownership and in the types of properties held. The predominance of 'small-scale' landlordism in low demand areas has already been mentioned. In high demand areas, the ownership structure tends to be more varied with individuals, small public and private property companies and financial and

charitable institutions represented in the market, as in Lambeth, Bristol and
Sheffield, for example. There is some evidence, however, of a growing
dichotomy in ownership patterns, with an increasing concentration of
individual, often residential, landlords at one end of the spectrum and of
large-scale investors at the other end. Forrest and Murie (1978) also noted in
Cheltenham a significant division in their methods of acquisition between
the owners of large and small holdings. While the former actively purchased
dwellings in the open market, the latter acquired their tenancies virtually
exclusively through inheritance. Great care needs to be exercised, however,
in interpreting these spatial differences. In the majority of studies, the
methods of selecting the sample of landlords introduced an inevitable bias
into the results. Apart from in Scotland, there is no accessible, representative
record of private landlords. Elsewhere the sources relied upon included a
combination of rating and rent officer records (Forrest and Murie, 1978;
Housing Monitoring Team, 1980; Short, 1979), lists obtained from a local
branch of the Property Owners Association (Short, 1979) or from their
National Association (Francis, 1971); contacts through estate agents (Harloe
et al., 1974); details from local authority surveys to establish housing action
areas (Cameron, 1978; Stuart, 1982) and a door to door survey in a small
area (Stuart, 1982). Each method resulted in the over-representation of a
particular category or categories of landlords.

The variation in dwelling stock between each survey area primarily is a
consequence of the different economic and social histories of these areas.
Despite the common predominance of nineteenth-century buildings, the
properties owned by landlords in different areas varied from granite
tenements (in Edinburgh), through Regency terraces (in Cheltenham and
Bristol), Victorian houses of many sizes (in Inner London) to redbrick
working-class terraces (in the West Midlands and Newcastle). In addition,
landlords' shares of the overall housing stock within each area also varied
considerably, reflecting both the demand for owner-occupation and the
local authorities respective commitments to council building and municipal
improvement. Thus the histories of different areas affects the current spatial
diversity within the private rented sector and is a crucial component in
explaining its decline. In the mid 1970s the absolute and relative importance
of private lettings was greater in the London survey areas (in Lambeth and
Islington, for example, private landlords still provided accommodation for a
third of all households) followed by the larger towns such as Sheffield,
Edinburgh and Bristol (up to 17 per cent of all households). Landlords were
less important in the smaller provincial towns, such as Lancaster (12 per
cent) and Dudley (6 per cent), although Cheltenham, with its large student
and retirement population and Conservative council, was an exception to

this generalisation. A fifth of all households looked to the private landlord in this town.

The political complexion of the different local housing authorities was the third major factor delineating the structure of decline. The extent to which each authority established an active municipalisation programme, encouraged public and private improvement and conversion or operated controls on private landlords' activities, such as registering properties in multiple occupation and/or insisting on adequate provision of amenities, influenced landlords' financial calculations, and their short- and long-term strategies. In Sheffield, for example, despite the fact that half the properties in Crook and Bryant's (1982) sample had been acquired in the previous ten years, there was evidence of a deceleration in the rate of new entrants, particularly to the furnished sub-sector, because of the local authority's growing stringency over the decade in operating controls on houses in multiple occupation. In a number of the inner London survey areas, direct acquisition by the authority of private lettings for subsequent improvement encouraged landlords to disinvest, whereas in Newcastle-upon-Tyne, the reverse effect was felt. Within housing action areas, Cameron (1978) found evidence of the growing importance of 'large-scale' absentee landlords, purchasing properties as long-term appreciating capital assets, despite legislation prohibiting in the short term the sale of rental dwellings to other than the local authority.

It hardly needs to be stressed, in conclusion, that the overall picture that emerges from our review of the existing studies of landlords' behaviour is one of diversity. Although the overall long-term trend in this sector of the housing market is one of decline, the pattern is uneven, both geographically and over time. Landlords' motivations and intentions, and their reasons for acquiring and maintaining domestic property as a form of investment, vary as do the opportunities open to them to disinvest and switch their capital elsewhere. In the next chapter, we shall argue that the national and local studies summarised here do not adequately deal with landlords' financial orientation to the market and also neglect landlords' conceptions of the rights, duties and obligations of property ownership. These factors, we believe, must enter into an adequate explanation of the structure of landlordism. Despite this, however, existing work does enable an anatomy of structured but uneven decline to be identified rather than the 'shadowy, ill-defined penumbra' discerned by Short (1978, p. 234) in his summary of the decline of the private rented sector.

3

The structure of private landlordism

The previous chapter traced the structured but uneven decline of the private rented housing sector and argued that three processes, disinvestment, investment and informalisation, were significant in accounting for the changing pattern of private renting. In this chapter we turn our attention from the processes themselves to the agents who are involved in these processes.[1] It is clear that private landlords are a diverse and heterogeneous social group and much of the literature on landlords and the rented housing market has attempted to reveal the diversity of their actions in the market place: the extent to which tenancies have been converted from unfurnished to furnished, the lack of amenities in rented housing, the number of improved properties, the extent of sales to owner-occupation, and so forth. Such studies, as noted in the previous chapter, have indeed contributed to our understanding of the changes that have occurred in the rented housing market, but they have often left us with little detailed knowledge of who is actually carrying out these actions or why they were undertaken. There is a methodological gap between the exhaustive detail with which landlords' activities are plotted and the analytical skills used to classify the nature and characteristics of different types of landlords.

In part, the problem is one of conceptualisation. Analyses of the structure of private landlordism do not go far enough; they tend to stop at the intuitive and the commonplace, for example, by identifying and distinguishing between landlords on the basis of the number of properties they own or their legal status – as a company, or a trust, or a charitable institution. In this chapter, we look first at a number of examples of these taxonomies and try to show their limited analytical value. We then outline an alternative mode of analysis based upon realist principles of explanation, one which directs our attention to the kinds of relations that structure landlords as distinct causal groupings; that is, as groups which because they are structured in a particular way act or have the potential to act in specific ways. Following this we identify six groups of landlords on the basis of the internal relations that structure their economic and social characteristics,

[1] This chapter is a revised version of Allen (1983a).

and conclude by outlining the role that classification performs in the construction of our explanation of the workings of the private rented housing sector.

Types of landlords: a critique

Many studies of landlordism have paid insufficient attention to the task of classification (see Cullingworth, 1963; Greve, 1965; Elliott and McCrone, 1976; Forrest and Murie, 1978; Paley, 1978; Short, 1979; Crook and Bryant, 1982). Landlords have tended to be classified along the lines of familiar, self-evident characteristics. For some subjects, classification along commonplace lines may prove a fruitful starting point, but in the case of landlordism it has often led to ambiguity and created a barrier to further understanding.

The categories of individual and company landlord often form the basis of an initial classification, and these terms are frequently further sub-divided along the lines of other pregiven categories: in the case of individual landlords for example, by sex, age, marital status, income, employment status, and the number of dwellings or tenancies owned, and in the case of the latter by their legal character: that is, by 'trust', institution, 'firm' and 'property company' as well as the number of dwellings or tenancies they own. This kind of classification has two main deficiencies. First, the taxonomies produced tend to draw their terms from the self-evident characteristics of landlords, with little or no justification for such a practice. Secondly, the taxonomies of how the types of landlord identified actually operate in the market appear to be drawn up in advance; there is little attempt to reason back from the actions of landlords that help to shape the market to the construction of particular taxonomies.

Even where a distinction is maintained between companies concerned mainly with residential property and companies for whom residential property is ancillary to their interests, the significance of the distinction is rarely made explicit. The apparent 'obviousness' of this distinction does not in itself indicate differences in the letting behaviour of the two types of company landlord. The fruitfulness of this distinction should be assessed on the basis of a detailed understanding of the types of companies involved in the market for rented housing. The same point may be applied to the common distinction drawn between resident landlords and non-resident landlords. Intuitively obvious and important as it may be, the reason for the distinction cannot be maintained simply on the grounds of residence. The case for this distinction, as we shall go on to show, encompasses factors above and beyond this sole criterion.

The apparent shortcomings of this type of reasoning and the ambiguity it creates can be illustrated by looking at the two main criteria used to classify landlords: the number of properties or tenancies owned by landlords and the legal title of landlords.

First, a size classification based upon the number of tenancies owned is frequently used to distinguish types of 'individual' landlords; for example, 'small landlords', 'medium landlords', and so forth. Yet it is possible that two groups of individual landlords holding the same number of tenancies may act and relate to the rented market in quite different ways. One group may be actively letting property in the market on licences, holiday lets or flat sharing arrangements to avoid the restrictions of the Rent Acts, whilst the other, perhaps a group of landlords who had previously held a larger number of rented properties, may be actively withdrawing from the market on the grounds that higher returns on capital are available elsewhere, say in the commercial lettings market. The fact that they both share the same legal status and both possess the same number of tenancies does not necessarily imply that they adopt a similar orientation to the market. The latter group may be working within a different set of economic and social parameters from that of the former. Differences in the size of the capital assets of the two groups, differences in their access to finance, variations in the scope of their investments, and perhaps contrasting ideologies of letting, may shape and mould their orientation to the market. Each of these factors, if not all these characteristics, are not revealed or reflected in a classification based primarily on a numerical criterion.

The problem arises through the *static* conception of the market that is produced by relying upon the number of tenancies owned by landlords as an unproblematic determinant of landlord's strategies. This snapshot effect may gloss over the presence of other perhaps more significant characteristics that shape and constrain the actions of different types of landlords in the market. We will take up this point shortly.

The dubious nature of relying upon a size classification of property ownership to distinguish between different types of individual landlord is highlighted by the seemingly arbitrary way in which the terms 'small', 'medium' and 'large' are often defined. In the surveys of Short (1979), Cullingworth (1963) and Greve (1965) respectively, 'small' varies from 1–2, 1–5 and 1–9 tenancies, 'medium' from 3–9, 6–20 and 10–99 tenancies and 'large' from 10+, 21+ and 100+ tenancies – an interesting display of numerical inconsistency. Elliott and McCrone (1976) fare no better by dividing individual landlords into unspecified categories of 'large' and 'small' property owners. The Environment Committee's report (1982, Vol. 1, p. 18) on the private rented housing sector take this a step further by drawing upon two 'self-evident' classifications that contain a series of vague numerical labels ranging from 'very small landlords', 'small landlords', 'medium sized property companies' to 'large estate owners'.

The ambiguity inherent in these studies cannot be solely attributable to poor analyses. After all, we have become accustomed to thinking about landlords in terms of their size. It has become common practice and therefore 'correct', and it is hard to break with custom and even harder to displace an apparently 'natural' classification. This practice has led to a largely unquestioned acceptance of the assumption that quantitative distinctions reflect real differences in the way in which landlords act and operate within the rented market. Yet this is not necessarily the case.

For example, in Short's (1979) survey of landlords in Bristol, he argued that 'large-scale landlords' were more likely to convert their tenancies from unfurnished than 'medium' or 'small-scale landlords'. Yet in *proportion* to the number of tenancies owned by the different types of landlord their actions were remarkably similar. It just looked as if 'large-scale landlords' were more likely to convert their properties because they owned a greater number of tenancies. But size was not necessarily the major determinant of their behaviour. 'Large-scale landlords' do not automatically exhibit profit-maximising behaviour whereas 'small'-scale landlords do so on odd occasions. The market is far more complex. 'Large-scale landlords' may adopt different practices in the various local markets that they hold property depending upon the nature of those markets: how they vary in terms of class composition, the tenure mix, the politics of the local authority, and so forth. There is nothing about their 'size' that necessarily tells us how they will act or are likely to act in the market. One further example is offered to conclude this point.

It is well-known that the majority of the estimated 500,000 landlords in England and Wales fall within the nebulous 'small landlord' category.[2] On the basis of evidence submitted to the Environment Committee (and summarised in their 1982 report, Vol. 1) we are told that small landlords, in contrast to large landlords, considered security of tenure legislation to be a major influence upon their attitude to letting residential property. Hence, it would not be unreasonable to assume that the repossession laws constitute the major deterrent to letting property for the bulk of landlords. Yet, if we turn to some of the largest surveys of landlord's attitudes that have taken place, we find a different picture. Paley's (1978) survey of landlords in the densely privately rented areas of England and Wales found only about a

---

[2] The estimated figure of 500,000 landlords is taken from the evidence submitted to the House of Commons Environment Committee on the Private Rented Housing Sector (1982) by the Small Landlords Association. It is difficult to gauge the accuracy of the figure in the absence of firm data; the reasons for which have been outlined in the previous chapter.

third who considered the repossession laws as a significant problem; and Crook and Bryant's (1982) survey of the private rented sector in Sheffield found that only about a quarter of the landlords in their sample considered repossession to be the most important factor. Of perhaps greater interest are the findings of the 'Empty housing in England' (1980) survey which concluded that only between 4 and 14 per cent of the 220,000 empty dwellings previously let in the private rented market could be attributed to the effects of the Rent Acts; and only 4 per cent to the perceived effects of the Rent Acts alone. It does not appear to be the case, therefore, that the security of tenure legislation is a significant problem for the majority of landlords. The evidence points to this conclusion but it does not appear to have been understood in this way.

Legal categories also fall short in their ability to unravel the diverse character of landlordism. Their weakness stems from an acceptance of the assumption that landlords of a different legal status will operate in a markedly different manner in the market place. In consequence, property companies are frequently distinguished from individual landlords with no explicitly empirical or conceptual justification. Yet private property companies, as opposed to public property companies, frequently perform a role as a tax front for individuals (i.e. their liability is reduced by operating as a private company). The same point may also apply to partnerships and private trusts which may operate a series of legal devices to reduce their tax burden. In general, fiscal reasons determine which legal vehicle is the most appropriate organisational form to trade under, but such labels are not in themselves a sufficient guide to landlords' actions, nor to any kind of structural similarity.

At worst a vague category of company landlords is offered; at best this category is broken down into either mainly residential and mainly non-residential property companies, or into public and private property companies. On most occasions, however, these sub-divisions disappear in the process of aggregating the empirical data. They are lost in the pursuit for representativeness. The number of types or kinds within a classification flow from the size and quality of the available data. If the data source is limited, the heterogeneity of landlordism tends to be squeezed into a small number of types; if the data source is rich, then sub-divisions within the general categories are admitted. In either case the lines of classification are rarely justified. The importance attached to the processing of statistical data is not extended to the task of classification construction.

So far then, we have argued that the practice of classifying landlords on the grounds of the number of tenancies they own or their legal status may indicate differences between types of landlords and between letting practices, but the justification for such a division may not rest upon either of these characteristics. Landlordism may be classified along a number of different lines, but not all lines are likely to be equally fruitful. Drawing upon the realist approach outlined in the introduction, we would argue that the justification for a particular classification of landlord rests upon its ability to individuate causal groupings. Classification, in this instance, is not a useful device for ordering a formless mass of data; it forms the basis of an explanation. Knowing what kinds of landlords there are in the market and how they are likely to act is a necessary prerequisite to an understanding of what is happening to the private rented housing market. In realist terms, if it can be established that certain landlords are constituted by a structure of relations that bind them as members, then landlords within that group may come to possess causal powers which tend to make them act in certain ways. And it is through a knowledge of these causal powers that the complexity of the rented housing market can start to be unravelled.

Landlords and residential property rent

The starting point for this kind of realist analysis is unproblematic; there is little choice, we can only start with the existing conceptualisations of the subject and, trite as it may appear at first glance, with the concept of landlord.

The concept of landlord possesses a commonplace meaning. Today it generally refers to particular agents or individuals who let residential or commercial property in exchange for a monetary payment. The attachment of the concept to land has withered and a distinction is often made between a landlord who lets a physical building in exchange for property rent and a landowner who lets land in exchange for ground rent. If we take this a step further, the necessary relation or basic characteristic of residential landlordism is residential property rent. The existence of money-rent (or interest on fixed-capital) in this generalised form presupposes the residential landlord-tenant relation. If a landlord were to offer a residential space to a tenant without exacting payment for the exchange, then the term landlord-tenant would be an inappropriate term to describe the relationship involved. The landlord would be acting in a non-landlord manner and is thus, by definition, not a landlord. Similarly, if capitalists were to remove their money-capital from the circuit of capital they would no longer be considered as capitalist. In this definitional form, residential property rent is the means by which agents become landlords; they sell the right to occupy residential space over time to appropriate an increase in their capital. Residential property rent, however, represents only one form of capital that may complete the circuit of house building capital. The development of loan capital this century, in the form of the Building Societies and the Banks, has effectively displaced the role of property rent in the circuit by enabling the commodity to be sold directly to the consumer (see Kemp, 1980). Nevertheless, the rent relation still performs a specific *economic* role in the circuit of house building capital and establishes landlords as a distinctive social grouping.

Residential property rent is not only an economic relation, it also possesses two distinctive *social* aspects; the first is an attribute of the general property rent relation and the second is peculiar to the residential property rent relation. First, the sale of the commodity, residential space, occurs *over time*. The tenant does not buy the property from its owner; the use value of the property, as Engels pointed out, is sold piecemeal. The letting relationship, therefore, is essentially a hire relationship. This relation has certain implications for the practice of landlordism. When a shopkeeper sells a commodity over the counter the property rights attached to the commodity are immediately transferred at the time of the transaction. In contrast, when a landlord sells the use of a particular space for a certain period of time the property rights of control and benefit attached to the space are uneasily divided between landlord and tenant. Both landlord and tenant represent conflicting claims to possession, one based on ownership and the other based on the hire of a commodity, residential space, and in legal terms this is reflected in the fragmentation of the rights of possession between claimants. This 'uneasiness' over property rights allows the intrusion of a personal relation into the ostensibly legal and economic relationship between landlord and tenant. It creates the ground, the possibility as it were, for a relationship of 'service' or 'tutelage' to be established between landlord and tenant. On one hand, the landlord considers the tenant to be under an obligation to take reasonable care of a property and return it in due course. On the other hand, the tenant has purchased the right of use of a property. The rights of control and benefit are unclear, and in consequence, may draw certain landlords into close surveillance of the use of a property.

Secondly, and relatedly, the letting of residential space possesses its own intrinsic ideological markings. Residential landlords do not sell any number of different commodities, they sell the use of a specific commodity over time; they sell 'homes'. Housing and homes hold strong associations; they attract deep seated emotions of security, warmth and enjoyment (Mellor, 1977, p. 88). This ideological characteristic shapes the constitutive meaning that landlords attach to their property which, in turn, has ramifications for their activity in the lettings market. A company, for example, which hires out heavy goods machinery operates upon a different ideological terrain to that of a landlord who hires out residential property. Housing touches a raw social nerve in the way that a 700 foot crane does not.

These two aspects of the rent relation: the ambiguous division of property rights inscribed in the hire relation and the ideological connotations of the commodity, housing, represent the *social* form of the residential property relation. The *economic* form of the rent relation is, as indicated, represented by the monetary payment between landlord and tenant. Diagrammatically, the two forms of the rent relation, the social and the economic, may be represented as two ends of a rental spectrum. At one end, the social relation between the landlord and tenant is signified by the opposing claims to possession and control over residential space. Landlords may draw support for their claim from a universal ideology of private property which conveys exclusive possession over things, and tenants, in contrast, may draw support for their claim from a particular ideology of housing which signifies the right of occupiers to enjoy their space, their 'homes', without threat of eviction or intimidation. At the other end of the spectrum, the economic relation between landlord and tenant is signified by conflicting interpretations of the landlord's right to benefit from and dispose of their assets for financial gain. The landlord does not possess an unrestrained ability to determine the level of rental payments, nor dispose of a property for capital gain at will.

In law, the state is the arbiter of this fragmentation of property rights: of control, benefit and disposal. In the case of private rented housing, the state, since 1915 when the first restrictions of landed property rights occurred in form of the Rent and Mortgage Interest (War Restrictions) Act, has enacted a series of legislative Acts which have restricted the landlord's rights of control, benefit and disposal. In practice, however, different types of landlords negotiate the social and economic forms of the rent relation in various ways depending upon how they are structured, historically, ideologically and economically. The legislative framework governing security of tenure provisions and rental gains at any one point in time represents a contingent constraint upon the activities of landlords and influences the negotiations, but does not determine their outcome. The manner in which landlords resolve the tension implicit both within and between the two aspects of the rent relation requires a knowledge of the characteristics which govern their market practice. In other words, the characteristics which cause them to act in certain ways and not in other ways in the market place.

The classification of landlords we propose in the next section is thus based upon a specification of the different characteristics that landlords display in their historical and ideological attachments to residential property, and their differences as economic agents; that is, in terms of the differences in the type and size of their capital, their sources of finance, and their investment practices. In what follows, we identify certain relations of landlordism which bestow a degree of coherence upon groupings, that is, a structure of relations which binds a group – distinguishes it from other groups – and, in turn influences their actions. For example, some landlords are constituted in such a way that the social form of the rent relation governs their letting practices; that is, they practice a service relationship with their tenants and consider their property as an extension of their personal possessions. Resident landlords exemplify this practice and are part of a group we have termed informal landlords. In contrast, the group we refer to as financial landlords, one which draws its members largely from insurance companies, pension trust funds and public property companies, displays a more explicit, impersonal financial orientation. It will be evident, however, that such a group is not untouched by the tensions implicit in the social form of the rent relation, particularly with respect to the ideological connotations of residential property as homes and the difficulty this poses for their investments in residential property.

In the remainder of the chapter we distinguish between six types of residential landlordism in Britain: traditional landlords, employer landlords, informal landlords, investor landlords, commercial landlords and financial landlords.[3] Each type exhibits an internal structure of relations that constrains the potential range and scope of their activities and distinguishes them from the other types of landlordism identified. The terms chosen to represent the different types of landlordism are familiar terms anchored within everyday discourse. The meaning of each term however, rests upon the shared position occupied by members of a structured group and the practices engaged in. More significantly, the lines of classification are not pregiven, as is the case with legal title, or arbitrary, as is the case with the number of properties owned by a landlord, or their age or sex. Nor are the groups intended to represent 'ideal types', an exaggerated accentuation of a phenomenon serving a heuristic function. Rather they represent an attempt to group the casual characteristics of landlords in the market place. As with 'ideal types' the characteristics of the groups identified are one-sided, but here the focus is casual, not taxonomic.

As with any classification of social groupings, it is historically specific and revisable in the light of changing conditions in the British housing market. The validity of the classification, therefore, should be judged on its ability to account for the basic characteristics which underpin the different types of landlordism in Britain in the 1980s and 1990s and its potential to act as an

---

[3] This is not an *a priori* classification. Its construction is discussed in Chapter 4, Research Design and Methods and in Chapter 5, Note 1.

explanatory framework for understanding the contemporary changes in the private rented housing market.

Types of landlord: a realist account

Traditional landlords

It is possible to distinguish traditional landlords by their somewhat anachronistic orientation to the rented housing market. The activity of letting residential property for this group does not amount to a straightforward commercial activity; it is modified by a service ideology, and a set of obligations and requirements that stem from their historical role in the rented market. Residential property for this group is not considered simply from the point of view of its potential economic return; this is only one element in the role that rented housing performs for this group. The calculation of profit, whether in the form of rental income or disinvestment, is shaped by a constitutive meaning of property that constrains and limits the flexibility of their investments; an aim that is further restricted by the group's financial liabilities, source of finance, and fiscal position.

This first group mainly comprises the Church, The Charitable Trusts, and to a lesser extent the Crown Estate who, despite their diminishing role as major residential landlords, still possess a significant number of properties. The group is structured by the tension between the economic and social aspects of rented housing. On the one hand the group requires a constant and increasing flow of income to meet its economic liabilities, the logic of which entails that they conduct either a policy of redevelopment of their existing stock to raise rental income, or a policy of disinvestment, with reinvestment in higher yielding assets. On the other hand, the properties in their ownership represent more than a block of capital for this group. The stock represents the physical embodiment of the institutions, a symbol closely allied to a philanthropic concern. Thus speculation with the homes of people carries the potential risk of a social scandal and places their privileged tax position in jeopardy. In essence, their economic needs and the constituted meaning attached to their property are in opposition to one another. The redevelopment of their assets is only possible through the sale of a proportion of their symbolic assets. Whereas, other types of landlords are able to raise the finance necessary for the redevelopment of their stock through the money markets, this option is closed to this group because of their charitable status. The privilege then, is also a constraint.

The dilemma has been resolved partly by the use of leasehold sales. Such a policy enables the group to realise capital on the sales: an income from the ground rent and a long-term freehold interest in what is potentially, in terms of site values at least, an appreciating capital asset (on the policy of the Church Commissioners see Furby and Skinner, 1981). However, not all landlords in this group adopt similar strategies. For example, the Crown, which has no major financial liabilities to meet, only a due regard to maintain the value of its capital assets, is less subject to the economic pressures outlined above. Yet the practices illustrated represent the limited options that stem from a particular structure of relations that constitute this type of landlordism. The practices stem from the structure and position of the group: the particular combination of the economic and social characteristics that structure the group and their position within a set of contingent circumstances that, when the two aspects are put together, creates a series of necessary possibilities for the group in the housing market.

Employer landlords

Employer landlords also operate with a set of historical practices, although they are of a qualitatively different form from those that structure traditional landlords. In the early nineteenth-century, industrialists occupied a dominant position in the rented housing market. The provision of tied housing offered a number of advantages to employers: an accessible and dependent workforce, and an element of control, coupled with a profitable outlet for their surplus capital (see Gauldie, 1974, Chapter 16; also Bedale, 1980). Only the first feature, the accessibility of labour now applies to employment-related housing. Rental income is no longer a significant factor in the provision of tied housing. Of greater importance is the need to provide accommodation for those employees who are required to labour outside of the normal working day; for example, hotel workers, security staff and the like. As this requirement decreases so will the stock of tied housing, although by the late 1970s such housing accounted for around 20 per cent of the total lettings in the private rented sector in England and Wales and covered a wide range of occupations – a sizeable proportion that receives scant attention in the literature on landlordism and rented housing (a notable exception is Ramsey, 1979).

The significant point to be raised about this type of landlordism is the absence of a profit motive. As higher rental yields can only be achieved by an increase in the wage levels of their employees, rent is, effectively, an extraction from the overall profits of an employer. Thus, it is not in the economic interest of this group of landlords to maximise rental yields. The distinguishing characteristic of employer landlords, therefore, is that they are constituted on a specific economic ground: the reproduction of their labour force – the need to house their workers. As a result they are not susceptible to the normal financial pressures for disinvestment in the private rented sector.

Nonetheless, employer landlords are susceptible to the ideological connotations attached to housing in general. Tied housing cuts across the wage relation between employer and employee, in so far as the pre-emptive claim to exclusive possession exercised by employer landlords (aside, that is, from the case of agricultural tied employees[4]) constitutes a potential area of conflict between employer and employee, in addition that is to potential labour disputes. As such, it brings into question the advantages that tied housing is supposed to offer. The efficiency and productivity of an employer's enterprise may be jeopardized by problems arising from their role as landlords rather than their role as employers. Where the particular relations that constitute this group of landlords, the reproduction of their labour force, is no longer strictly necessary to the working requirements of employers, the provision of accommodation with a job is likely to be dropped.

Informal landlords

Informal landlords embody the contradiction between the economic and social roles of rented housing in its sharpest form. Informal landlords make up a significant and growing proportion of landlords in the rented housing market. The structure of relations that bind this group primarily encompasses resident landlords, but also includes a large number of non-resident landlords, letting perhaps one house or flat.

Resident landlords, in particular, are a by-product of the increase in owner-occupation that has taken place in Britain since the Second World War. As noted in the last chapter, the actual number of resident landlords in Britain is difficult to pin down, as they are often classified in official data as owner-occupiers. Nevertheless, in the last decade or so rising unemployment levels, coupled with high mortgage rates and maintenance costs, have seen an increase in owner-occupiers sub-letting part of their property. The structure of relations that bind the individual landlords in this group, however, are not only based upon the limited number of properties that they

---

4 The Rent (Agriculture) Act of 1976 gave agricultural workers in England and Wales who have worked for more than ninety-one weeks in a prior two-year period the statutory right to a protected tenancy. If, however, the Agricultural Dwelling House Advisory Committee judges that a farmer requires the tied accommodation for reasons of efficiency the employee loses that protection. In such cases the local authority is requested to provide alternative, secure accommodation.

own, they also include their orientation to the market and to a lesser extent their source of finance.

Property rent, for this group of landlords, does not fulfil a strict commercial role. The act of letting property is primarily grounded upon a social and not an economic basis. Property is considered as a series of social rights over personal possessions and not, in any clear sense as a form of capital. The property relation is 'lived' as a form of authority; that is, as an individual's right to the unfettered power over their personal possessions. This 'lived' experience is not the product of an ideological distortion, it is rooted in the nature of the letting relationship. Unlike a normal commercial transaction, letting property, as noted earlier, involves a 'hire' relationship which divides the property rights of control and benefit between landlord and tenant. For informal landlords this right of control comprises an integral part of the letting relation. Informal landlords do not simply rent the commodity housing to regain the capital they have advanced plus a profit; they 'lend' their houses. They sell the use of personal space over time, but the right of control is not included in the package. The close personal relationship of control that is often established between informal landlord and tenant represents another dimension of the rent relation.

This is not to imply that the rent nexus is altogether unimportant for this group. For resident landlords, letting accommodation is often a necessary requirement to meet their mortgage repayments and running costs. In other cases, however, rent is virtually incidental to the security or company gained through letting accommodation (see Stuart, 1982). Where this type of personal relation exists, rent is usually assessed on an informal and not a commercial basis. Despite the differences in the basis of rent assessment between informal landlords, however, this type of landlordism is principally structured by the tension between the role of rented housing as a source of economic gain and their right to control the commodity after its use has been 'sold'. The constitutive meaning of their property is locked into the notion of housing as an extension of their personal possessions. Hence the informal landlord 'lives' the economic and political forces that shape the rented housing market at a distance. The rights and duties in law that govern this sector of the rented housing market are largely incidental: complex, and inapplicable in the face of what is essentially a personal letting contract.

Earlier we represented the economic and social forms of the rent relation as a tension between rights of financial gain at one end of a spectrum and rights of possession and control at the other end. In this diagramatic sense, the three types of landlords identified so far, traditional, employer and informal, all negotiate the tension towards the latter end. The issues of possession and control, in essence the social form of the rent relation, strongly influence the manner in which they resolve the tension between residential property as capital and residential property as possession. Within the remaining three types of landlordism, the tension between the two aspects of the rent relation is resolved at a point closer to the economic pole of residential property. That is not to deny, however, the pressures exerted by the opposing social pole upon the three groups of landlords. These groups experience them as *limits* to their general financial orientation in the lettings market.

Investor landlords

Investor landlords are among the best known and the most researched group of landlords in this half of the spectrum. The disappearance of this type of landlord from the sector has frequently been documented (see Stafford, 1976; Wareham, 1977; and Kirkwood, 1979). And perhaps it is because their demise has been closely charted that the actions of the remnants of this group who still let property tends to be neglected.

An interesting feature which distinguishes this type of landlordism from the other groups discussed is the source of their capital; in most cases the properties owned are a legacy from the more profitable era of private rented housing in Britain. The properties owned are often inherited capital, and at the risk of stretching the point, they represent a 'burdensome asset' for their owners, whether the owners operate in the market place as private property companies, private trusts, or simply as individuals. Even though reasonable rates of return on capital may be realised due to the low debt repayments incurred on long-term property ownership, their upkeep and development is limited by the restricted access this group has to adequate sources of finance and the ability to repay financial loans. Investor landlords possess a limited financial asset base.

A second factor which has structured the activity of this group of landlords is the change over the last thirty years in Britain in the ideological connotations attached to the image of landlordism. The social position of landlord is one that now predominantly carries a negative status. The effect of this ideological shift is that the letting of property is no longer considered as a 'way of life', or the only form of 'real' investment. One consequence of this shift is that the post-war generation of landlords who inherited rented property find themselves with the *wrong* asset and hence tend to dispose of it at the first available opportunity, even if it implies, as it does in some cases, selling their properties at tenanted and not vacant possession value.

The landlords within this group are, in one sense, the 'victims' of a changed ideology. At a general level, their interests are expressed by the pressure group, the 'Small Landlords Association', who consider 'the landlord' to be discriminated against for attempting to provide a service at a profit. The Rachman stereotype, the 'folk-devil' image of the landlord hurts this group. The image hurts because, in a sense, they are constituted as an anachronism. Although their prime motive for letting residential property is profit, a factor which they may still realise, the service role in which they operate is no longer acknowledged by their 'clients'. The loss of a legitimate social role, plus an increase in maintenance, rates and insurance costs, equals an exit from the letting market for the investor landlords. More importantly, this particular type of disinvestment is not caused by an 'upturn' in house prices on the domestic property market, nor by the availability of alternative investment opportunities. Such phenomena merely facilitate a tendency inscribed in the characteristics of this type of landlordism.

Commercial landlords

Commercial landlords represent the post-war manifestation of the investor ideology and are closely linked to the preceding group. Commercial landlordism, however, differs from the investor landlordism in one marked sense; rented housing is considered solely as a commodity, unsullied by the ideology of the home. Commercial landlordism encompasses individuals, private companies and partnerships, and owes its growth to the disinvestment policies of investor landlordism. Rented housing is an attractive commodity for commercial landlords to trade in for two reasons; first, it is a speculative activity suitable for small capitals reliant upon private or bank loans for their finance, and secondly, it is a profitable venture. The group's requirement to meet short-term loan repayments is achieved either by letting outside of the restrictions of the Rent Acts, particularly through licences or flat-sharing arrangements, or through the sale of properties on receipt of vacant possession. It is a financially risk-laden activity; one that stems directly from the limited size of the capitals involved and their source of funding. This type of landlordism represents the practice of commercial capital – the rapid turnover of commodities, the repeated buying and selling of commodities in order to realise capital in the form of money. It is found in its purest expression among trading landlords, for whom the letting of property is simply a moment in the process of the realisation of their capital, a phase of the disposal process. The tension that exists between housing as capital and as possessions is firmly resolved by this group in terms of the former. This group of small-scale entrepreneurs have inherited the Rachman mantle, albeit adjusted to fit contemporary market conditions.

Financial landlords

The final group of landlords to be discussed, *financial landlords*, share the developed capitalist orientation towards housing exhibited by commercial landlords but they are distinguished from the latter by a number of characteristics:[5] first, in terms of the size of capital available to the institutions in this group; secondly, and relatedly, by virtue of their different source of finance; thirdly, by the minimal role that rented housing performs in their investment portfolios; and last, by their vulnerability to the negative stigma attached to the role of private landlords.

Both public property companies and financial institutions – insurance companies and pension trust funds – are included within this group. The inclusion of the two within the group may, at first sight, appear surprising given the differences in the origins and the position of property and financial capital within the sphere of circulation. Such a classification is justified, however, on the basis of their shared economic relation to rented housing. The commodity, rented housing, for this group, is assessed primarily in terms of both its capital to realise rental income and its potential capital asset value. The financial return in either dimension of the investment are keenly compared to other forms of investment to evaluate their worth. The comparative financial disadvantages of residential property to other forms of investment such as fixed interest securities and equities are well known and quite correctly identified as one of the main reasons for the withdrawal of this type of landlordism from the rented housing market. This process of disinvestment, however, cannot simply be explained by the availability of more lucrative fields of investment, nor by attributing an economic logic of profit maximisation to this group. The process is more complex.

Straightforward economic factors alone do not constitute the rationale of this type of landlordism. In the late 1970s the gap between the investment yields on industrial property, offices and in particular shops, and the investment yield on residential property narrowed. Yet a recognition of this changed situation did not halt institutional disinvestment from rented housing. The reason for this lies in the nature of the commodity, rented housing. First, management of residential property is qualitatively different

---

[5] The characteristics of financial landlords sketched here draws upon Massey and Catalano's (1978, chapter 6) discussion of public property companies and pension trust funds' involvement in the land market in Britain.

from say, the management of commercial property. The units of residential property are smaller than commercial portfolios and this has management implications for both rent collection and maintenance responsibilities. Both functions are time consuming and potentially troublesome for the management of residential property, particularly for a type of landlordism based upon large-scale capital. Secondly, investment in rented housing has attendant problems; it touches a political raw nerve. The spectre of Rachmanism hangs over this type of investment and few large institutions can afford to risk the potential dangers attached to it. Commercial property, on the other hand, does not carry the same political connotations. Eviction for default of a lease on a shop, unlike housing, is not likely to reach the public eye. This is not an incidental point, the social meanings attached to landlordism and rented property shape the orientation of financial landlords in the rented housing market.

The market characteristics, however, which bind this group of landlords are economic in the narrow sense. The size of the capitals involved, the sources of their finance and their particular economic liabilities distinguish them from the preceding types of landlordism and orientate them towards a policy of disinvestment from the rented housing sector. The reasons for disinvestment within this group do, nevertheless, spring from different grounds. Public property companies have withdrawn their capital from rented housing at a faster pace than financial institutions. The reason for this phenomenon may be found in the differences in the financial structure of the two forms of capital.

Public property companies are dependent upon short-term financial loans and share issues for their funding. Their ability to raise the former rests upon the health of their liquidity and yield ratios to sustain a credit-worthy position and the ability to meet their short-term financial liabilities. Hence, the capital value of their assets has to be maintained and high profit yields have to be sustained. Rented housing currently fulfils neither of these requirements, and, in consequence, has produced a rapid policy of disinvestment by public property companies from the residential lettings market.

In contrast, financial institutions operate within a different set of financial constraints. Their liabilities are long-term; the sheer volume of their capital derived from annual premium income or pension contributions has to be maintained in value over a considerable length of time. A policy of risk-minimisation stems from the nature of this type of capital. The stable appreciation of capital asset values is of greater importance than short-term profit maximisation for balancing long-term liabilities. In consequence, insurance companies and pension funds are less vulnerable to short-term fluctuations in the rate of return of their investments. Despite this difference in structure, however, financial institutions cannot sustain low profit yields indefinitely. A strategy of long-term capital appreciation is not inconsistent with a judicious short-term financial policy. Selective disinvestment from the less profitable areas of private rented housing, albeit at a slower pace than property companies, has formed part of the institution's overall strategy of investment rationalisation. It is interesting to note, therefore, that despite the different time scale on capital returns held by financial institutions and public companies their actions tend toward the same result, major disinvestment from the mainstream of the lettings market.

At the same time, institutional capital has been reinvested in the more profitable, luxury end of the residential lettings market. At the risk of oversimplifying, this type of capital will move in and out of the different sectors of demand in the rented housing market if its basic orientation of capital risk-minimisation can be satisfied. This will, of course, depend upon the prevailing economic and political circumstances that characterise the market at any one point in time.

This account of the structure of financial landlordism concludes the classification. The strength of the classification, however, lies with its potential to act as an explanatory framework and we now outline what such a framework would look like.

Explanatory framework

The argument of this chapter has been that a classification of landlords based upon the size of capital at a landlord's disposal, their source of funding, the type of capital involved – commercial, financial, industrial, inherited and so forth – and the historical relations exhibited by the different types of landlordism, in particular the constitutive meaning they attach to the ownership of residential property, has considerable potential to explain what has been happening in the rented housing market. Broadly speaking, different types of landlords will tend to act in certain ways by virtue of the causal powers they possess. Whether or not the causal powers inscribed in the different types of landlordism are realised, however, will depend upon the particular features of a local housing market. It is not possible therefore, to 'read off' the activities and strategies adopted by the different types of landlords from the causal powers they possess. The processes of investment and disinvestment that are shaping the market are not linked directly to particular types of landlord, although it is possible to discern *potential* rather than *actual* links. The causal powers inscribed in, say, financial landlords who tend towards a strategy of disinvestment will only be realised in certain local circumstances. Hence detailed studies are necessary to trace the actual impact of the powers held by the different types of landlordism in any one locality. And this will involve addressing the differences between areas in terms of the kinds of landlords present, the structure of the local housing market, local state policies, the type of rented housing stock and the demographic and class profile of tenants.

From this standpoint, it follows that the variation in the types of landlords in different areas are likely to lead to different kinds of rented housing market where the circumstances of the areas are similar, and *pari passu*, variations in the circumstances which pattern two or more markets are likely to give rise to different events where such areas are characterised by a similar structure of landlordism. In one sense then, the character of a local private rented housing market is shaped by the relationship between certain local circumstances and the kinds of landlords that operate in that locality. In Chapters 5 and 6 we attempt to illustrate this process of structured unevenness by looking at the six groups of landlords and their activities in two inner London boroughs characterised by a wide variation of their histories and their structure. First, however, it is necessary to detail briefly our research design and data sources.

4

Research design and methods

In the preceding chapter we outlined our critique of the existing classification of the structure of private landlordism and proposed a new classification. In the succeeding chapters we present the results of empirical research into the structure of landlordism in two inner London boroughs – Hackney and Islington – at the end of the 1970s and in the early 1980s, followed by a chapter that tackles the difficult question of policy recommendations to effect change in this sector of the housing market. In this chapter we outline the methods that we adopted in the empirical research. Before doing so, we wish to point out that in this type of social science research there are important interconnections between classification, empirical research and policy recommendations. Despite presenting the chapters in this order, the different processes are interconnected and we found it difficult to separate them completely.

In fact, the chapters follow a 'logic' of presentation rather than the overlapping sequence of our method of working. The reconceptualisation of the workings of the private rented housing market and those who organise and shape it did not take place in some autonomous realm separate from or prior to submersion in empirical detail. Working with a selection of secondary sources such as the publications of the British Property Federation, the Small Landlords Association, Shelter, government surveys, in particular Paley's *Attitudes to Lettings* (1978), and a number of academic sources, we built up a tentative understanding of types of landlords operating in the market. Together with the largely descriptive results of the extensive statistical survey (Chapter 6) we were able to construct a clearer picture of the different processes reorganising the market and which types of landlord were active in producing this pattern of change. Over the same time period, although not in tandem, we identified and interviewed individual members of each potential grouping to ascertain the actual relations entered into by these agents and why they acted in a particular manner (Chapter 5). In turn, the qualitative results of these interviews shed new light upon the patterns of housing change revealed by extensive analysis. While it was possible to discern patterns of disinvestment, investment, and informalisation through extensive research methods, their explanation remained largely at a speculative level. Through a qualitative reanalysis of the findings, these patterns became explicable, not as a matter of course, but slowly and rather painstakingly in terms of identifiable causal groupings. The process of reconceptualisation was thus one in which the categories of landlords were formed and modified in the light of empirical evidence, and, in turn, were used to represent this evidence in a theoretically informed (rather than determined) manner.

This sketch is an overview of our general method of working; we now return to the starting point of the research and the specific methodological criteria we needed to fulfil in order to construct a realist explanation of housing change:

(1) to identify a sample of landlords through whom we were able to scrutinise empirically our tentative classification.

(2) to identify landlords all of whom were faced by a similar situation in order to uncover the similarities and differences in their actions when faced by a set of similar circumstances.

(3) to select a geographical area or areas that enabled us to identify the actual effects of local housing circumstances upon the activities of different groups of landlords and to uncover how their potential ways of acting were realised, modified or negated.

(4) to decide the type of empirical research methods appropriate to such an investigation.

The ways in which we met these criteria are outlined below. The first and second criteria were met together and so are not discussed separately.

Selecting the sample and identifying landlords

One of the major methodological difficulties facing all analysts of the private rented sector in England and Wales is the absence of a complete record of the owners of private lettings from which to select a sample.[1] This problem has been tackled in a variety of ways; sources such as local authority rating records or rent registration records have been used in some studies. Other analysts have undertaken door-to-door surveys in areas where private tenants are concentrated as revealed by the decennial census, or they have used lists of a sub-sample of private tenants, such as students in higher education. Finally, property owners or landlords' associations have been used as contact mechanisms. We chose to use a different source and one which, to our knowledge, has not been utilised before. This was the housing

[1] In Scotland, the register of Sasines included full information about house ownership.

waiting list records held by local housing authorities. The majority of applicants for council housing in inner city areas are tenants of private landlords and when registering on the waiting list they are required to provide details of their personal circumstances, of their current accommodation and their landlords. Thus, such lists provide a sample of private landlords operating within the inner city, albeit partial and incomplete, but with the major advantage of providing a set of names and addresses of the landlords, or in some cases of the agents of a set of private tenancies.

There are, however, two biases in such a sampling frame. These biases are logically apparent but unfortunately unverifiable. Because local authorities restrict applications to certain categories of household, those landlords who do not house prospective Council tenants will not be included. The main category of exclusion from eligibility for rehousing includes young, single and mobile people. Single people under forty-five are generally not considered for rehousing, except in special circumstances. Mobile households also tend to be excluded as they find it difficult to accrue sufficient years' residence within a single housing authority's area to meet the commonly demanded residence requirement before being eligible to register on a housing waiting list. Thus, landlords who specialise in the provision of lettings for mobile young people, such as students, apprentices and single workers will tend to be under represented in a sample drawn from housing waiting list records.

There is a second bias, too, in a sample drawn from housing waiting lists and that is towards landlords who let inadequate properties in poor physical condition. Households who register on the waiting list are awarded 'points' according to a bureaucratic set of definitions of housing need.[2] The physical inadequacy of the applicant's dwelling and the extent of shared amenities and over-crowding typically are accorded considerable significance.

The great advantage of using housing waiting lists as a sampling frame, however, lies in their unique ability to allow us to satisfy our second criterion for selecting the sample. By selecting our sample from that group of landlords whose tenants recently had been rehoused, we were able to construct a group of landlords who had all experienced the same change at the same time: viz the creation of a vacancy in one of their lettings. Thus, unlike most previous studies of landlords' behaviour which have relied on a 'what if' type of question (see especially Bone and Mason, 1980 and Paley, 1978), we were able to investigate landlords actual behaviour and their decisions whether to relet, disinvest or leave their vacancies empty. All the

[2] See Appendix 1 for the 'points' scheme in operation in Hackney and in Islington in 1980.

landlords in such a sample, whether they were traditional, employer or one of the other six types, were faced with the same choice.

Selecting the geographical area

The next major decision was to select the case study area for the empirical investigation in order to uncover the ways in which contingent factors interact with the causal mechanisms structuring each of the six groups. We argued earlier that landlords of a particular type have a capacity or tendency to act in particular ways. However, these causal relations or mechanisms that bind them together as a group do not automatically lead to the same strategy being adopted when faced with vacancies. The ways in which landlords of particular types actually act in specific circumstances are mediated by the actions of other causal agents and by variations in local and national housing conditions at the time. In Sayer's terms 'whether a causal power or liability is actually activated ... depends on conditions whose presence and configuration is contingent' (p. 97). Whether a landlord actually relets under similar or different conditions, or disinvests will depend upon the particular circumstances in a particular place at a certain time. In one sense, the choice of location was unimportant as we were not concerned with searching for an area that would be 'representative' of the structure of private landlordism, which in itself, as we have just argued, is unascertainable. However, we were concerned to choose an area or areas where the contingent circumstances were such as to create the opportunity for a wide range of possible actions for private landlords. Thus we were interested in areas where, first, demand for private rented accommodation remained high so that landlords might choose to relet, secondly, where there were opportunities to disinvest, either through sales to the local authority in its improvement programme or through its sponsorship of housing associations or sales to private individuals for home ownership, thirdly where there was some evidence of informalisation, and finally, where we might expect all of our tentative categories of landlord to be represented. All these factors led us to consider several inner London boroughs.

As we argued in Chapter 2, the private rented sector is a spatially concentrated phenonomen. The greatest concentrations of private tenants are found in particular parts of the largest towns and cities in England and Wales, in a number of coastal and 'university' towns and, if tied accommodation is included, in some rural areas. However, over one fifth of all the tenants of private landlords were, in 1981, living in Greater London: 415,289 households in all. Seventeen per cent of all households lived in this part of the housing market in Greater London, compared with an average of 13 per

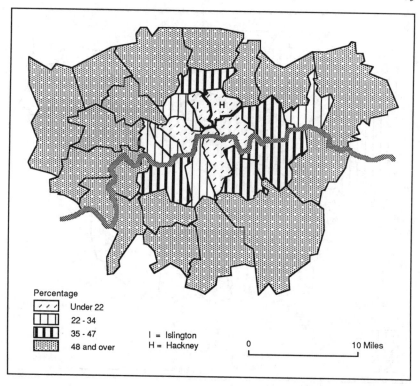

Percentage

✓✓✓	Under 22
	22 - 34
	35 - 47
	48 and over

I = Islington
H = Hackney

0   10 Miles

Figure 4.1a The tenure distribution of the housing stock in Greater London, 1981:
households in owner-occupation

cent in England and Wales. At the metropolitan scale too, there is a marked spatial concentration in the distribution of each housing tenure. Changes in the structure and location of employment in Greater London and in the class composition of the population in different areas have produced areas that seem to be becoming increasingly polarised on the basis of social class and housing tenure distributions (Hamnett and Randolph, 1986), and also by political allegiance. The suburban boroughs of outer London tend to be dominated by Conservative voting, home-owning families; the inner boroughs, and particularly those in the east, by working class Labour voters living in low and high rise council housing. The private rented sector is, to a large extent, a residual category in both these areas (see Figures 4.1a, 4.1b and 4.1c). It is an historical legacy of earlier social relations of building production and housing provision; Victorian homes stranded by the inter-war and post-war spread of suburbia and by the actions of the post-war state and its urban bulldozer.

The size, scale and impact of urban redevelopment programmes varied,

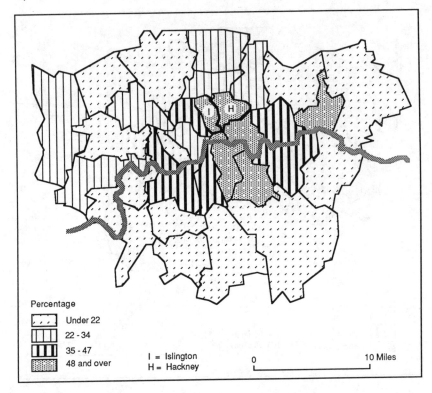

Percentage

⠿ Under 22
▭ 22 - 34
▥ 35 - 47
▦ 48 and over

I = Islington
H = Hackney

0   10 Miles

Figure 4.1b The tenure distribution of the housing stock in Greater London, 1981: households renting from the local authority

however, partly because of the political complexion of the inner London boroughs. The Labour controlled authorities embraced the high technology, modernist philosophy of the 1960s with greater enthusiasm than their Conservative counterparts and have reaped the whirlwind in the form of a vast inheritance of unpopular and, in some cases structurally unsound, high rise flats. However, their stock also reflects a longer period of municipal socialism and state provision of housing; the locally owned stock reflects pre-war as well as post-war building, and in some areas almost all the properties are council owned. In Tower Hamlets, for example, over 80 per cent of all dwellings are state-owned.

Where municipal development has been relatively unimportant, in Hammersmith and Fulham, Kensington and Chelsea, Wandsworth, for example, and in Westminster to a lesser extent, the private rented sector has remained correspondingly large (see Figure 4.1b). Because we wanted to be able to evaluate the impact of local state actions on the choices and options open to landlords we excluded these boroughs from consideration. In Chapter 2 we

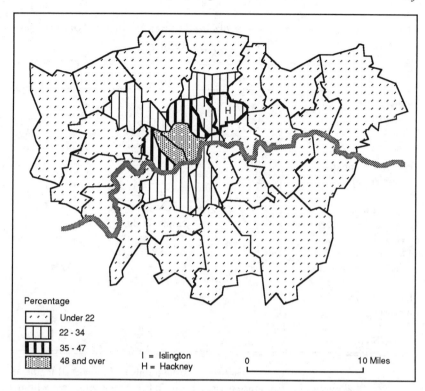

Figure 4.1c The tenure distribution of the housing stock in Greater London, 1981: households renting from private landlords

argued that, through compulsory purchase and redevelopment and through tenure transfers in improvement programmes, municipal actions have played a significant role in the decline of the private rented sector. Thus the choice of survey area was narrowed to include boroughs where these programmes have been significant. We also, however, were interested in areas where the private rented sector remained relatively bouyant, with a continuing high demand for such accommodation and so opportunities for existing landlords to reinvest and for new landlords to enter the market. A number of boroughs met these criteria: Camden, Brent, Hackney, Islington, Lambeth and Lewisham among them. Several authorities were interested in cooperating with us and in making their waiting list records available. Eventually, we decided to undertake survey work in two spatially contiguous boroughs: Hackney and Islington in North East London. There were two reasons for adopting this comparative approach. First, in a preliminary investigation it became apparent that many of the landlords represented on the housing waiting list records of these boroughs operated across the whole

Table 4.1 *Ownership structure of private lettings in Greater London, 1963, 1976 and 1977 (percentages)*

	(a)	(b)[1]	(c)
Individuals			
resident	18 ⎫	14 ⎫	11 ⎫
non-resident	33 ⎭ 51	40 ⎭ 40	41 ⎭ 52
Property companies			
residential	27 ⎫		⎫ 22
non-residential	3 ⎬	26	⎭
New property companies	6 ⎭	employer co.	7
Charitable trust and			
housing associations	4	24	14
Executors and other			
trusts	6	4	other ⎫ 5
Public bodies	3	6	⎭

Notes: [1] Paley seems to have under-estimated the number of individual landlords and over-estimated housing associations in her survey compared with the other two sources. One of the explanations might be that she contacted landlords through tenants, omitting the landlord from the sample if tenants were unwilling for their landlord to be contacted. Perhaps in the highly competitive private rented sector in London, tenants of individual landlords preferred their landlords to be excluded.

Sources: (a) Gray, P. E. and Todd, J. (1965) p. 313.
(b) Paley, B. (1978) p. 9.
(c) DoE (1978b) pp. 120, 122 and 124.

area, thus enabling us to evaluate the impact, if any, of differences in the housing markets in the two boroughs upon landlords' actions. Local authority boundaries obviously are an administrative construct rather than significant local housing market boundaries. Indeed, each of the two boroughs was created by the amalgamation of a number of smaller areas in 1965 under the Local Government Act 1963. The second reason for choosing two adjacent boroughs was that such a choice increased our ability to assess the impact of contingent conditions on landlords' strategies in a particular way. The nature of the housing stock and the administrative and political context of the two boroughs were similar, whereas there were differences in the demand for particular types of housing in the areas. These factors will be

Table 4.2 *Ownership structure of private lettings in Hackney, Islington and Greater London 1977 (percentages)*

	Hackney	Islington	Greater London
Individuals			
resident	12 ⎫	16 ⎫	11 ⎫
	⎬ 54	⎬ 54	⎬ 52
non-resident	42 ⎭	38 ⎭	41 ⎭
Property companies	17	11	22
Employer companies	4	6	7
Charitable trusts and housing associations	20	19	14
Other	5	10	5

Source: The percentages are calculated from three tenure and ownership tables in the DoE (1978b) pp. 120, 122 and 124.

outlined in detail in Chapter 6. Thirdly, Hackney and Islington had a similar profile of landlordism and, particularly important, all the categories of landlords we had tentatively identified appeared to be represented in the areas, although, of course, in the absence of a complete sampling frame and because of differences in the way in which previous studies have classified landlords, adequate comparable information was not easily available. In the tables below, the main information that is available about the structure of the private rented sector in Greater London as a whole, and within Hackney and Islington during the 1960s and 1970s, is presented.

It is clear from the table that individual landlords each owning a small number of properties predominate in Greater London, although smaller numbers of other types of landlords own substantial numbers of properties. The National Dwelling and Housing Survey also included estimates for each London borough based on a sample survey of approximately 10 per cent of households renting privately. In Table 4.2 the structure of ownership of private lettings in Hackney and Islington is compared with the Greater London average. Whereas the percentage of households with tenants of individual landlords is similar, in both Hackney and Islington, property companies seem to be under-represented and housing associations over-represented compared with Greater London average. The profile of landlords within Hackney and Islington, however, is remarkably similar and so reinforces our arguments about comparability between the boroughs.

The final task was to select a sample of landlords from the housing waiting list records of the two boroughs in order to compare the strategies of

Table 4.3 *Private landlords in Hackney and Islington*
Percentage of households renting from different types of landlord

| | Hackney | | Islington | |
	NDHS*	Sample	NDHS*	Survey
Individuals				
resident	14.5	41.9	19.6	29.8
		67.0	80.5	66.4	77.6
non-resident	52.5	38.6	46.8	47.8
Property companies	21.8	13.0	14.2	11.4
Employer companies	4.5	2.0	6.8	2.0
Other	6.7	4.5	12.6	9.0

Note: * The figures look different from those in the previous table as housing
associations have been excluded. In the rest of the chapter, and indeed the
book as a whole, we are concerned solely with private landlords who,
theoretically at least, are market entrepreneurs, profit makers, rather than
non-profit institutions like housing associations.
Source: DoE (1978b) and Hackney and Islington sample surveys 1981 and 1979

different types of landlords when presented with one or more vacant
lettings. A 25 per cent sample of all private tenants who were rehoused over
a two year period at the end of the 1970s was selected.[3] This resulted in a
total of 235 vacancies in Hackney and 302 in Islington which formed the
basis for an intensive and extensive study of landlords' behaviour and the
consequences of the strategies that they adopted for the structure of this
stock in the boroughs and for access to private tenancies in general.

Considerable detective work was involved in actually piecing together the
histories of the dwelling spaces and properties included in our sample,
especially in tracing the landlords or agents. Each property was visited up to
six times by a team of interviewers who undertook a questionnaire survey of
the new occupants, when there were any. A number of other sources also
had to be used to identify a proportion of the owners of empty dwellings.
These included information from neighbours, from estate agents, from local
authority rating lists and from rent registration records. In addition we
contacted all known landlords by letter, administered a postal survey to
those living outside London and personally interviewed a sample of
landlords living within the Greater London area.

The sample was selected randomly as there were insufficient details of
landlords' holdings to enable us to select a sample that might mirror the

[3] Further details of the sampling procedure are included in Appendix 1.

Table 4.4 *The six-fold classification of landlords in*
Hackney and Islington
Percentage of households living in each category

		Hackney		Islington
Traditional		0.5		1.6
Employer		9.8		4.3
Informal		40.4		34.1
resident	39.1		29.1	
non-resident	1.3		5.0	
Investor		33.6		42.0
Commercial		15.7		15.2
Financial		–		2.6
Total number of households*		235		302

Note: * The number of landlords was smaller than the
number of household spaces as in several cases
more than one tenant household was rehoused
from a landlord's properties. We have presented
the results on the basis of households or household spaces, however, as the actual strategy
adopted by landlords in a particular case affected by the type and location of the household
space and the property within which it fell.
Source: Hackney and Islington sample surveys, 1980
and 1979.

overall pattern of lettings by different types of landlords in the two
boroughs. As Table 4.3 demonstrates, the final sample was biased towards
individual owners compared with the overall borough averages. This
reflects the ways in which waiting list schemes operate. The types of
landlords owning properties in poor condition that are inhabited by
households in housing need, as defined by each borough, inevitably will be
over represented in a sample based on local authority records.

In Table 4.4 the sample is represented on the basis of the six-fold
classification of landlords described in the previous chapter. In the table, the
sample landlords are presented in an order that reflects their orientation to
the market. In Chapter 3, we argued that a significant characteristic of
landlords was their negotiation of the tension between the social and
economic aspects of the rent relation for different types of landlord.
Traditional landlords resolve the tension between the two aspects at the

'social' end of the spectrum, financial at the 'economic' end. As the table shows, we found in these two areas that it was landlords for whom the tension between the two aspects of the rent relation was the greatest – the informal and investor landlords – who were the most heavily involved in housing the type of tenants who qualified for council housing. This was, perhaps unsurprising. Traditional landlords, concerned with their 'image', tend to provide at least adequate accommodation in terms of its physical condition and so their tenants seldom appear at the top of housing waiting lists, given the significance that is accorded to such factors as the absence of basic amenities. Commercial and financial landlords, on the other hand, are also less likely to house tenants who qualify for rehousing, although commercial landlords are represented in reasonable numbers in the sample. For these landlords, the reason for their relative absence is economic. They are primarily interested in high rates of return and tend to prefer affluent tenants who can afford to pay for reasonable accommodation. Thus we have a sample that is composed, in the main, of landlords whose motives for investing or disinvesting are less clearcut. The advantage of this for evaluating our arguments about the importance of contingent relations is that factors such as the structure of local demand, the nature of the housing stock and the area in which it is located will make a significant difference to the strategies adopted by landlords in each of the six categories. We investigated these strategies in two ways – by means of a detailed intensive case study of a small number of representative landlords in each category and by an extensive questionnaire survey of all landlords, new tenants and new owners in the total two borough sample of 537 lettings.

Intensive and extensive research methods

The distinction between intensive and extensive research design is one borrowed from Harré (1979) and utilised by Sayer and Morgan (1985) in their study of the electrical engineering industry in South Wales. In general the distinction is based on the 'depth' or 'breadth' of analysis, but different methods are also utilised in each case. Intensive research deals in depth with a small number of cases, usually using interview techniques, which often are relatively unstandardised, interactive and semi-formal. The results tend to be open to interpretation and are qualitative rather than quantitative. Extensive research, on the other hand, is more formal, often based on large-scale questionnaire survey work and numerical analysis. Sayer and Morgan have argued that whereas each type of research is valuable, they fulfil different functions. Intensive research is primarily explanatory and extensive primarily descriptive and synoptic. We produce below a table from Sayer

Table 4.5 *Intensive and extensive research: a summary*

	Intensive	Extensive
Research question	How does a process work in a particular case or small number of cases? What *produces* a certain change? What did the agents actually do?	What are the regularities, common patterns, distinguishing features of a population? How widely are certain characteristics or processes distributed or represented?
Relations	Substantial relations of connection.	Formal relations of similarity.
Type of groups studied	Causal groups.	Taxonomic groups.
Type of account produced	Causal explanation of the production of certain objects or events, though not necessarily a representative one.	Descriptive 'representative' generalisations, lacking in explanatory penetration.
Typical methods	Study of individual agents in their causal contexts, interactive interviews, ethnography. Qualitative analysis.	Large scale survey of population or representative sample, formal questionnaires, standardised interviews. Statistical analysis.
Are the results generalisable?	Actual concrete patterns and contingent relations are unlikely to be 'representative', 'average' or generalisable. *Necessary* relations discovered will exist wherever their relata are present, e.g. causal powers of objects are generalisable to other contexts as they are necessary features of these objects.	Although representative of a whole population, they are unlikely to be generalisable to other populations at different times and places. Problem of ecological fallacy in making inferences about individuals.
Disadvantages	Problem of representativeness.	Lack of explanatory power. Ecological fallacy in making inferences about individuals.

Source: Sayer and Morgan (1985).
  A modern industry in a declining region: links between theory, methods and policy in Massey, D. and Meegan, R. (eds.) *Politics and Method*, Methuen.

and Morgan summarising the characteristics of each type of research. Sayer
and Morgan have argued that *in isolation* 'extensive research often fails to
indicate what processes have produced the patterns it reveals. Conversely,
intensive research does not tell us how widespread or "representative" are
the results produced by the particular process on which it is focused'
(p. 152). It thus seems clear that the two methods of research may be
complementary. As Sayer and Morgan have argued 'if a particular kind of
mechanism or process has already been identified by intensive research, then
provided adequate data exists it might be possible to use extensive methods
to discover its incidence and extent' (ibid., p. 151–2). Equally, it is possible
to discern general patterns of groupings through extensive research and to
identify members which are taken to be typical, which are then subjected to
intensive investigation to reveal any substantive, causal powers. In practice,
there is no prescriptive order in which to proceed; it depends largely upon
the nature of the object under investigation. Research into the structure of
private industrial companies within a particular region, for example, could
very likely proceed from intensive to extensive, primarily because descriptive information on the types of company in a region is likely to be known.
In the case of private landlords, the numbers involved and their general
characteristics in any particular area are rarely known in any sufficient detail
to identify potentially typical members. Thus the starting point was
pregiven; the need to construct an extensive picture of the kinds of landlords
in the two areas, their similarities and differences, and the type of activities
they were involved in. On the basis of this information, as noted earlier, we
undertook intensive interviews with a small number of landlords in order to
investigate in detail how they interpret and make sense of their actions. This
was an essential element of constructing and evaluating the six-fold
classification and uncovering the basic relations of residential landlordism.
Having done so, we were then in a position to represent the results of our
extensive survey in a manner akin to Sayer and Morgan's view above; that
is, as a causal rather than a statistical explanation. Because we uncovered
the specific substantial and causal relations each category of agent entered
into in the intensive phase, we are able to argue that the results of the
extensive phase also reveal causal relations of connection rather than formal
or statistical relations of similarity or dissimilarity. The results from both
types of research will not be 'representative' in the sense that they reoccur
elsewhere in the same form. The actual strategies practised by the landlords
interviewed in Hackney and Islington were dependent upon the distinctive
characteristics of the two housing markets at the end of the 1970s and early
1980s. Thus, the results we uncovered are unlikely to be either representative
in the usual sense of the word or generalisable to other areas. However,

insofar as our research uncovered the causal characteristics that constituted each group of landlords wherever these types are found in the present conjuncture, these characteristics will also exist, predisposing these landlords towards particular forms of action. In this sense our research methods are replicable.

5

Landlords in profile: an intensive survey

This chapter is based on the results of in-depth interviews with different types of landlords owning and renting residential property in Hackney and Islington. In Chapter 3 we argued that attempts to classify landlords have often been marred by inadequate conceptualisation; that analyses have tended to accept rather uncritically the convention of classifying landlords by the number of properties they own and their legal status. We then proposed an alternative classification of landlords based upon the differences in their historical, ideological and economic characteristics, and identified six causally structured groups. Here we focus upon each of these groups in turn, to show how the actual characteristics of individual members within a group combine to admit the possibility of emergent causal powers.

If we take seriously the idea that landlords may be considered as a series of structured groups then we should be able to subject such a notion to empirical scrutiny. Indeed this is the rationale for intensive research; it offers the possibility of investigating the structural relations that bind particular groups and identifies certain social practices that would very likely be glossed over in more formal, extensive modes of research. There are, of course, attendant risks connected with this approach. The most significant risk is that of distortion; the individual member identified as 'typical' from our preliminary extensive research may turn out to be atypical. It is not entirely possible to overcome this danger; however, it is possible to minimise it by selecting a sufficient number of members who ostensibly fall within the same group and to use each member in turn as potential falsifiers of the view that each is typical.[1]

---

[1] By looking in detail at landlords in the context of the housing market or markets in which they operated and investigating the nature of their activities, we were able to discern the structure of relations that lay behind their actions. In turn, we were able to use the results of the case studies to assess the validity of our initial six-fold classification of landlords identified from the findings of our extensive research. The results, in our view, corroborated our initial classification, but as anticipated also revealed differences between practices of landlords which we had placed within the same group. We then had to address the possibility that our guiding preconceptions on the structures of landlordism had foreclosed our analysis of the case studies and yielded corroborative evidence. It would be naive to deny that our initial conceptualisation of landlord types did not influence our interpretation of the case

The following case studies of individual landlords have been chosen from a total of thirty-nine open-ended interviews; nineteen from the Islington survey and twenty from the Hackney survey. Both sets of interviews, the former in 1981 and the latter in 1982, were conducted on a cumulative basis, one by one, with the intention of slowly building up our understanding of the membership of each causal group.

Each landlord was interviewed along similar lines, with certain variations to allow for the different operating characteristics between types of landlords; for example, the visible difference in characteristics between the operation of a pension trust fund and a resident landlord. The major areas of investigation were:

the rationale for their role as residential landlords and why they originally entered the private lettings market,
the source of their funding and financial liabilities,
the amount of capital at their disposal and their investments, if any, outside of the private rented market,
the social meaning they attached to the ownership and letting of residential property, and
their attitude towards government legislation relating to the rented housing sector.

In this chapter, with the exception of employer landlords, we have selected three case studies of each type of landlordism. Our selection of the case studies was based on three considerations. First, that they exhibit the economic and historical characteristics that distinguish them as members of a particular group; secondly, that they illustrate that landlords of a different legal status and of different property holdings may share a similar structure

studies, indeed the situation could not have been otherwise; but this statement is rather different from accepting that our preconceptions determined the research findings.

The criteria for deciding the number and boundaries of groups of landlords was the identification of the causally significant characteristics within and between groups. Thus each case study was analysed for the substantive relations that made sense of why they actually did operate in a particular way and which, in turn, rendered explicable some of the patterns of investment and disinvestment revealed in the extensive survey. Despite differences in the time scale and location of activities of landlords structured in a similar way, we found no substantive evidence to suggest our initial six-fold classification of landlords should be extended or compressed.

Our first attempt to devise a classification of landlords from the results of the extensive survey yielded an initial division between informal and formal landlords. Within the latter broad category we subsequently identified the possibility of six types of landlords: traditional, investor, employer, financial, commercial *and* trading. Further analysis of the extensive results indicated that commercial and trading landlords were possibly structured in a similar way despite the variation in the nature of their activities. At root they both appeared to share a similar commercial orientation to the rented housing market based upon a similar economic and ideological constitution. The findings of the intensive survey corroborated this hypothesis.

of relations and general orientation to the market; and thirdly, that they highlight the different ideologies of property to be found among private landlords.

This last consideration is significant in as far as the intrinsic meanings that landlords attach to their property and their rights over property are constitutive of their social action. How landlords interpret their role, define their rights, and legitimise their activities, influence and indeed constrain their actions in the market. In this sense, the social meanings that landlords attach to their property represent the ideological character which, in combination with their historical and economic character, structure the activities of the different groups. Ideas are no less causally significant than the financial constraints that influence landlords letting activities. We thus draw particular attention to the different practical ideologies held by landlords in this chapter. And we do so because it is possible to convey the consequences of such ideologies through case study materials in a manner that was not possible in the kind of analysis conducted in Chapter 3.

Unfortunately, our research base limited our ability to examine in depth a sufficient number of members within each group. It would appear that landlords such as public property companies and the financial institutions who specialise in the provision of letting for higher income groups are under represented in a sample drawn from housing waiting list records. In addition, employer landlords are also under represented in the records[2].

In respect of the companies and institutions initially identified as financial landlords we were able to obtain a sufficient number of interviews to gauge the validity of attributing a causal structure to such a grouping. Naturally, not all of the companies and institutions that comprise this group exhibit identical characteristics or hold an identical set of beliefs about property and housing. We have tried to preserve these differences in the case studies without, we hope, losing sight of the general 'logic' which motivates and binds them as a group. We leave it to the reader to judge the extent of our success.

In the case of employer landlords, we are unable to make a similar claim. Only a small number of employer landlords were identified from the sample and only one agreed to be interviewed in depth. We were therefore unable to assess the typicality of members of this group or corroborate the validity of this grouping. For the remaining four groups of landlords identified – traditional, informal, investor and commercial – we were able to identify and interview a significant number of potential members, from which we

---

[2] A discussion of the sources we drew upon and the nature of the difficulties that we encountered in selecting our sample and identifying landlords is included in Chapter 4.

have selected those that meet the aforementioned considerations. Fortunately, these four groups constitute the majority of private landlords in the British housing market today which, as is known, are predominantly private individuals. Turning to the case studies, we start with accounts of the activities of three traditional landlords.

Traditional landlords

In the previous chapter, we spoke of traditional landlords as an anachronism. In an ideological sense this is quite true. Of the ideas held by landlords within this group – ideas of patronage, of guardianship, of stewardship, and the obligation that each entail – few are widespread in the housing market today. The state provision of housing has largely eroded such notions, in particular, that of the 'deserving poor', and, indeed, few traditional landlords today hold these attitudes with the same intensity. Nevertheless, the residue of ideas embedded in the past practices of traditional landlords still possess an influence upon how such landlords interpret their rights of ownership and continue to shape their attachments to residential property.

Different aspects of these points are highlighted through these case studies – an established charitable trust in Islington, a private trust representing one of the older nineteenth-century housing estates in Islington and a large philanthropic body that has extensive properties throughout London. Despite the differences in their legal status, it is of particular interest to note that all three adopted a similar orientation to their property. The properties themselves represented the physical embodiment of the various institutions and as such limited, within bounds, the *extent, form and pace* of their investment activities.

The charitable trust

The trust dates back to 1517 and has been administered by the trustees as a developed residential site since 1811. In that year the trustees of the estate – 'six men, honest and discreet' – had successfully petitioned Parliament to develop the fourteen acre site and the land was subsequently developed – mainly residential, with a few shops – on a leasehold basis. In 1938, however, nearly three quarters of the estate was sold in lots by public auction for £110,000. The remaining property, approximately sixty houses, each divided into two unfurnished flats, and forty-eight purpose built flats, plus two shops, represented the better property of the estate. The reasons for the sale are interesting.

By 1938, the properties on the estate were between 100 and 120 years old, and in poor condition. To maintain the property, the trustees, now seventeen in number as a result of the rising income of the charity, needed capital. The only way they could raise capital, however, was to sell part of their capital assets, part of the estate. Legislation governing the activities of charitable trusts was until 1961 excessively restrictive. Up to that date concern about the investment activities of trusts had limited investment opportunities largely to government stocks and property. Such institutions, as charitable concerns, could not be seen to be involved in speculative ventures. The only option available at the time to this particular charitable trust, therefore, was to raise capital through the sale of some of the very assets which they wished to preserve.

After the cost of the maintenance of the remaining properties had been met, the remainder of the proceeds from the sale was invested in government securities. Up to 1938 the sole source of income for the trust had been from ground rents. This departure, however, represented the beginning of a diversification of investments as alternative opportunities were opened up by changing legislation governing charitable trusts. In recent years the trust's investment portfolio has included stocks and shares, and local government loans, most of which are in equities. Its current investment return from the remaining residential properties is minimal, after costs of management, maintenance and rates have been met. Why, then, has the trust not sold the remainder of its residential properties? The answer is straightforward. The properties represent more than investment capital to the institution. This point deserves elaboration.

The trust is over 460 years old. The fourteen acre site, and the dwellings upon it, including a church, represent the physical embodiment of the trust: a social symbol, not so much to the philanthropic nature of charitable trusts in this instance, but to piety. The benefactor could have given the land outright to the church, but instead chose the legal device of a trust to ensure the continuance of certain religious observances and practices (including an annual memorial service for the benefactor on the anniversary of his death). The surplus income, after payment to the district churches, is directed to the 'sick poor of the ancient parish of Islington': hospitals, medical and nursing charities. Over time, the inscribed religious character of the trust has given way to a more concerted philanthropic concern, but the physical character of the site still represents the external symbol as it were, of the trust. In turn, this particular constitutive social meaning attached to their property has constrained both the investment and the letting strategy of the trust. The trustees have shaped their guardianship policy to meet both their economic and social needs. Their management considerations are threefold: the beneficiaries' concern, a community concern and concern for their tenants.

The first two concerns are met by the income of the trust, the third, however, is met by a specific lettings strategy.

First, rent levels must not be seen to be exploitative. In consequence, all rents are registered as 'fair' rents. There is no attempt to exercise the right of financial benefit over and above a level deemed acceptable by established authorities. Rent control legislation, therefore, is not an issue for this type of landlord.

Secondly, the legislation governing security of tenure is not disputed. A preference for long-term tenants, including the encouragement of succession right to sons and daughters, is compatible with the wishes of stability and peaceful enjoyment (peace that is for the trust) sought by the trust. The less attention drawn to the trust's activity of letting residential property, the more thankful the trust. As a charitable trust, their public image cannot afford to be tarnished by public scandal.

The Church Commissioners

A considerable amount has been written about the role of the Church Commissioners as landlords of private rented housing (Sutherland, 1968; Harloe *et al.*, 1974; Furbey and Skinner, 1982). Recent discussion of the Church Commission's role as a residential landlord has focussed upon the disposal of part of their higher-rented residential stock, mainly on the Maida Vale Estate. The residential portfolio of the Commissioners is in fact quite varied. It ranges from a series of smaller 'Octavia Hill' estates, 1,900 flats and houses in total, to the more prestigious Hyde Park Estates which include a number of period buildings in terraces and squares. In 1983, the Commissioners managed approximately 8,000 properties, the majority on the Maida Vale and Hyde Park Estates.

In terms of the Commissioners' overall net income from property, however, residential property made up only 16 per cent in 1982, or £5.8 million. Moreover, income from land and property represented 35 per cent of total income in 1982. Alongside investments in equities and offices the residential property component is relatively unimportant as a capital asset for the Commission. Whilst this is true in economic terms, the same cannot be said for its social 'value'. The Commission is extremely sensitive about its management and control of residential housing, and not without reason. Housing is after all a socially raw issue. The image of the Church as a slum landlord is a well-known slander and acts as a considerable pressure upon the activities of the Commission.

The Commissioners' recent financial strategy towards housing incorporates attempts to balance, or resolve the tension, between both economic and social interests. The freehold sale of nearly one-third of the properties on the Maida Vale Estate and the extensive improvement programme represents part of its financial strategy to meet the ever-increasing costs of the salaries, pensions and housing of the Church of England clergy. This strategy has attracted criticism for its neglect of the interests of low income tenants. As the estate undergoes gentrification, lower income tenants have experienced higher rent levels. In consequence, the Commission has been accused of putting monetary concern before social concern. This is not an accurate portrayal, but nor is it entirely misplaced. In fact, it could be argued that the Commission is 'trapped' by its very structure, an obligation to meet both investment and social aims, in consequence it has acted to realise these aims. The solution has taken a spatial form.

Although the Commission is steadily decreasing their investment in rented housing, on the grounds of better yields on other forms of investment and the social displeasure that rented housing brings if mismanaged, one part of their residential portfolio continues to fulfil philanthropic principles of social concern and social need – the 'Octavia Hill' estates. Numbering 1,900 houses and flats, they represent the 'housing conscience' of the Church. They fulfil the traditional charitable need of the Church to 'house the poor'. With the development of public housing, albeit decreased in stock under the Thatcher administration, it could be argued that such a felt obligation is anachronistic. Be that as it may, this ideological legacy still has an impact today. A liking for traditional assets dies hard for the synod. Even though housing has significantly decreased as a percentage of the Commission's assets, the Church is unlikely to completely disinvest from residential property. Housing possesses the 'marks' of philanthropy in a way that offices or stocks and shares do not and never will. The erection of a new housing estate in South London in the late 1960s bears testament to this need.

The Commission, then, controls two different types of housing, two different types of asset; one, the high value property, is subject to a judicious economic policy of profitable gain, and the other, the lower value property, appeases their social concerns. On the 'Octavia Hill' estates legislation governing security of tenure and rent controls does not restrict the Commission's management of these properties. Stability, conformity, thriftyness, still pervade the management's ideology. The value of these estates as an asset is social not economic. Short-term profitability is a poor second to the values of the extended family network, the social significance of making regular rent payments and community values. It is the philanthropic estates that represent the historic endowment of the Church as a landlord, and not the Maida Vale and Hyde Park developments.

Nevertheless, the sum total of the Commissioner's activities as a residential landlord is open to the public gaze. The advantageous tax position they enjoy (they receive all the benefits of charitable status, yet they are not a registered charity), the financial subsidies they receive (on the basis of a housing association status, yet they are not a registered housing association), and the image of the Church as one of social concern, all operate as constraining pressures upon the actions of the Commissioners. The estates they own and manage are no longer as extensive as in the inter-war years, but the flow of disinvestment is likely to stop at the gates of the philan-thropic estates. The fashionable Hyde Park Estate still carries with it the possibility of conveying the 'wrong image' for the Church as a 'luxury' landlord and could well depart from the Commission's investment port-folio. The mixed portfolio that would meet the Commission's approval is a minor stake in housing that reflects their benevolent image and a much larger series of investments in anonymous, impersonal assets such as stocks and shares and commercial property. The power of both the Church's socially inscribed meaning of housing and the predominant negative image attached to residential landlords acts to modify and shape the economic policy adopted by the Commissioners.

The Private trust – a family estate

In the mid-nineteenth century the hillsides of Islington provided a dormitory for city executives, merchants and clerks. As Jenkins in his book *Landlords to London* states, 'these were the great days of the Thornhill, Milner Gibson, Henry Penton and Northampton Estates' (1978, p. 94). An extensive sequence of squares and terraces sprang up to meet market demand, a demand that dramatically increased the population of Islington from 37,000 in 1831 to 155,000 in 1861. One of the estates built to meet that demand for rented accommodation still currently occupies a distinctive sloping site overlooking much of Central London. The attractive facades, the hillside terraces and the squares are still evident. The period since the mid nineteenth century and especially in recent years, however, bears witness to both social and physical changes.

First, much of the estate was in an advanced state of dilapidation by the 1970s. Lack of amenities and inadequate maintenance turned once attractive properties into a run-down series of dwellings. In 1979, three-fifths of estates, the properties in the poorest condition, were sold by the agents of the trust to the local authority. The remainder of the properties have been subject to a policy of leasehold sales since that date. The second change, therefore, is one of tenure. The estate is now a mix of predominantly public housing, owner-occupation and a smaller number of privately rented properties. The remaining tenants are mainly low income older tenants, originally on controlled rents, but now subject to registered rents. As the rented properties become vacant, they are put up for sale on the open market on a leasehold basis.

What factors, what characteristics about this particular type of landlord, a family trust estate, have shaped this contemporary policy? The obligation of the agents under Trust Act legislation to obtain the best investment for their clients is obviously a major determinant. By 1980, the trust had diversified its investments into commercial and agricultural property on the basis of the higher financial returns available from those assets. The agents had no intention of reinvesting their capital in housing. Nevertheless, the social meaning of their housing, still plays an important part in shaping the disinvestment and letting strategy of the trust.

Disinvestment, for example, is not on a freehold basis. The 'family' has an historical association with the area, the site is the physical embodiment of the family, and as such the image of the area and the housing within it represents the window, if you like, through which the public and other institutions judge it. A policy of leasehold sales allows the continuance of the family name in the area; it allows control over the type of owners and their activities, and, in a more economic vein, it allows the trust to retain an appreciating asset in potential land value.

In terms of their letting policy, the management and control of the remaining tenanted properties continue in an historical 'benign' manner, but with a difference. There is no sincerity in the relationship. The letting of properties is simply a temporary expedient, a treading water exercise, until the whole estate is sold on leasehold. The pace at which such a policy may be pursued, however, is limited by the possibility of scandal becoming attached to the family name of the trust. The past, in the form of a benign, estate landlord limits contemporary action, but it is not strong enough to forestall an eventual policy of disinvestment from the lettings market. In this case, unlike the philanthropic or guardianship gestures of the two previous landlords within this category of landlords, the constitutive meaning of property for the trust may be preserved outside of the rented tenure. The 'good' name of the family is maintained without the patronage associated with certain landlord-tenant relationships.

For all three landlords within this group, however, the constitutive social meaning attached to their property structures their activity in the rented housing market. The ideological dimension modifies and translates their economic practices, a dimension that has its roots in the past, but one that lives on as a causal legacy.

Employer landlords

We turn now to the second of our six types of landlords, looking at the letting strategy of a brewery company. Because of our limited data on employer landlords, for reasons already referred to, it is useful to situate the case study in the context of the wider group.

Employer landlords in the private sector are an anomaly among residential landlords. Letting residential property, or what is commonly known as tied accommodation, for this group is not undertaken to derive financial benefit from the properties themselves, it is solely and often reluctantly undertaken to accommodate employees who are deemed essential to the running of a business. Essential, in the sense that particular types of business require labour to be on 'call' at irregular times or at regular periods throughout a seven-day week. In geographical terms and in the size and nature of the enterprises, the tied accommodation sector is diverse, ranging from a predominance of the hotel, catering and licenced trades in urban areas to the preponderance of farming and land owning interests in rural areas. It is impossible to do justice to this complexity here and for our purposes it is not entirely necessary. Our concern here is to illustrate how, in general, employer landlords operate within a different set of ideological constraints from other types of landlords. That said, the urban focus of our study does not stretch our findings to include employer landlords in non-urban areas.

Elsewhere, Newby *et al* (1978) in their study of agricultural property relations in East Anglia, have shown how some of the various ideological strands woven around a unitary conception of private property are drawn upon by small, large and institutional agricultural capital to justify the ownership of land. Although their discussion of ideological relations only refers to landed property and not to residential property, it is of interest to note the authors' indication of a stewardship ideology which was held by a number of the larger landowners with regard to all of their property, including that of tied housing. Central to this idea of stewardship is the characteristic of guardianship, a notion of holding and protecting property on behalf of the community. An obligation to others that is conferred by the right of ownership. We have met this characteristic before in the case of the charitable trust landlord and it is one that is shared by traditional landowners and traditional landlords alike. Both groups are, in a sense, representations of a past age of landlord and tenant relations, yet it is an age which still colours the lives of their tenants today.

For the majority of private employer landlords, however, service sector employers, small farmers and the like, the rented housing within their ownership is only a means to a business end; a facility provided by the employer which is considered necessary to the efficient and smooth operation of an enterprise. Yet as a facility it is quite unlike the employer's provision of protective clothing or catering facilities; as the 'home' of their employees it holds the potential to disrupt business efficiency and hence profits. The following case study of a Brewery company illustrates the tension between the social and economic role that rented accommodation plays for the enterprise, and, although it is not typical of employer landlords in all respects, it serves to highlight how this group of landlords evaluates and negotiates its rights of possession.

The Brewery company

The Brewery company is just one of a number of breweries that has lost its independence as a result of the monopolisation of the licensed trade by the large food and drink conglomerates. It is a managing company for the parent company, located in the Northern Home Counties serving much of that area and parts of North London. The company owns 600 public houses and five off-licences, of which 490 of the public houses are let on a 'tied' basis to self-employed 'landlords' who rent both the public house and the accommodation, and purchase their stocks solely from the brewery. A further eighty-three public houses are managed directly by employees of the company who live and work on the company premises, but pay no direct residential rent. The small remainder of public houses, often connected to restaurants, are let on annual leases to private companies and individuals and are for all intents and purposes outside of the scope of this case-study.

Strictly speaking, neither the self-employed tenants, nor the employee tenants are representative of normal landlord-tenant relations insofar as the element of residential rent is virtually insignificant to the owning company. Yet for both types of tenant the security of their accommodation is dependent upon their ability to realise a profitable turnover of trade for the Brewery. Moreover, a certain percentage of this turnover is basically considered as residential rent, although no distinction is made in accounting terms. Despite the blurred nature of the landlord-tenant relation, there is a contractual obligation to live in a particular premise as a requirement of employment or agreement with the Brewery.

Two reasons were offered by the Brewery to justify this obligation: first, security, the need to protect the company's stock, and secondly, the hours of the trade, the need to call upon labour to work outside of normal working hours. Interestingly, neither reason was considered to be a necessary justification for the company to provide accommodation on the premises for their tenants. This represents a shift in company policy. The representative of the company spoke of a move towards an 'American model': the employment of 'professional landlords', employees working in newly constructed public houses without accommodation; the idea of landlords operating on a 'time-share' basis, a form of shiftwork for landlords; and the decreasing importance of security as an issue as new methods of protecting stock became available. The thinking behind this model is not hard to understand. The problems carried by the tied employment system for the employer are no longer balanced by the need to ensure an efficient business operation. In particular, the right of the employer, the owner, to dispose of the property, or more correctly in this instance, to repossess the living accommodation in the case of a tenant dismissed, fairly or unfairly, represents a potential three-month disruption to the business as the tenant works out his/her notice to quit. A disruption that is no longer considered by this particular company to be entirely necessary.

Nevertheless, the vast majority of the company's public houses do possess 'built-in' accommodation and this disruption is a feature of their enterprise. This raises a significant difference between the economic interests of employer landlords and say those of commercial or financial landlords; whereas the latter groups exercise their right of disposal to sell housing on the domestic property market, employer landlords seek repossession to relet the accommodation in order to continue their business interests. This, in part, accounts for the relatively slow rate of decline of tied accommodation compared to the rest of the private rented market. Tenants of employer landlords are dismissed for employment related reasons, and not for increased rental yield or capital gain on residential property. In essence, the Brewery company is a business landlord, not a residential landlord. Together, the public house and the accommodation represent a joint business proposition.

Thus far, the business logic of the situation – the dismissal and the hire of new tenants appears to be a relatively straightforward affair. The logic is broken, however, by the fact that the facility transferred with the job is also a 'home', and is thus susceptible to public outcry – 'a cross to bear' in the eyes of the company. People, after all, may lose their jobs through inefficiency, but surely not their homes. The truth of this statement was acknowledged by the company and is itself an additional reason why employer landlords such as brewery companies are beginning to reconsider the necessity of providing tied accommodation to their tenants. A disruption of the company's business activities is not only caused by a change in the occupancy of residential tenancies, the change in itself may result in further disruption if a large Brewery conglomerate is publicly seen to have acted uncaringly towards the plight of those rendered homeless by *their* employment policy.

Informal landlords

In comparison with the other groups of landlords identified, informal landlords represent the most heterogeneous category. At first sight, the inclusion of landlords within this group may appear self-evident on the basis of the few properties owned by the individuals or because of the fact that resident landlords would fit uneasily into any other category of landlords. Indeed, there is an element of truth in this rather obvious categorisation. Of greater significance, however, is their limited financial orientation and their sharp experience of the tension between their property (or properties) as personal possessions and as a source of economic gain. It is for these reasons that these landlords fall within the informal category of landlords. The case studies in this section exemplify these characteristics, although, it should be pointed out that they are not identical; they merely share the basic characteristics that bind them and distinguish them from the other types of landlord. Two of the case studies are resident landlords, the other is a non-resident landlord letting a property adjacent to the family dwelling. All three landlords identify closely with their right to 'control' their property during the period in which the use of it has been 'sold'. In common with investor landlords, as we shall see, they share a strong sense of individualism and independence. Unlike investor landlords, however, this characteristic often manifests itself as a resentment of their economic need to let accommodation and an attempt to deny tenants any right to treat the hired space as other than the owner's possession. Interestingly, few landlords within this group felt dissatisfied with the level of rental income received, despite, as we shall show in the next chapter, the generally low returns in this group. Their antagonism towards their tenants resulted from disputes over their right to supervise the use of their properties, rather than their right to benefit financially from them.

Mr C.

A first-generation Jamaican migrant, Mr C. purchased a four-storey nineteenth-century house in a quiet cul-de-sac in North Islington in 1950 through the financial help of relatives and a loan from a bank. At that time the property was considered an extended family home for himself, his wife, their children and close relatives. With the subsequent break up of the family, Mr C. retained possession of the property and lives in part of it with only one of his children. He lets the two upper storeys of the house as furnished flats to two separate tenants. His rationale for letting the accommodation was straightforward – he could not afford the upkeep of the mortgage repayments on his house, nor could he meet the costs of insurance and rates. The income from his occupation as a painter and decorator did not cover his financial obligations and his only other source of income was the house. In consequence, he hired out rooms and adopted the role of landlord.

At the risk of a caricature, Mr C. could be described as an 'involuntary' landlord; involuntary in the sense that he had little choice but to utilise the only other resource available to him to meet the costs of keeping and maintaining his home. The word 'home' is deliberately used here, because the house possessed a meaning for Mr C. over and above its role as a type of shelter or an investment. The property expressed his identity; it was his possession, all that 'he owned' in the world. In comparison to his other possessions, the property was 'the' possession; it endowed him with a sense of belonging. This sense of having roots shaped his actions, the house had to be retained at all costs. As a result, the idea of selling the property and purchasing a smaller property suitable to his reduced needs was unthinkable. The house was decorated in his image and it stood out from the rest of the street.

The predicament of Mr C. expressed itself in a particular letting relation. First, the rent levels set by Mr C. were privately agreed and calculated on a blend of moral and economic grounds. Set at below market value, a standard of which Mr C. seemed unaware, the rent levels were calculated to meet both a contribution to the financial upkeep of the house and to justify Mr C.'s own moral sense of what the accommodation was worth. This attitude was coupled with a concern that the tenants within his home were not simply contractual partners, they were also there to 'help' both him and his son if any 'trouble' should befall them. This was, then, a complex calculation and one that he arrived at almost as a bribe to induce guilt in his tenants. A bribe to meet *his* requirements in *his* home.

Secondly, a conflict of interest between the landlord, Mr C., and his tenants presented itself in the use of the residential space. The landlord recognised it was equally the tenant's 'home' as well as his own 'home' but only in a qualified restricted sense. He, the landlord, owned the home, whereas the tenants 'only rented' the home. The difference, as perceived by Mr C. justified his right of control, his right to police his possessions. The point at issue was not one of excessive concern for the lifestyle of his tenants, but one of concern for 'their' use of 'his' possessions. The fact that he had sold the use of such objects for a period of time did not appear to enter into his perception of the situation. The right of ownership etched in a unitary ideology of private property overrode any considerations he may have had over the division of property rights between landlord and tenant.

Challenged on this issue, this type of landlord withdraws under the ideological shield of private property and exercises the ultimate form of control – eviction. The right to dispose of one's property is not at issue here, for this type of landlord has little choice but to relet the accommodation to meet their chosen needs: the ownership and preservation of their home.

Mrs P.

The second case study is also an illustration of the close control exercised by informal landlords over their perceived possessions. Indeed, this appears to be *the* marked characteristic of informal landlords and perhaps, the root of an inescapable conflict between this type of landlord and their tenants. The differences between the landlord discussed here and the landlord cited in the previous case are to be found in their different economic situations and the symbolic meaning they attached to their property.

Purchased through a bank loan in 1966, the property, a three-storey dwelling, remained in the owner-occupied tenure for over a decade until the death of her husband led Mrs P., the owner, to let two of the three storeys on a furnished basis to two separate tenants. The rental payments, which were agreed on a private basis, initially supplemented Mrs P.'s income and covered the mortgage repayments. A change in her financial circumstances, however, which arose through her employer declaring her redundant, altered the economic significance of the rental payments from a secondary source of income to the ·major source of income. As in the previous case study, the letting of accommodation became a real economic necessity for Mrs P. and was simply no longer a useful source of finance which eased her financial obligations.

Unlike Mr C., however, no moral considerations entered into her calculation of rent levels. Her property was indeed perceived as a home, but it was not considered as a source of identity, nor as a source of status; it was a home plain and simple, the place where she happened to live. And a place which, if the rent levels were set high enough, could offer a reasonably high financial remuneration. It is difficult to estimate the financial return on vacant possession value but in comparison to registered rents in the same street the rents obtained were in excess of those set by the rent officer for broadly similar accommodation.

Of perhaps greater interest in this case, is that the high degree of formality that she exercised with her tenants led her to an excessive concern for the supervision of her possessions. Resentment was expressed by her, not merely towards the lack of care exhibited by tenants towards her property, but also to the extent that tenants who, on their departure, failed to redecorate the accommodation were regarded with disdain. Resentment over tenants' *use* of landlords' possessions, despite their payment for such usage, was a common feature identified among informal landlords and points, once again to the degree of protection exhibited by the individuals within this group towards their property. Obviously, the felt need to protect property is also present in other types of landlords, but the intensity with which it is felt, in particular by resident landlords, owes much to the ideology of the 'home' and the fact that they as a group often have little economic choice but to open their home to 'outsiders'.

Mr & Mrs F.

The last case study in this group, a Greek family, arrived in Britain shortly after the end of the Second World War, and entered the private lettings market in 1963. They raised the capital to purchase the property adjoining their own dwelling from a number of friends and through a short-term bank loan. The reasoning behind their purchase of a nineteenth-century three-storey dwelling with one sitting tenant did not spring from a clear desire to enter the rented housing market. The stimulus came from two directions: the prestige accorded to property owners and the value of property as an asset for their offspring. In the latter sense, they share the investment orientation of a number of other landlord types, in particular that of the investor landlord. What locates Mr & Mrs F. within the informal category, however, as opposed to one of the other groups is first, the limited extent of their investment and the financial resources available to them, and secondly, the indirect role that letting accommodation fulfils for them as property owners. The purchase of a second residential property was undertaken by them, not for the explicit reason of capital gain, either through rental returns or potential sales value, but to extend the *family's* assets, assets which are enjoyed by the family and act as a source of status for the family. The notion of enjoyment and status were thus linked to housing as a specific form of property by Mr & Mrs F. and were not extended to *every* form of property. In effect, the dwelling purchased was considered as an extension of the family's personal possessions.

The implications of this conception of their investment can be seen by their attitude towards both rental income and tenants. Rent levels for the three furnished tenancies were not particularly low; they were calculated to meet all financial outgoings on the property, in particular the cost of mortgage repayments, rates and insurance. Costs, they stated, generally exceeded the rental income, especially when maintenance and repairs to the property were taken into consideration. Whether this was a true depiction of the circumstances or not, the role that rental income performed for this particular landlord had less to do with any economic gain than with the preservation of the property until the house was required by the family. As Mr F. expressed it: 'the tenants occupy the property and pay for it, until it is wanted for our own use'. In other areas of the family's economic life (they owned a small café) a strictly economic orientation was adopted, and the two types of property, commercial and residential, were not equated.

The attitude of Mr & Mrs F. resulted in a specific letting strategy. Tenants, in general, were friends of the family, people who would tend to look after the property and acknowledge the ownership rights of the landlord. In effect, the tenants met the landlord's main objective: to finance, maintain and return the property when required. The scale on which this type of transaction was conducted, the *one* property, allowed for the possibility of such a relationship. Owners who let a number of properties on a commercial basis would have to face the issue of a tenant's right to security of tenure. In this case, the issue was not significant for Mr & Mrs F.; the needs of the family dictated the extent of house ownership, not the potential financial gains that such ownership can entail. It is perhaps no surprise, therefore, that the family involved in this letting relationship did not consider themselves as landlords but as property owners. The letting of property formed an integral part of their concern to own and enjoy a prestigious possession – a house.

Investor landlords

This group of landlords carries the collective image of the landlord, which over the years has fed the stereotyped impression of landlords as 'folk devils'. As with any stereotype, a number of traits have been locked into a fixed image – the unscrupulous individual, preoccupied with status and their power over others, and usually male. Stereotypes are always partial, never completely accurate, but the image of the investor landlord as a 'folk devil' possesses a grain of truth. It is more appropriate today, however, to attribute this image to the commercial, rather than the investor landlord. Vulnerability is one of the main characteristics that describe the investor landlords that remain in the rented housing market; vulnerability to change, vulnerability to a world that no longer recognises their status, nor their moral authority.

The case studies within this group comprise a partnership, two private property companies and one individual landlord. The number of properties let by each landlord varied from three houses up to sixty self-contained flats. Each had been letting residential property for over twenty years in varying numbers and in varying types, ranging from houses, flats, to maisonettes. Each has limited access to sources of finance, mainly bank loans, and all three possess an orientation to the market that is rooted in housing as a 'real investment'. This ideological orientation shapes their perception of their assets and influences the manner in which they conduct their relationships with their tenants. As with traditional landlords, investor landlords are an anachronism, yet their ideology of 'service' still lingers on and shapes their activity in the market place.

An individual landlord – 'The Property Man'

As the title suggests, property, more correctly residential property, is the favoured investment of this individual. In 1938, he purchased his first property and now owns and lets three houses, and a shop with a flat above. His initial purchase was obtained through a building society mortgage, and his subsequent purchases, the last of which was in 1953, were obtained through short-term bank loans.

In 1938 his rationale for investment in private rented housing was uncomplicated – property was a secure investment. The rental income would provide him with a pension in his retirement. Forty odd years on, his faith in the residential lettings market is still firm. Firm, despite the fact that the landlord was aware of less troublesome investments in commercial property and stocks and shares. Nor was the landlord unaware of the returns from these alternative investments. Is this a case of property 'blinkers'? Not entirely.

For this landlord housing was considered primarily for its rental income and not its capital value. The properties were considered for their future sales value, but this did not influence either the calculation of rent levels or the current assessment value of the investment. Rents were privately agreed, and achieved a rate of return on capital equivalent to investment in shops. This is a high rate of return for residential property, but it is high because of the low debt repayment attached to property purchased thirty to forty years ago and also because of the minimal standards of maintenance carried out over the years.

The properties were not dilapidated, but they were not maintained at a level considered adequate by the tenants. Indeed, maintenance was inadequate but the landlord refused to see this state of affairs. He interpreted the situation as one of the tenants demanding proprietary rights, of failure to recognise who controlled the affairs of the properties. In effect, the landlord believed that the 'service' he provided was inadequately recognised by the tenants. This 'service' ideology has its roots in the period before the Second World War and has no legitimacy in the housing market today, yet it still clouds certain landlord-tenant relationships. The social status that the ownership of property once brought is no longer applicable. Nor was it ever an extensive positive status, but it is still 'lived' as such by certain landlords. A strong streak of individualism characterises this type of landlord and it is expressed through the ownership of property and the 'service' ideology. Other types of investment such as stocks and shares were looked upon with distaste by this landlord. The impersonal nature of the investment did not bestow the social status he sought to gain from property.

Locked into this sense of individualism was a reaction against bureacratic authority. Legislation governing the private rented sector was known in detail, but avoided if possible. Rent controls were evaded in preference for privately agreed rents, and the security of tenure provisions played down in preference for personal tenancy agreements. The denial of tenants rights that results from these personal agreements was not considered as a loss by this type of landlord; rather their replacement by a personal bond was deemed to be mutually beneficial to both landlord and tenant. The unequal power vested in the landlord by these personal agreements does not appear to figure in the landlord's perception of the arrangement. This type of landlord desires both respect and status as well as an economic return, and is at a failure to understand why they are not forthcoming.

A private property company – a family concern

Despite the company status attached to this landlord, the individuals concerned showed a similar orientation to the rented housing market as the previous landlord. In effect, the company status acted as an appropriate legal vehicle for tax purposes. The shareholders of the company, the husband and wife, set up the private property company in 1965 to reduce their tax burden on the rental income received. In payment, as it were, for lower tax rates on retained profits, the shareholders had to meet certain book-keeping requirements to present annual audits. The formation of a private company was certainly to their financial advantage, but other landlords operating as individuals, dealing with approximately the same income (as we shall see) preferred to use evasive practices rather than cumbersome, and administrative legal practices to reduce their tax burden.

In common with the 'property man' the number of properties they owned was small. At the time of the survey they let two multi-occupied dwellings split into fifteen units, and two self-contained flats. Financed through building society mortgages and bank loans, they had built up to this number since their initial purchase in 1960.

The purchase of all their property took place in the following five years and it represented a long-term investment for an income in their retirement years. They are now both pensioners and derive the majority of their income from letting property and interest on their bank deposit accounts.

Their initial decision to invest in residential property reflected the 'obviousness' of property as a secure long-term investment. Managed and maintained correctly, the properties were considered a befitting manner to realise investment income. Letting property was not considered simply as an exercise in providing 'roofs over peoples heads', it involved 'a way of life', an investment that entailed 'paternal' obligation and responsibilities. The corollary of this benevolent approach was the close supervision – up to fourteen hours a week management – and a detailed interest in tenants lives. At its most extreme form the role of landlord as 'father confessor' was raised. Underlying this form of landlord-tenant relationship was a contradiction in the right of control. The landlord was at pains to point out that the tenants had a 'home'; this encouraged respect for both property and the landlord. At the same time the landlord pointed out that 'it's my house, but it's their home'. The relationship between landlord and tenant was not perceived as an informal, social link, though it was perceived as more than a business transaction. From the tenants' viewpoint, the relationship was seen as one of excessive, patronising concern: less to do with them as individuals than with their adopting a 'correct lifestyle' which, in turn, would maintain the upkeep of the furnished dwellings.

Once again, the legislation governing tenants rights were sidestepped by the landlord if possible. Rents were privately agreed and tenants encouraged to stay, assuming that is, that a correct lifestyle was maintained. The image of the landlord as an unscrupulous person was strongly resented by this type of landlord. Such caricatures did not mesh with their own notion of 'benevolent service'. The economic relationship between landlord and tenant was closely monitored, rents were by no means lower than the market rate, and the regular payment of rent eagerly sought. Yet the idea of the relationship as a simple cash nexus was abhorrent to this type of landlord. Landlordism as an economic relationship does not convey to them the full meaning of letting property. By covering the rental transaction with a layer of benevolence, the act of monetary gain is rationalised as a service.

A partnership – the hire firm

Three generations made up the partnership which had its roots in a decorators and builders firm established in 1870. Their move into the rented housing market started with the purchase of fifteen properties in the early 1930s from capital generated by the family business and was built up into a stock of sixty-two houses over the two subsequent decades. In 1970, the firm branched into plant hire and changed its legal status from a private company to a partnership to reduce its tax liabilities. In 1982 the partnership had a turnover of £50,000 per annum, of which the letting of residential property formed a minor component. The partnership is first and foremost a plant hire business and second a 'house' hire business. The contrast between the two forms of hire associated with the two commodities makes an interesting comparison.

The move into the lettings market in the 1930s stemmed from the grandfather's concern for a financial provision for his old age and as a legacy for his offspring. In effect this foresight was never required. The rental income provides only a small percentage of their current overall income and the properties have fulfilled an alternative function of providing security for a series of bank loans for the partnership, particularly in the transition stage, when they changed the nature of their operations. Before 1970, the properties also provided work for the employees of the firm in the seasonal slack periods of the building and decorating trade. Conversion into self-contained flats and redecoration continued over a number of years in the post-war period to realise a greater rental income from the properties. By 1970, sixty of the sixty-two houses had been converted into self-contained flats, all unfurnished. After 1970, with the change from a building firm to a plant hire firm, the relationship between the two activities of the firm was no longer complementary.

Yet, although the relationship was no longer compatible, the mode of commercial activity was identical: both involved a hire operation. This, of course, is qualified by the fact that machinery is hired on a short-term basis, whereas, in contrast, housing is hired out over a longer time period. Nevertheless, both involve a letting relationship, and both involve rights of control and benefit over the commodity lent. The nub of the difference between the two operations, however, lies with the ideological nature and use fulfilled by the different products. Houses are consumed as 'homes'; heavy machinery represents a form of capital put to use in a productive capacity. Rented housing involves a contested terrain of property rights and interpretations; with heavy machinery the contract of rights of hire is largely undisputed. The difference in the ideological nature and the use value of the two commodities has implications for the orientation adopted by the bailor towards the respective commodities.

As a provider of plant machinery, the firm expressed satisfaction with the conduct of the hire business. The 'service' to industry was acknowledged as a legitimate business concern and the rental income justified by virtue of the capital invested in the machinery. In contrast, the role of the partnership as a landlord did not receive the same degree of legitimacy. The 'service' to tenants was not acknowledged by the tenants, nor by the local authority. The hire of machinery conducted in a free market, largely unfettered by legislative control (aside from health and safety regulations) contrasted sharply with the hire of housing caught in a web of legislative controls and regulations. This interference was resented as a detraction from the firm's ability to provide a 'service' to tenants. It undermined the landlords' 'role' as a 'provider'. It is interesting to note that the firm did acknowledge the different uses which the two commodities performed, but failed to grasp the differences in legitimacy accorded to the different roles.

The lack of legitimacy accorded to the provision of rented housing as a service had influenced the partnership's decision to disinvest from the rented housing market. As vacant possession is realised a policy of sales has been adopted. Offers have also been made to tenants to encourage them to purchase their dwellings at tenanted value. It is obviously difficult to disentangle the extent to which the lack of legitimacy accorded to landlords has shaped this policy, but the decision does not reflect a simple economic rationality. Rents reflected market values, the majority were privately agreed, and a financial return comparable to commercial property was received. This high rate of return is almost certainly due to the low debt repayments incurred on the long-term ownership of property that has been passed down through the three generations of the firm. Equally, the inherited nature of the properties has also shaped the 'service' mentality adopted by this type of landlord. A mentality that is no longer accommodated in the contemporary rented housing market. What is of interest, then, is that the way in which the tension between the social and economic roles of rented housing has been negotiated by this landlord has resulted in a policy of disinvestment, despite the reasonable rate of return on capital achieved.

Commercial landlords

The activities of commercial landlords are different again. They are structured predominantly by an economic set of relations. Rented housing for them as a group is assessed for its profitable return, almost to the complete exclusion of any notion of service or consideration of enjoyment connected to the provision of housing. The notion of rented property as people's 'homes' does not modify their economic calculation and judgement. Housing, like any other commodity, is considered as a form of capital, from which a profitable gain may be successfuly realised. As a group commercial landlords exercise a form of impersonal control over their assets; a control that is geared towards the straightforward execution of their rights to benefit financially from their properties. Largely petty bourgeois in orientation, ownership is the only form of legitimate control recognised. No fragmentation of rights between landlord and tenant is acknowledged.

The commercial landlords interviewed ranged from a builder landlord owning 150 properties, mainly houses and purpose built flats; a property group incorporating a private property company and private trusts with control over 362 dwellings, and a private individual who let fifty-nine properties. The characteristics they share in common are both economic and ideological. First, all were dependent upon private loans or short-term bank loans for capital; secondly, all required a reasonable rate of return on their investments in the short term to meet their financial liabilities; and thirdly, all exhibited an indifference to the ideological connotations that mark housing as a separate commodity. Together, the three characteristics stem from the initial rationale of this group's entrance into the rented housing market: an objective of short-term profit maximisation as opposed to either a long-term capital investment or the provision of a service.

The trading landlord

Although this landlord was operating as a private individual at the time of interview, he had previously traded under five different private companies, all of which had dealt with property in the capacity of both landlord and builder and decorator. The decision to operate as a private individual, and not as a limited company or partnership, stemmed from the nature of his operations – a practice which involved covert, illegal payments, and hence difficulty in presenting formal, accurate accounts. A strong sense of individualism shaped his preference for a free market in rented housing and strengthened his reaction to the state's regulation of company activities and also the letting of property.

This type of landlord is first and foremost a small-scale entrepreneur. Letting property was a means simply to realise a capital gain. This particular landlord took this orientation to its logical economic conclusion and treated the letting of property as merely a phase in the overall process of buying and selling property. Since he had entered the rented housing market in the early

1960s, he had continually bought, converted and sold a large number of properties.

A considerable percentage of these properties were bought with sitting tenants at below vacant possession value. In such cases, the landlord did offer alternative accommodation in one of the hundred odd dwellings he tended to own at any one point in time. On his own admittance, the alternative accommodation was rarely of a comparable status, usually smaller in size, although often with the same low level of amenities and in the same poor condition. If tenants refused to move, a policy of payment to tenants or harassment was practised. On obtaining vacant possession of a property, the dwellings would be modernised and placed for sale on the domestic property market, or, if the market was depressed, let as unfurnished on the rented market, pending a later sale. The different activities amounted to an overall strategy in which both rental income and sales income met financial liabilities (both loan repayments and tax payments), increased capital growth, and produced a high rate of profitability over time. Rental yields in effect represented a tide-over to meet loan repayments in periods of recession in the domestic property market. In general, income from rents represented approximately 15 per cent of total annual business income.

Housing, for this type of landlord therefore, is simply considered as an economic commodity; it is not considered as someone's 'home'. In consequence, the legislation governing the rights of control and use of a property by tenants is widely disregarded by this type of landlord. Security of tenure provisions and rent control legislation are known, but ignored. They amount to a series of obstacles which can be overcome either by harassment, tenants' ignorance or fear of exercising their legal rights, or by recourse to the courts by the offer of alternative accommodation. If the latter action is taken, all those landlords interviewed in this group anticipated a court ruling in their favour for between 50 and 70 per cent of their actions.

Of the three landlords discussed here, however, only this particular landlord openly justified harassment as a means of overcoming 'bureaucratic interference, in what should be a free market'. Without recourse to such measures he considered the buying, letting and selling of residential property would not realise the degree of financial turnover required to meet loan repayments and further reinvestment in housing. Adherence to the legislation governing the rented sector implied a disruption to the cycle of investment and disinvestment. The tenants rights, the other half of the letting relationship, do not figure in this economic rationale. Nor has the public image of the private landlord as a shady and unscrupulous character affected his mode of operation. The cap fits, and it is certainly worn.

The property group

A private property company formed the backbone of this group. The major shareholders of the company were the landlord and his wife; the company was directed by the landlord and the managing agents were another limited company run by the same individual. For over forty years an estate agent, the career of this individual as a commercial landlord had developed in the early post-war years and had mushroomed in the late 1960s and 1970s. Much of his initial property was bought from one of the larger, traditional estate landlords in Islington who, in the 1950s, was under financial pressure to sell property, and also from a private trust in the same area who decided to disinvest in the late 1960s. Throughout the 1970s the landlord adopted a strategy of concentrating the sitting tenants in his properties into a small number of the poorer properties he owned. The remaining vacant properties were sold on the domestic property market, either as 'town houses' or self-contained flats, to high income, middle-class owner-occupiers who represented part of the demand to move back into inner city areas. The tenants of the properties were either offered money to leave or offered alternative accommodation in the poorer properties.

By 1982 the landlord had continued to purchase, let and sell properties, both within and outside of the London Borough of Islington. In recent years, the majority of his lettings were to be found in the more fashionable boroughs of London, let on a furnished basis, through licence agreements, to young, single tenants. The majority of this accommodation was to be found in multiple occupied dwellings.

This particular landlord, then, operated two strategies. In one area where demand for owner-occupation was high, properties were sold on the open market at the expense of tenants' rights and wishes. In another area, where a demand for furnished lettings offered high rental returns a strategy of letting property was operated. In both strategies, however, the legal rights of tenants were displaced. A decanting procedure operated to the disadvantage of sitting tenants on the Islington estate, and a policy of licenced agreements with privately agreed rents operated in areas of high tenant demand. Some sitting tenants had had their rents registered, but a number of these had been phased out after they had lapsed.

The long-term orientation of this landlord, however, was to buy and sell property, rather than to let accommodation. The state of the domestic property market in a particular area dictated which strategy – to sell or to let – was adopted at which particular time. In some instances, property was let in anticipation of greater capital gains from sales at a later date. Moreover, only a limited number of sales would be made by the landlord each year to distribute the tax liability on sales (Capital Gains Tax) evenly over a number of years.

It is also important to note that as the property group grew in size in terms of both its capital assets and the number of properties it owned, its financial constraints eased. This allowed the group to exercise a greater flexibility in the timing of its sales, insofar as the pressure to repay bank loans in a short period of time did not dictate the necessity of immediate sales. Nevertheless, there is a considerable difference between the sums of capital available to this type of commercial landlord and, say, a public property company or financial institution. This difference in the size of capital assets and sources of finance is an important determinant of the letting and disposal strategy operated by commercial and financial landlords. Commercial landlords buy, let and sell properties to enhance their capital growth and profitable returns; financial landlords tend to sell property because they do not wish to be seen to be involved in a speculative activity that may damage their public image. They have other options available. Financial landlords are primarily disinvestors, commercial landlords are investors *and* disinvestors. The process for commercial landlords is cyclical and unlike financial landlords it is virtually restricted to the residential property market.

An individual landlord

Not all landlords within this group exhibited the clear abuse of tenants' rights displayed by the two previous commercial landlords but all the landlords within this group operated with a wide knowledge of tenants' rights and of ways they could be circumvented. Their rationale for investing in the market is economic gain, the ability to repay financial loans and obtain a rate of profit well above the 2–5 per cent return on residential property with vacant possession that was considered acceptable in the late 1970s and early 1980s. The role of a commercial landlord, as noted above, is essentially that of a speculator, but it is an activity that is not restricted solely to the speculation of residential property in the housing market. It also involves speculation with rental income; that is, the ability to realise a high rental income through the avoidance of rent control measures and the ability to move out tenants who either cannot afford speculative rent levels or refuse to pay them.

The commercial landlord in question entered the lettings market in 1960 and since that date has bought and sold property through funds generated by a restaurant business and bank loans. In the early 1980s he let fifty properties, half in the Hastings area on the south coast of England and half in the London Borough of Islington.

Between 1972 and 1982 he had sold more properties than he had bought and he intended to further reduce his stock. The pace of disinvestment was dependent upon his ability to achieve vacant possession of his properties. Unlike the previous two commercial landlords he had not been as successful in ignoring tenants' rights of security of tenure. In part, this is because this aspect of private rented housing legislation had not concerned him. Unlike the trading landlords, the letting of property did not represent a mere phase in the overall process of investment and disinvestment. His business acumen was directed towards the maximisation of rental income on furnished lettings, provided on the basis of six monthly licence agreements. In the properties that he purchased with sitting tenants, who would have possessed security of tenure, his concern was to increase rental income rather than to obtain vacant possession for the sale of the properties.

An adequate rent level for this particular landlord had to cover maintenance costs, rates, the renewal of furniture and fittings, a provision for bad debts, and it had to keep up with the current rate of inflation plus a 10 per cent profit margin. Rents, where possible, were privately agreed, but at a figure well in excess of registered rents for similar properties in the Islington area. More importantly, an inability to secure binding rental contracts across the majority of his properties was one of the major reasons behind this commercial landlord's decision to disinvest. This inability to secure an agreement was perhaps unsurprising, given the high levels of rent demanded and the possible awareness of their right to a registered rent among his predominantly young, single tenants.

It was not the case, therefore, that this landlord took a decision to disinvest when vacant possession was achieved because he had experienced financial loss. Rather, it was the lower level of financial return received and the management difficulties experienced in 'patrolling' his commodities that informed his decision. In effect, the practice of speculation with rental income did not lead to the stable financial rewards that he had anticipated. Selling the use of housing over time through rental agreements can realise a high rate of financial return, particularly in the luxury lettings market, but in the mainstream market this aim is usually achieved at the expense of tenants' rights. Not all commercial landlords, however, are equally successful at exploiting their tenants, despite their orientation.

Financial landlords

As a group, financial landlords include a diverse collection of institutions ranging from some of the major representatives of finance capital to the more established public property companies. Within this group are to be found the large insurance companies such as the Prudential, Norwich Union and the Legal and General; the pension trust funds of institutions such as British Petroleum and the Post Office; and the funds of Building Societies, most notably the Abbey National. Also included in this group are the familiar names of the property world such as Freshwater, Peachey Property Corporation, London City and Westcliffe, and New London Properties.

In the previous chapter this group was attributed a predominantly economic orientation towards investment in the rented housing market, although one that did not follow a straightforward logic of profit maximisation. Despite the different financial constraints that these various institutions operate within, investment in private rented housing has little to offer this group either by way of investment yield or social status. Looking in turn at a major insurance company, a pension trust fund, and a national building society we show how the economic activities of large-scale capital in the residential lettings market has been shaped by an engraved ideology of property as 'homes' that is rarely acknowledged. The absorption of this ideology has mediated what has, therefore, largely been considered as the straightforward economic practices of disinvestment and investment carried out by large-scale capital in the rented housing market.

A major insurance company

In contrast to the housing markets of Western Europe, Britain's corporate institutions have not contributed to the development of a rented housing market in the post-war period. With insurance companies, their investment in property has been concentrated in the commercial rather than the residential property market, and indeed in recent decades, their investments in this area have continued to grow.

The insurance company discussed here may be considered as typical of this pattern of investment. An increasing proportion of its investment portfolio involves commercial property, and in recent years new property purchases have been concentrated in the retail sector. Residential property is of diminishing importance to the company, and for this reason a policy of sales is pursued for those properties no longer considered appropriate to the company's portfolio. This trend fits in and confirms the well-known scenario of institutional disinvestment from the residential lettings market.

This general scenario, however, fails to reveal the presence of two different types of residential property in the company's portfolio – and only one type is considered 'inappropriate'.

The 'acceptable' type of residential property entered the company's portfolio as part of larger packages of commercial investment which included a combination of shops, offices and industrial units at different sites. The majority of the residential properties are flats, mainly grouped in blocks. The reason for their acceptable nature, however, does not rest with the properties themselves; it lies with the whole commercial package of which they are a part. The packages represent neat, tidy blocks of capital in sought after locations where the combined development has a greater long-term asset value than the sum of the individual components. As a result the company has made no attempt to break the packages by disposing of the residential units. Nor has the company shown concern about the Rent Acts which govern the flexibility of their residential assets. Such a concern was considered unrelated to assets that are part of a wider investment strategy. A different yardstick, however, has been applied by the company to the evaluation of its remaining, separate residential properties.

The properties, some two hundred, two-storey, nineteenth-century working-class family dwellings in Islington, form the remnants of an investment decision taken in 1946. At that time the company purchased the freehold of the properties from a local clothing manufacturer who had owned the dwellings since 1850. The company's rationale for the purchase of the properties in 1946 is a little unclear. They cited 'an historic link with those who paid their insurance premiums', a reference to the tenants of the dwellings at that time. The truth of the sentiment, which may possess some substance, is perhaps best understood in the light of the sharp rise in house prices that occurred in the 1930s and continued to rise after the war. Between 1939 and 1948 house prices rose by just over 75 per cent, a dramatic rise and in stark contrast to the decline in house prices that occurred after the 1914–18 war. In 1946, despite the decreasing real return on rental yields in the post-war years, the purchase of housing as a long-term asset represented a viable investment proposition and one that was in line with the long-term economic interests of insurance companies to maintain the value of their capital over time to meet their long-term liabilities. Some thirty years later, in a different climate of investment opportunities and set against a significant increase in the company's investment capital, such assets were 'no longer considered appropriate to the company's portfolio'.

Since the early 1970s the company has actively pursued a policy of selling the properties in the domestic property market – mainly unmodernised and where possible with vacant possession. Two reasons were offered by the company for adopting a policy of selling this type of property and for not selling the lettings previously discussed: the low rental yield and the difficulties involved in the management and maintenance of a number of old, small family dwellings. On closer examination, the rental yield from the properties did not differ markedly from some of their commercial interests, nor was the management undertaken directly by the company. The properties were managed by agents. Yet the properties were still considered inappropriate to the company's portfolio of investments and the main reason why they were considered inappropriate is because they did not match up to the company's notion of a 'clean' investment.

The ideal 'clean' investment is a neat package of impersonal, stable, trouble-free assets that realises a steady rising income. Commercial property fits this model nicely, and so too does a certain type of residential property that is not readily perceived as a domestic 'home'. An assortment of small, family dwellings with long established residents, however, is subject to a degree of control and instability that is anathema to corporate investors. This sort of investment attracts public attention, which indeed it did, with frequent mention of the company's role as a landlord and 'speculator' in the local newspaper. Such publicity is a problem in as far as it cuts across the company's smooth execution of its property rights of benefit and disposal. Moreover, in contrast to informal or investor landlords, the right of control that property ownership offers is interpreted by financial landlords as the right to economic control over their assets, not personal control over their tenants. In the case of this particular insurance company, it was not residential property *per se* that carried a series of legal, economic and organisational disadvantages, but the ideological packaging in which certain types of rented housing were wrapped.

The pension trust fund

The amount of investment capital of this large multinational company tied up in residential property represents a tiny fraction of their total investments, some £500 million, which covers a vast range of property and non-property interests. Unlike the case history of the insurance company discussed, the pension fund of this company has never had a specific investment interest in residential property. Yet, as a result of their acquisition of public property companies and investment in commercial property, the fund is now a major landlord – by default. It owns three different types of dwellings in three different housing markets.

The first, some 6,000 properties, entered their ownership in 1969 when the pension fund acquired a public property company with a mixed portfolio of property investments, of which less than 20 per cent was residential. The vast majority of this residential inheritance is made up of nineteenth-century terraced housing located in South Wales and let on a leasehold basis. The remainder of this package is to be found in Islington and, in contrast with the Welsh property, consists of a small number of prime flats and houses that were formerly part of one of the nineteenth-century estates designed to accommodate the growing middle-class spilling out of Central London. Another of these estates was mentioned earlier in connection with the property owned by traditional landlords.

The third component of the fund's residential portfolio comprises 400 flats in Central London, also let on a leasehold basis, together with fifty luxury flats, with a rateable value that is sufficient to exclude them from the protection of the Rent Acts. The 400 flats were acquired from a large public property company in 1977 who, at that time, were experiencing financial difficulties.

The amount of residential property in the trust's investment portfolio is therefore both substantial and varied. And to match this variety in the letting relation, in the type and in the location of property the trust has devised different economic strategies. Each of which, it should be noted, is guided by a unitary ideology which signifies that property is property, and property is capital, and capital has to achieve an economic, not a moral return. Only in the case of the residential property in Central London, however, has the pension fund been able to maintain this ideology. In respect of the other two types of property, the commercial ethic has been modified by an opposing ideology of residential property that puts homes before economic gain.

In South Wales, the policy of the pension fund has been to dispose of the dwellings under the terms of the 1967 Leasehold Reform Act by selling the freehold to the residents at a price which one observer has estimated at ten times their real valuation. To 'encourage' the residents to purchase the freehold at this price, the fund raised the ground rents by an excessive amount. Such an act received considerable attention in the press, all unfavourable. For a pension fund, with apparently socially desirable aims, the effect of adverse publicity upon a minor part of its investments simply hastened their move out of residential property.

In this respect, it is interesting to contrast the way in which the fund disposed of its properties in Islington to the economic practice of a commercial landlord (cited earlier) who owned similar properties, adjacent to those of the trust. In the 1970s the commercial landlord rapidly moved tenants from one property to the next, either through financial incentives or 'passive' intimidation, in order to sell the properties on a thriving domestic market with vacant possession. The pension fund, however, was unable to adopt similar practices, despite the obvious financial advantages. The reason was clear. The risks attached to this kind of strategy were too great. A pension fund with a multinational profile cannot be seen to be associated with speculative practices for fear of its public image. Over an eight year period, however, the fund achieved a result similar to the commercial landlord; the properties have been sold, albeit in a relatively quiet manner and with less lucrative results. The rights of the trust's tenants were respected in the process of disinvestment and the letter of the law was seen to be obeyed. For example, the small blocks of purpose-built flats in the holding were not broken for sale; they were sold to a small private property company who, in turn, sold them to another company and they 'broke them up'. Indeed, this process is a microcosm of the phenomenon of 'flat break-up' in London, in which financial landlords, such as insurance companies and pension funds, provided the property for the commercial landlords to 'break' and thus receive the speculative profits.

In this instance, it is not that the fund wished to be involved in illegal speculative activities but could not do so by virtue of its visible profile. Rather, it is because of its visible profile that the mere ownership of residential property by this type of institution is a sensitive issue. It is the image of the 'big' company using people's 'homes' for financial gain. For the pension fund of a multinational company to be identified as a residential landlord – to be 'tarred with the same brush', as one representative of the fund referred to it – is a strong disincentive to invest or to retain a financial interest in rented housing. Unless, of course, the residential property in question falls outside of an ideology which identifies only certain properties as 'homes' – as, for example, properties in the luxury lettings market which appear to be free of this association.

A national building society

In contrast to the general policies of disinvestment adopted by financial institutions in the rented housing market, the third financial landlord to be discussed – a housing association set up by a national building society in the early 1980s – is something of an anomaly in post-war Britain; it is investing in newly built private rented housing. It is included here to illustrate how one particular institution has *used*, rather than reacted against, an ideology that locks housing into the imagery of the home. In this instance, a domestic ideology has enabled rather than constrained the actions of the institution to improve its public profile. Its exceptional nature also illustrates the limits of intervention in the rented market likely to be undertaken by financial institutions.

In a strict legal sense, this is a case study of a housing trust, not a housing association. The trust is internally financed by the funds of the Building Society and represents a legal device through which the Society can engage in the wider aspects of housing provision, in particular that of house building. Legislation at present does not permit Building Societies to hold land directly and the formation of a linked, yet separate trust circumvents this legal restriction. It is within the overall context of the Society's move into house building that the investment by the trust in private rented housing should be judged.

By 1983, the trust had built some two hundred houses in three inner London sites, of which the vast majority, over 90 per cent were constructed for owner-occupation and their purchase financed by mortgages from the Society. Future development plans were drawn up for a number of urban sites throughout the country and a controlled expansion of the programme was envisaged in successive years. In each of the completed developments, a small percentage of the properties have been let under the 'assured lettings' scheme. This scheme was introduced under the 1980 Housing Act and was designed to attract institutional investment in the rented housing market. Initially the scheme was applicable only to 'new build' property and it operated outside of the restrictions of the Rent Acts. Security of tenure provisions were relaxed under the scheme to allow landlords easier possession of their properties and rents were set independently of the Rent Officer. The initiative was welcomed by the British property lobby as a first step on the deregulation of the rented housing market. On closer examination, however, the motives behind the trust's adoption of the scheme revealed a token, rather than a major commitment to the initiative. It was a calculated token that owed more to improving the public image of the Society than to any regeneration of the rented housing market.

Each of the projects completed by the trust have been guided by a financial policy of risk-minimisation. As a non-profit making body, the investment aims of the trust have been promotional, not financial. Building houses for the lower end of the owner-occupied market in areas of low income ownership is the major objective; an aim close to the interests of the parent Building Society. The provision of a small number of properties for rent through each of the projects represents an additional element of publicity; that is, for providing accommodation in a declining market. The gesture, however, was far from philanthropic; the exact percentage of houses built for rent through each of the projects has varied according to the costs incurred on the purchase of the land, the construction of the dwellings and the type of demand for rented property in the area. Rent levels were calculated on an open market basis and were sufficiently high to exclude most people earning an average or below average income. Overall, the exercise appears to have been designed to obtain the maximum publicity with no financial loss. In the long term, private rented housing is peripheral to an institution whose future rests with further expansion of the owner-occupied market.

The way in which the trust has administered its assured lettings would appear to support this view. The selection of tenant's for example, was a carefully monitored exercise. Only savers with the Building Society were considered and only those tenants who would blend with the values of the adjoining home owners were selected. As a safety-valve, in the case of a mis-selection, tenants were subject to a two-year renewable tenancy. In contrast to the indifference exercised by other financial landlords towards the behaviour of their tenants, aside that is from their ability to pay rent, the trust exercised a surprising degree of personal control. In doing so, however, it has been able to draw upon an ideology of housing for people, not for profit and still maintain a strategy of capital risk minimisation.

Ideology and its limits

In each of the case studies we have attempted to show that the rented housing market is cross-cut by a number of ideological strands. In particular we have tried to show how the difference between types of landlord owes much to the way they interpret the rights vested in the ownership of private property and how they 'make sense' of the images that surround the home and landlordism in general. These practical ideologies which enable land-lords to legitimate their activities in the market are, of course, influenced by the economic relations that bind them as a group, but the ideas cannot be reduced to these relations. There is no simple correspondence between the economic relations which structure a particular type of landlordism and the ideas that they hold about their property and their tenants. Differences of interpretation, for example, over property rights, are to be found within the same group of landlords and this reflects the diversity of circumstances that similar landlords face in the market and the various past experiences of letting property that inform the current activities of landlords.

Nevertheless, it is possible to assert that certain practical ideologies are associated with particular types of landlord. The constraints in the 'worlds' inhabited by the six different types of landlord, the nature of their financial operations and how those operations are actually experienced and interpreted and the imagery they attach to their actions in the market are sufficiently clear to discern a series of practical ideologies.

By the term practical ideology, we are not referring to a set of isolated images which landlords draw upon to make sense of their actions. Isolated images do not make an ideology, rather it is the combination of the different images held by particular types of landlord that makes sense of their actions. Investor landlords, for example, particularly those who entered the lettings market before the Second World War, tend to define their right of control over their property through their interpretation of the moral worthiness of their tenants to occupy their investment. The fact that this notion of power and control is not acknowledged and is, quite correctly, resented by tenants who have purchased the right to live in the property free from such impositions has led many investor landlords to disinvest. Resentment over the perceived loss of legality attached to their control, their belief that tenants 'no longer' respect the rights of landlords, and their recoil in the face of what they perceive as an 'unfair' stereotype of the landlord as a 'folk devil', have all helped to shape a specific practical ideology which is lived by a number of investor landlords. In their heads, as it were, the 'way things are' is not 'the way things were'.

This is obviously true; the housing market has significantly changed in Britain since the 1940s and 1950s, with the rise of owner-occupation and the growth of public housing to rent. Such changes have altered people's attitudes towards private property to rent and have exacerbated a long-standing resentment of the landlords perceived right to control, both economically and informally, people's 'homes'. The existence of alternative tenures offering a greater degree of control and security, whether obtainable or not by tenants, has in general aggravated the inescapable conflict of interests between private landlord and tenant. The point, however, is that landlords have interpreted the objective changes in the housing market and the changes in people's attitudes towards private property to rent in quite different ways. Commercial landlords, as we have seen, have 'made sense' of the altered circumstances in quite a specific manner. The practical ideology that guides their letting strategies is not informed by the notion that tenants should respect their landlords or that tenants should in some way be morally worthy. Letting residential property, for commercial landlords is an activity which means something quite different from the image of service perpetrated by investor landlords. They legitimise their activities by drawing upon a quite different set of ideas, of which the most important is their right to treat housing on a par with any other commodity: an impersonal asset from which a profit can be returned. At the risk of caricature, commercial landlords 'live' a free market ideology, whereas investor landlords 'live' the tension between liberalism and the market.

In sum, the practical ideologies associated with the different types of landlord enable them to interpret and 'make sense' of their activities in the rented housing market. Such ideologies are not mere ephiphenomena; they are grounded in experience and thus have real consequences for how landlords react to changes in the rented market. The constitutive meanings that landlords attach to their residential property, together with the image of landlords and of tenants that they hold, influences but does not determine their practices of investment or disinvestment. Rather, they set *limits* to the possible range of actions that they may take in different local housing markets. We now turn to an extensive assessment of the practices of the six groups of landlords in the two local housing markets to discern their general patterns of investment and disinvestment.

6

Landlords in the inner city: an extensive survey

The main purpose of this chapter is to show how the particular characteristics of local housing markets at a point in time, modify, realise or constrain the emergent causal powers landlords possess by virtue of their membership of a particular group. Whether and how the causal powers of different groups of landlords operate depends upon certain social conditions, that is, upon their interaction with certain kinds of contingent circumstances and events. This chapter will attempt to unravel several different strands of this type of explanation. The first strand is the association between the different groups of landlords, inscribed with potential ways of acting, and the three possible courses of action outlined in Chapter 2: reinvestment, disinvestment and informalisation, and their various sub-trends. Whatever strategy or strategies are pursued by groups of landlords cannot be known in advance of the second strand, the nature of the housing markets in which they operate. Landlords in our extensive study, with certain exceptions, mainly operated across two local authority areas – a geographical space that is differentiated by type of property, degrees of environmental attactiveness and by accessibility to a range of local goods and services. In turn these different characteristics affect the way in which rents and house prices vary across space and so rates of profit from reletting or sale. This last set of factors, in association with the structure of demand for different types of housing in different parts of the boroughs, are the contingent factors that influence which strategy or strategies, or variants of them each category of landlord actually adopted at a certain time. Thus the chapter is structured around landlord types, showing how the particular local housing circumstances result in the same or different strategies being adopted by landlords in each of the six categories.

The context

The options open to each category of landlord are, to a large extent, dependent upon the nature of demand and the structure of supply of housing in a local market. Hackney and Islington, our case study areas, are inner London boroughs located in North and East London. The London Borough

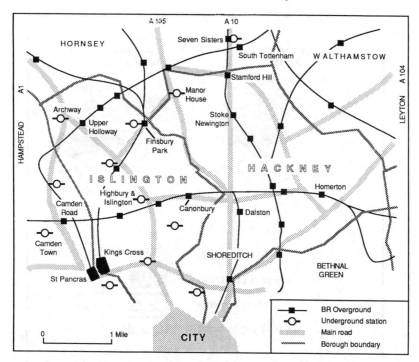

Figure 6.1 Location of the Boroughs of Islington and Hackney

of Hackney covers an area that stretches from Bethnal Green in the South to Stamford Hill in the North and from the River Lea in the East to Finsbury Park in the West. The borough of Islington abuts Hackney on the East. It stretches North from the City of London to Hornsey and extends West to King's Cross in the South and to the edges of Hampstead in the North (Figure 6.1). Both boroughs have a shared history of Victorian expansion and gradual decline in this century. Hackney's population peak was reached in 1901 and Islington's in 1911. By 1981 their respective populations had fallen to approximately half the maximum figures – 179,529 in Hackney and 157,522 in Islington. The decline was particularly rapid in the 1960s and 1970s and, in common with other inner London boroughs, it was encouraged at the time in association with policies to assist the departure of industry and office employment.

The two boroughs' history of Victorian development is reflected in the nature and condition of their current housing stock and in the continued significance of private landlords. Over half the dwellings in both boroughs in 1981 had been built before 1919 and large numbers of these properties have now reached or are reaching the end of their useful life.

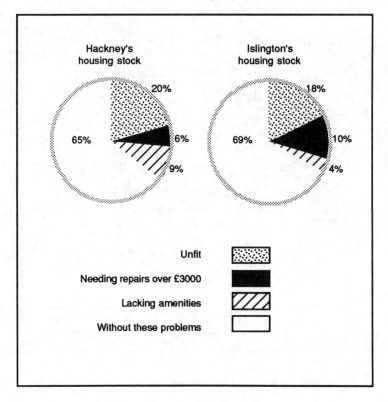

Figure 6.2 Housing conditions in Hackney and Islington in 1980
Source: London's Housing Shelter

In the pre-1919 stock, the percentage of inadequate properties is extremely high, for example 33 per cent of all pre-1919 dwellings in the two areas lacked one or more basic amenity. A large proportion of these dwellings are concentrated in the private sector as this was the common ownership pattern when these dwellings were built.

Successive reoccupation by generations of households, often in multiple occupation as household size declined and expanding employment opportunities reduced the domestic workforce, lack of investment and maintenance and changing ownership produced, in large parts of both boroughs, areas that were officially designated as ones of 'housing stress' in the 1969 Greater London Development Plan. Conditions are still inadequate for many households; overcrowding and sharing of physical amenities is common in both areas (see Figure 6.2).

The municipal response to poor conditions has been, in the decade immediately prior to our investigation, demolition and rebuilding, particu-

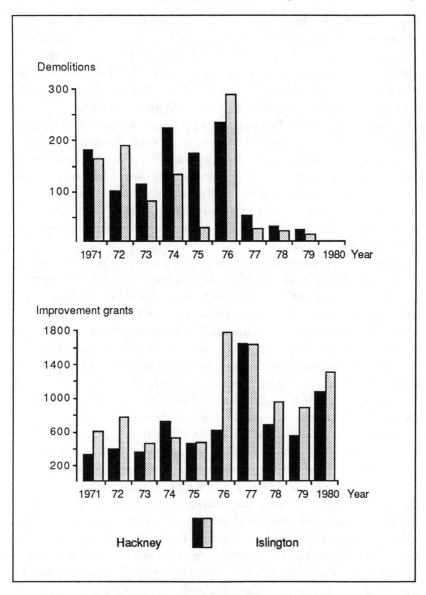

Figure 6.3 Indicators of municipal response to poor housing conditions
Source: Local Housing Statistics

larly in the early years of the 1970s, and the purchase and improvement of privately owned properties by the local authorities. In Hackney, 1,137 properties were compulsorily purchased and demolished between 1971 and 1979, in Islington the figure over a comparable period was 949. A large proportion of these dwellings were owned by private landlords. From the mid 1970s, however, partly in response to a changing emphasis in national housing policy and partly because of the struggles by local communities against redevelopment programmes, improvement of the existing stock gathered pace. In Figure 6.3, the number of demolitions and improvement grants granted each year in the 1970s are compared. General Improvement Areas, introduced under the provisions of the 1969 Housing Act, and later Housing Action Areas under the 1974 Act, were designated in both boroughs to facilitate the improvement of properties within particular small areas comprising up to a hundred houses. In 1981 there were ten GIAs and seven HAAs in Hackney and eleven HAAs in Islington. GIAs defined by Islington in the early 1970s had reached the end of their designated life by 1981, although the borough had had an active small area improvement policy during the decade.

Improvement programmes also have an impact on the conditions of operation of private landlords; within improvement areas their properties are subject to regulation and even compulsory transfer into local authority ownership, although a series of incentives to improve, such as higher than average grants in housing action areas, are initial mechanisms to raise the average standard of the housing stock. In addition, sale to local authorities or to housing associations has been an option within the specially designated small areas. However, as Harloe *et al.* (1974) have shown for Lambeth, an inner London borough south of the Thames, bureaucratic delays and generally lower valuations make this a less attractive prospect than sale to an individual household or to a speculator. Small area programmes also have an impact on private tenants as improving conditions generally involves reducing the density of occupation. Tenants who remain in the improved properties may thus have better accommodation; other tenants may have to move. Overall, the number of private tenancies has been reduced by both demolition and improvement programmes during the 1970s. In Hackney the number of households living in this sector of the housing market declined by 17,600 between 1971 and 1981 and in Islington by 25,700 over the same period. In Figure 6.4 the declining proportionate share of the housing market of private landlords is illustrated.

Demand for housing in these boroughs remains high. Between 1971 and 1981 despite falls in total population of 17 per cent in Hackney and 19 per cent in Islington, the decline in the number of households in each borough was smaller, especially among single person households. Overall, the decrease in the number of households in Hackney was 14 per cent whereas single person households actually increased by 1.4 per cent. In Islington the overall decrease in households was 16.5 per cent but the number of single

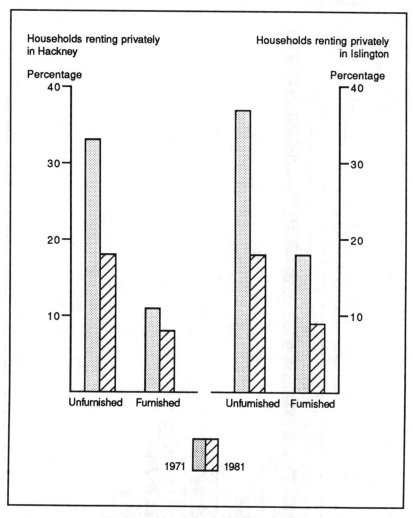

Figure 6.4 The decline of the private rented sector* in Hackney and Islington, 1971–81
*These figures include housing associations as tenants of private landlords and of housing associations who were not distinguishable separately in the 1971 census
Source: Census, 1971 and 1981

person households fell by less than half this figure (6.7 per cent). This is partly a consequence of rising household formation rates. These rises (an increase in the number of individuals in particular age groups who become household heads) have been an important element in housing demand in England and Wales since the 1950s (Cullingworth, 1979). They reflect demographic, social and economic changes in Britain, such as increased life

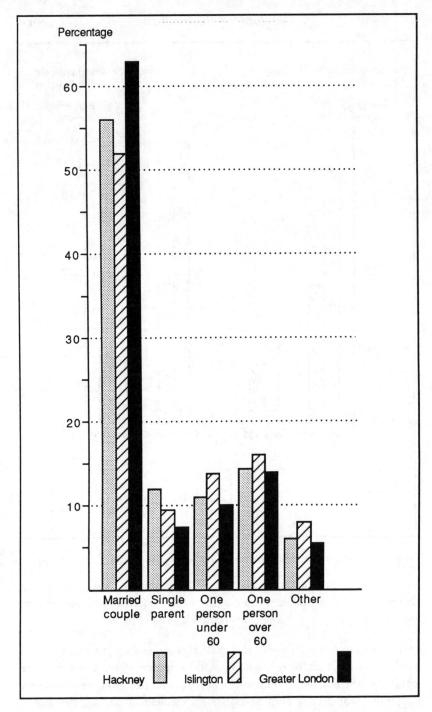

Figure 6.5 Household types in Hackney, Islington and Greater London, 1977
Source: National Dwelling and Housing Survey, 1978, DoE

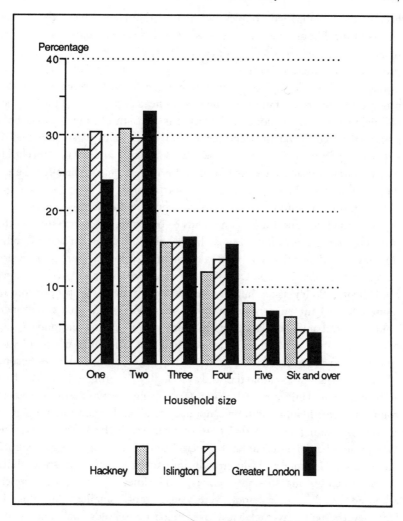

Figure 6.6 Household size in Hackney, Islington and Greater London
Source: National Dwelling and Housing Survey, 1978, DoE

expectancy, rising divorce rates, the growth in real incomes throughout the post-war period, the greater propensity for young people to leave home for a period of independent living in a non-family household and, until recently, rising student numbers. All these factors have increased the number of households, particularly small households, at either end of the age spectrum. These factors are reflected in the distribution of household types and sizes in Figures 6.5 and 6.6. As the figures show, in both areas there are large numbers of households of a 'non-traditional' kind. Just over half of all households are married couples, with or without children – the typical clients of local housing authorities – whereas between a quarter and a third of all households are single people. There is also a higher than average proportion of single parents in the two boroughs compared with Greater London as a whole. Indeed, Hackney has the highest percentage of this group in the metropolitan area. The rises in headship rates and the number of single people living alone are reflected in the figure showing household size. In the two boroughs 40 per cent of all households was comprised of either one person or five or more people. Both large and small households tend to find it difficult to become local authority tenants as typically it builds 'family' houses and flats of two or three bedrooms.

Within Inner London in general and Hackney and Islington in particular, the continued demand for housing tends to be expressed as pressure on the private rented sector, often because households searching for accommodation have no alternative available to them, at least in the short term, if not permanently. Inner London was officially described in the 1977 Green Paper on Housing Policy as a 'high demand' area where the proportion of households reliant on private landlords was increasing. This situation is quite unlike that facing landlords in many towns in England and Wales, particularly in the North and in parts of the Midlands where private landlords have been faced with declining demand since the end of the Second World War (see for example the study of Dudley undertaken by researchers at Birmingham University, Housing Monitoring Team, 1980). Access to council housing in inner London is not open to all and in addition there is an enormous waiting list for this type of property in both boroughs. The average number of households registered on the waiting lists for council properties in Hackney and Islington during each year in the 1970s was about 9,000 in each borough, rising to 14,000 in Hackney in 1980.[1] The numbers rehoused on the other hand, were considerably smaller than this. In Hackney the figure averaged just over 3,000 households each year in the peak years in the middle of the decade, but was down to only 2,000 a year by the end; in Islington, large numbers were rehoused but there was a similar decline, from 5,000 in the peak years to under 4,000 in 1980.

In London as a whole, and indeed in the country more generally, waiting lists have been expanding since the 1970s, at the same time rehousing programmes have been declining. This is partly a consequence of successive Conservative governments' preference for owner-occupation rather than

---

[1] Housing waiting lists are not an accurate reflection of total housing needs in an area as many people fail to register, or are ineligible to do so under the points schemes in operation. They may also include households who have moved, died or otherwise changed their circumstances and so there is a degree of over – as well as under – estimation.

state provision of housing; a preference that is being enforced by a combination of incentives to purchase council housing and by cuts in local authorities' housing revenue accounts. Hackney and Islington have suffered severe reductions in housing expenditure since the end of the 1970s, with the result that their building programmes have been reduced to virtually nothing. In 1981, for example, thirty-five new council houses were started in Hackney and fifty-three in Islington. For the majority of applicants registered on housing waiting lists, the chance of being offered housing became an even more remote possibility during the years of our investigation.

There is also a sizeable proportion of households in housing need in the two boroughs that are not represented on waiting lists. Many households fail to register for local authority rehousing either because of ineligibility for reasons of marital or family status, mobility, or the sheer lack of the knowledge needed to register on the local authorities' housing waiting lists. These households include recent immigrants, single parents, the mentally or physically handicapped, young single people, students and others who traditionally have looked to the private landlord for accommodation. There is a large ethnic minority population, for example, in both boroughs. In the maps overleaf the percentage of household heads in each ward who were not born in the United Kingdom is shown. In the Northern and central parts of each borough there is a sizeable minority population. In Hackney, the largest 'non-white' ethnic group is West Indian – many of whom, of course, were born in the United Kingdom and so not represented in the figures (6.7 and 6.8). There are also many people from the less developed parts of western Europe in both boroughs – particularly from Eire and from Greece, Turkey and Cyprus. Overall 40 per cent of Hackney's household heads and 20 per cent in Islington were not born in the United Kingdom. Because of factors such as their generally below average incomes, mobility and sometimes language difficulties, members of minority groups tend to find it difficult to gain access to local authority housing or to purchase property in a good condition. In both boroughs, therefore, but particularly in Hackney, the housing needs of such groups of people have provided potential tenants for private landlords and so created the opportunity for reinvestment, with or without changes in the condition and legal status of the lettings. Increasingly, however, ethnic minority household heads are becoming owner-occupiers of properties at the bottom end of the market and so are also providing landlords with the alternative of selling their properties.

For most of the households in housing need, owner-occupation was seldom an option. In both boroughs, the share of the housing market accounted for by households owning or purchasing their own homes was significantly below the national average – 13 per cent in both Hackney and

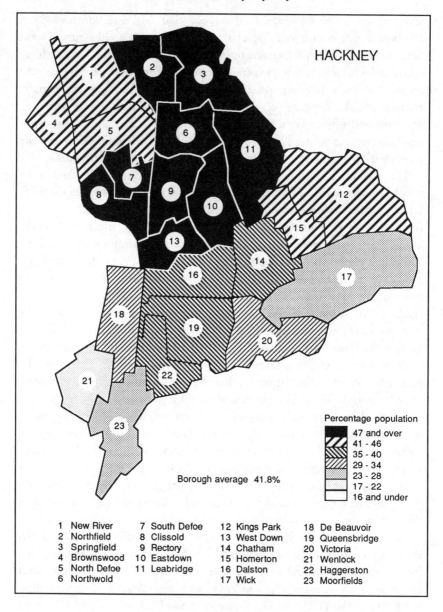

Figure 6.7 Percentage of the population born outside the UK (heads of households),
Hackney
Source: Census of Population, Small Area Statistics 10 per cent sample

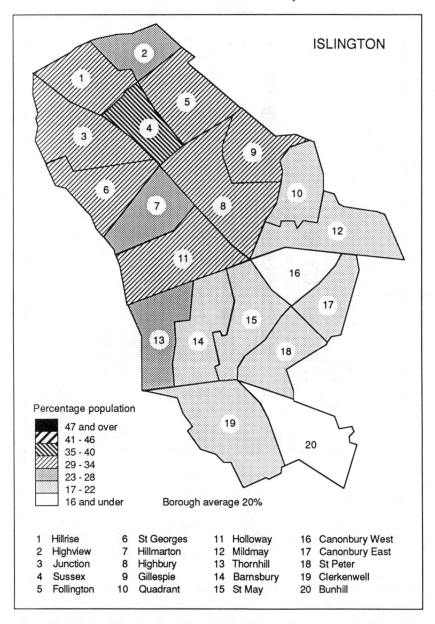

Figure 6.8 Percentage of the population born outside the UK (heads of households), Islington

Source: Census of Population, Small Area Statistics 10 per cent sample

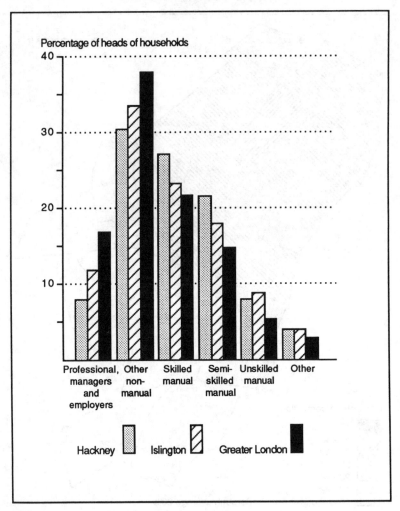

Figure 6.9 Socio-economic structure of Hackney, Islington and Greater London
Source: Census of Population, Small Area Statistics 10 per cent sample

Islington compared with 56 per cent in the country as a whole in 1981. In both boroughs the high cost of land puts home ownership beyond the reach of households on average wages and, indeed, makes the construction by private capital of new houses for sale unlikely as profit margins are low. In 1981, only 127 dwellings were started by private builders in Islington and none at all in that year in Hackney. Thus most of the increase in home ownership levels in these areas in the decade 1971 to 1981 predominantly have been through the mechanism of tenure transfers within the existing

Table 6.1 *Dwelling types in Hackney and Islington, 1977*

	Percentage of all household spaces	
Type of dwelling	Hackney	Islington
Detached house	0.5	0.4
Semi-detached	1.8	1.0
Terraced house	16.2	15.6
Purpose built flat or maisonette	53.8	43.3
Other flat or rooms	25.9	36.5
Other	1.9	2.2
Total	100.0	100.0

Source: DoE (1978b).

stock, in the main from the private rented sector. The extent of council house sales to sitting tenants during the 1970s was insignificant in these boroughs, in the main because the majority of the council owned stock is in the form of flats and maisonettes rather than single family houses. Indeed, the housing stock as a whole in both boroughs consists mainly of flats, maisonettes and rooms. Only 18.5 per cent of Hackney's dwellings and 17 per cent of Islington's are houses whether terraced, semi-detached or detached (see Table 6.1). During the 1970s, owner-occupation increased by 2,036 households in Hackney and by 560 in Islington.

A number of housing researchers (see particularly Hamnett, 1982 and Merrett and Gray, 1982) have argued that sale to owner-occupation is the preferred strategy for 'economically rational' landlords. They have argued that the gap between the capital value of residential properties and the rates of return from rents, less maintenance and management costs, is so wide that it makes reletting unlikely. Accurate information about these relative costs and benefits in particular cases is, however, virtually impossible to obtain. In 1981 the Department of the Environment published a series of estimates of registered rents for particular types of properties as a percentage of the capital value of these properties with vacant possession. The data for Hackney, and for Greater London are included in Table 6.2. Unfortunately, Islington was not included in the DoE survey. As the table shows, estimated registered rents per annum in London are an insignificant percentage of capital values. In reality the situation is even more unfavourable as these figures do not take account of the costs of repair and maintenance, or of the phasing of rent reviews. The DoE has estimated that maintenance costs

Landlords and property

Table 6.2 *Estimated capital values of dwellings and rent as a percentage of capital value as at 1 January 1981*

Registration area	Estimated capital value of property (£000s)			Estimated registered rent as a percentage of capital value		
	A	B	C	A	B	C
Hackney	16.2	19.5	26.4	2.6	4.5	4.1
Greater London						
Median	17.3	25.8	31.7	2.4	2.9	2.9
Upper quartile	20.5	27.1	34.8	2.6	3.2	3.0
Lower quartile	16.1	20.1	29.3	2.3	2.6	2.6

Notes: The dwellings were A – 2 storey, mid-terrace, unimproved built about 1870
B – as A but up to improvement grant standard
C – 2 storey, semi-detached, built about 1930
Source: Supplementary memorandum by the Department of the Environment, *House of Commons Paper*, 40, part 5, 1981

normally account for 15–30 per cent of the full registered fair rent depending on the age and condition of the property and that, because of time lags in the rent review periods, actual fair rent payments in 1980 were about 20 per cent lower than the new fair rents registered in that year. These adjustments would give the landlord a pre-tax return typically 35–50 per cent lower than the return in the full registered fair rent. Of course, these are all ideal calculations. The landlords in our sample in Hackney and Islington were seldom included in the fair rents scheme nor did many of them let their property as a single self-contained dwelling unit. Consequently, rent returns would be considerably higher than these estimates. However, despite this, capital values of houses are rising in these boroughs and the prospect of sale is an attractive one to many landlords. In England and Wales as a whole the average price of second hand houses for owner-occupation rose by 375 per cent between 1970 and 1980, compared with a 125 per cent rise in registered rents over the same period and an enormous 420 per cent rise in repair and maintenance costs. But these are estimates for all landlords and arguments that sale is the overwhelming likely option fail, like earlier and less sophisticated versions of the reasons for decline, to consider the heterogeneity in landlords' motives and in the stock that they hold. In fact many landlords in inner areas and in Hackney and Islington, as we shall show, choose to relet.

As we have shown, there are evident similarities between Hackney and Islington in the condition and structure of the residential stock and in the nature of demand for housing. Landlords owning property in both boroughs have opportunities to relet or to disinvest. However, there are also differences between the boroughs that need to be clarified as these too are part of the contingent factors that affect landlords' strategies and need to be distinguished to interpret the results from the questionnaire survey.

One of the main differences between the two boroughs in the 1970s was in the nature of the local state. Although both authorities were Labour dominated during the decade, Islington has consistently had a larger programme of public spending than Hackney. Its domestic and business rates were higher and so it raised a higher proportion of its total revenue locally than Hackney (63 per cent compared with 33 per cent in 1980). One of the effects of this has been higher expenditure on the housing programme and a more flexible and innovative approach to the use of its own stock and acquired private rented properties. In Islington during the 1970s greater attention was paid to the needs of non-nuclear families and to less-traditional methods of provision than in Hackney. Islington has been more prepared to experiment with rehabilitation, housing associations, licenced squatting and various forms of local area initiative than Hackney, and to rehouse a wider range of applicants, both from the general waiting list and under special schemes such as the key workers or young singles programmes. In Hackney, on the other hand, during the 1970s there was no policy to allow short life groups to use empty properties acquired by the Council for rehabilitation, despite the authority having the third highest percentage of dwellings empty for over a year of all local authorities in England and Wales in 1981 (4.5 per cent of the total housing stock, third after Knowsley and Corby). In Islington, by comparison, several hundred properties had been handed over to short life groups by the end of the decade. Hackney relied to a much greater extent on redevelopment programmes, and rehousing from the general waiting list was the most typical method of gaining access to local authority property. These differences have an impact on landlords' strategies and on the changing tenure divisions in the two boroughs. In Islington there were more opportunities for private landlords to relinquish their dwellings to the local authority.

There were also differences between the boroughs in the structure of demand for housing, partly because of the relative geographical accessibility of the two boroughs, but also reflecting differences in the population and in income distributions. Hackney, at the time of our survey, was very poorly served by public transport. There were no underground stations in the borough whereas Islington is crossed by the Northern, Piccadilly and Victoria lines. The opening of the latter line in the late 1960s, in particular, improved the communications of certain parts of Islington. One reflection of this has been a higher demand for owner-occupied property at the top end of the market in Islington. The percentage of the population in professional and managerial occupations in Islington is half as high again as in Hackney, although in both boroughs the averages are well below the overall figure for Greater London (see Figure 6.10). In Islington, too, but not in Hackney, there are several institutions of higher education, creating buoyant demand from students to rent property for shared accommodation.

However, despite these differences, as we emphasised earlier, administrative boundaries between boroughs are not necessarily congruent with the spatial boundaries of housing markets, with the exception, that is of the local authority sub-sector. In this case each borough's housing stock, its allocation and management is controlled under a set of specific policies that apply throughout the borough. But for the private rented and owner-occupied sectors the boundaries of the housing market may be either smaller or larger than the borough boundaries. In general, housing markets tend not to be spatially contiguous areas, but rather take the form of a ragged pattern with holes and peaks. These areas are defined by that set of properties that potential occupiers regard as acceptable alternatives. To take an illustrative example, inner city owner-occupation is now seen as desirable by a sub-set of relatively affluent householders who may see small areas within Hackney, Islington or, indeed, other north London boroughs, as equally possible places to live. Their market will be defined by characteristics of the stock and by a set of desired local attributes, such as open space, access to transport facilities and to other amenities. Thus areas such as Canonbury and Barnsbury in Islington, De Beauvoir and Mapledene in Hackney, but also certain small areas in perhaps Haringey or Camden might equally well be alternative residential locations. Within the private rented sector, there are similar patterns and sub-markets, each defined by the set of characteristics seen as desirable by particular fractions of demand. Thus the strategies adopted by each type of landlord, outlined in the forthcoming pages, were in part a reaction to the spatial distribution and interaction between these diverse housing markets, but also to the borough defined political framework. Political decisions made by local government politicians and officers about demolition, rehabilitation, purchase of on-street properties or improvement of estates, and the economic power of potential owner-occupiers together make inroads into the private rented sector, producing the fragmentary and diverse structure that is its current defining characteristic. Overall, inner city housing in the case study boroughs, and in those like them, may perhaps be best regarded as a mosaic whose complicated pattern is shifting over time, unlike the more uniform and static pattern of the outer

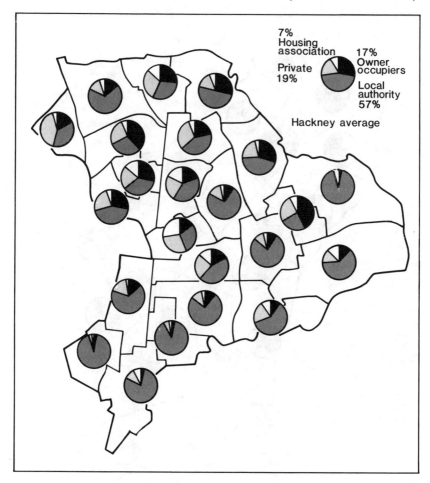

Figure 6.10 Hackney Housing Tenure, 1981
Source: 1981 Census of Population, Part 2

suburbs that largely are dominated by owner-occupied housing in a relatively narrow range of type, price and condition.

In Figures 6.10 and 6.11 the tenure structure within each ward in Hackney and Islington is shown. The significance of the local authority sector is apparent. It is especially dominant in the southern end of both boroughs. In the north of the boroughs, the tenure distribution is more heterogeneous, although in a small number of wards owner-occupation now dominates the tenure distribution. These are the areas where, as we explain in the next section, landlords were particularly able to sell to individual owner-

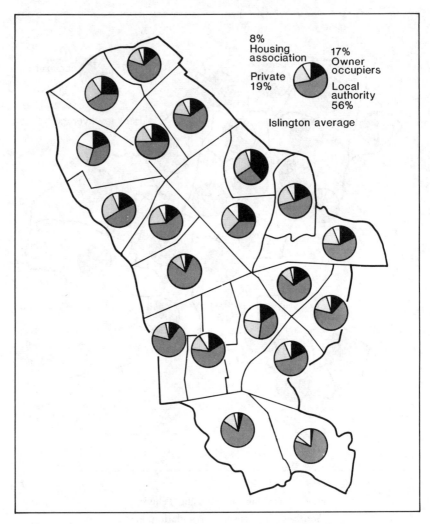

Figure 6.11 Islington Housing Tenure, 1981
Source: 1981 Census of Population, Part 2

occupiers and leave the rented market in relatively profitable circumstances. Elsewhere especially in the group of wards in the north east of Islington and north west of Hackney the rented market remained bouyant and landlords had the opportunity to relet, often to a different type of household from the ones which the local authorities had rehoused.

The survey findings

In Table 6.3 strategies adopted by landlords when presented with vacancies in their properties are outlined. This table is the lynchpin for the ensuing discussion where the results of the complex interaction between the causal relations constituting each landlord type as a distinctive category and the contingent circumstances affecting their choices are presented. It is immediately apparent that the overall impact of local authority rehousing on the private rented sector in these areas has been to significantly reduce the number of vacancies. Only a third of all the vacated tenancies had been relet at the time of our survey, in many cases up to two years afer the vacancy was created. Consequently access to the private rented sector appears to have been reduced in these areas. Reletting of these vacancies occurred without any monitoring of the process by the relevant local authority in order to enforce improvements in physical conditions or to control rent levels. Thus local authority action presents landlords with an opportunity either to reinvest or to disinvest. Landlords taking the second option may or may not realise a profit. Whichever option the landlord chooses, however, is not subject to local authority control. The implications of this policy will be addressed later. The table also reveals significant differences between the activities of different categories of landlord. These variations and the range of explanation for these will now be discussed. As the numbers of traditional, employer and financial landlords were small, reflecting both the local and national pattern, detailed statistical information will be presented only for the other three types: informal, investor and commercial. The variations in the strategies of the former group of three will, however, be outlined where appropriate.

Informal landlords

Our sample included 198 informal landlords, 95 of whom were selected from Hackney's waiting list and 103 from Islington's list. In Chapter 2 we defined informalisation as the continuance, and indeed expansion, of that section of landlords who trade as individuals, either living in and renting part of their own dwelling as a resident landlord or deriving all or a major part of their income from the rental receipts from a relatively small number of tenancies. In general these landlords regard their tenancies as, first and foremost, their own personal property. It is this personal relation with their tenants that is the most significant characteristic of informalisation. Landlords are actively involved in choosing their tenants and in controlling, in a variety of ways, their behaviour in the accommodation, which is often

Table 6.3 Landlords' reactions to vacancies in their dwellings

Strategy	Landlord category						
	Traditional	Employer	Informal	Investor	Commercial	Financial	All landlords
Reinvest in private rented sector i.e. relet	16.7	33.3	31.3	28.6	55.4	12.5	33.7
Disinvest							
(a) with profits	83.3	8.3	24.2	38.8	28.9	75.0	31.3
(b) without profits	—	55.6	40.4	31.1	15.7	12.5	32.8
Disinvest (a + b)	83.3	63.9	64.6	69.9	44.6	87.5	64.1
Informalisation i.e. relet to relatives or friends	—	2.8	4.1	1.5	—	—	2.2
Total numbers	6	36	198	206	83	16	537

shared, in part or in total, between landlord and tenant. Informal landlords are a diverse group with changing membership, as individuals owning one or a small number of houses enter and leave the lettings market according to the exigencies of their financial circumstances. For many of the landlords whom we identified in this group letting was a short-term expedient, others had been landlords for many years. Some of them let solely to friends and relatives, whereas others advertised or let through word of mouth to individuals or households whom they did not know personally. For all these landlords though, the ensuing relationship with tenants was a personal one, despite the significance of the cash nexus. Indeed for many of these landlords, the rental receipts were an absolutely essential prerequisite of retaining and maintaining their homes. As Kemeny (1981) has pointed out, the diffusion of owner-occupation down the income scale has led to the growth of 'owner-occupier landlordism' by low and medium income owners who are unable to meet their mortgage repayments without additional income from rental receipts.

Table 6.4 shows what strategies these landlords adopted during our survey period. Almost a third of the informal landlords identified in our sample decided to relet the vacancies created by rehousing. This group consisted of landlords who had been in the lettings market for between one and ten years at the time at which their existing tenants were rehoused by the local authorities. The landlords owned between one and four properties of which the majority still had substantial loan repayments outstanding. Thus both resident and non-resident informal landlords were reletting. For most of them the combination of financial obligations and sitting tenants left little option but to relet.

Most of the informal landlords who reinvested, let properties to several tenants. Houses in multiple occupation in association with ownership and renting, are still an extremely significant part of the housing system in both Hackney and Islington. In 1981, for example, 5,053 households in Hackney lived in non-self-contained accommodation. This number represented 7.4 per cent of all the households in the borough, but as a proportion of households in private lettings accounted for 39 per cent. The vast majority of accommodation that is not self-contained is found in the private rented sector. The same figures for Islington are 5,481 in total, 8.5 per cent of all households and 44.6 per cent of private tenants. Multiple occupation is an inadequate form of housing into which many of the poorest households in these boroughs are forced because of the absence of accessible alternatives. Amongst the informal landlords who relet vacancies in multi-occupied dwellings, we came across many examples of properties that were in an extremely poor state of repair. In most cases, no improvements had been

Table 6.4 *The strategies of informal landlords*

	Landlords in	
Strategy	Hackney (%)	Islington (%)
Reinvestment i.e. reletting	30.4	32.0
Disinvestment		
A *With profits* (in order of declining profits)		
(1) Sale to an individual owner-occupier*	21.1	19.4
(2) Sale to another landlord or speculator	1.1	1.9
(3) Sale to a sitting tenant		
(4) Sale to local authority or housing association	2.1	3.9
B *Without profits*		
(1) Left empty but hope to sell	5.3	8.7
(2) Left empty/abandoned	8.4	12.6
(3) Compulsory purchased		1.9
(4) Returned to sole owner-occupation by the landlord	25.3	14.6
(5) Demolished	2.1	1.0
Informalisation	4.2	3.9
Total numbers	95	103

Note: * Where the dwellings were converted and/or improved before, the rates of return probably were higher than if sold without improvement as in most cases the purchase price of improved dwellings less the cost of improvement would be greater than the price of unimproved properties.

carried out before the rooms in these houses were relet. Many of the new tenants shared the bathroom, when there was one, and often had no cooking facilities. Other tenants had to manage with a gas ring in their rooms or share a communal cooker on the landing. Single men, in particular, were found in spartan conditions. Several of these tenants were middle-aged or elderly Irish men who had emigrated after the war and had moved from one inadequate room to another within inner London over the decades. The younger single male inhabitants in our sample tended to be members of other ethnic minority groups, often from the 'new Commonwealth' countries. In other cases, reflecting the changing employment situation of inner London and the shift in patterns of in-migration towards married couples and families, informal residential landlords relet their rooms to 'family' households, often young couples with babies and toddlers. For these families, informal landlords provided accommodation that was totally inappropriate to their needs. However, most of these families were faced

Table 6.5 *Household structure of previous and new tenants of informal landlords in Hackney and Islington, 1977–81*

Household structure	Hackney		Islington	
	Old	New	Old	New
	tenants		tenants	
Pensioner couple	1.0	—	6.8	—
Single pensioner	13.7	—	26.2	—
Non-pensioner	23.2	18.2	18.4	16.7
Non-pensioner single person	31.6	42.4	16.5	55.5
Family with dependent children	27.4	27.3	31.1	16.4
Group of single unrelated people	3.1	12.1	1.0	11.1
Totals	95	32	103	36

with no alternative in the 'tight' and expensive private rented market in these two boroughs.

In Table 6.5 the household structure of the 'old' and 'new' tenants of informal landlords in Hackney and Islington is compared. In both boroughs the move away from elderly tenants was clear. In Islington, however, landlords were less likely to relet to families than landlords in Hackney. This was partly the consequence of the differences in the structure of demand from young people. Within Islington there is a greater number of students and young workers who, by pooling their rent paying capacity, can outbid poorer, family households. In both boroughs, however, informal landlords let predominantly to households without dependent children. In all cases, the properties were relet as furnished tenancies. This mirrors the general shift towards furnished lettings that has occurred in Inner London as a whole. In Case studies 1, a number of case studies are outlined that demonstrate in more detail some of the changes consequent upon the rehousing of the original tenants.

Among ethnic minority informal landlords who relet we found some evidence of a preference to let to tenants of the same nationality. In Hackney 31 per cent of all ethnic minority informal landlords who relet, let to households who were from the same country of origin as themselves. The proportion in Islington was exactly the same. Overall, the proportions of informal landlords in the sample who were from minority groups were 27 per cent in Hackney and 39 per cent in Islington but the proportions rose to 69 per cent and 76 per cent respectively of those landlords who relet. The countries represented included the West Indies, Nigeria, Ghana, Guyana,

Case studies 1

The impact of reletting by informal landlords: 5 case studies

1   An elderly British man living in a terraced two-storey Victorian house in Stoke Newington rented two furnished rooms to a couple in their forties who had two children in care in Derby. The man was a painter and decorator, and his wife was a shop assistant at the time they applied for council housing. They paid £14 a week for the rooms and shared the bath and WC with their landlord. On rehousing, both rooms were relet to single unemployed men, each paying £9 a week and also sharing the bathroom with the landlord.

2   An Indian landlord in North Hackney rented two furnished rooms to an unrelated fellow countryman who was a minicab driver. These two rooms were shared by the man's wife and his three children and his two younger, single brothers. They shared the bathroom with two other tenant families as well as with their landlord's family and paid £15 a week rent. After rehousing the same rooms were relet to another Indian couple and two children, this time related to the landlord.

3   A middle aged Irish man who had bought a large Victorian house in NW Islington in the 1950s let it out as bedsitting rooms to single men from Eire. Each tenant occupied a sparsely furnished single room and paid about £5–6 a week rent. There was one shared bathroom and no cooking facilities at all in the property. The vacated room in our sample was immediately relet to a single Irish building worker for £8 a week in 1980.

4   A West Indian family who had bought a four-bedroomed terrace house in Highbury, central Islington, had to let rooms to meet their mortgage repayments. The rehoused tenant was a single woman with three children who worked as a hospital domestic. She had rented two unfurnished rooms for £15 a week and had shared the kitchen and bathroom with the landlord and his family. This tenant had complained of harassment to the local authority housing department. She was rehoused in 1978 and one of the two rooms was then let furnished to a young single West Indian man who was unemployed at the time. He shared also the amenities with his landlord, had no rent book and again paid £15 a week rent, though for only one not two rooms.

5   The British owner of a three-storey end of terrace house in N1 rented the house to four sets of tenants and by providing breakfast evaded the provisions of the Rent Acts. In 1978, Islington rehoused a young Maltese couple who worked as a chef and chambermaid in a West End hotel. They had lived in a furnished bedsit, sharing the kitchen and outside WC with all the other occupants of the property – ten people in all. They paid £9.30 a week rent in 1978. The room was immediately relet to a Philipino couple who barely spoke English. Although the conditions of the let remained the same, the rent increased to £26 a week.

Cyprus, Mauritius, India and Bangladesh, Poland, Spain, Turkey and Italy, Sri Lanka and Eire. It is clear that for ethnic minority groups in Hackney and Islington the private landlord remains an important provider of accommodation and that, for ethnic minority landlords, informal landlordism is both a way of meeting the initial high housing costs incurred through inner area purchase and, for many, a way of making short-term profits. Indeed, given the extremely high rates of unemployment in Hackney and Islington, income generated from renting may become an increasingly important part of the survival strategies of many inner city households. Over 1 in 6 working-age men in each borough were unemployed in 1981 and the rates have increased since then. In certain small areas unemployment among young people, especially blacks, is as high as 50 per cent. Many of these landlords had no choice but to let part of their home.

For the tenant, on the other hand, this form of accommodation is seldom ideal. Even for those tenants who were reasonably content to remain in the private rented sector or, more realistically, recognised their inability to gain access to either of the other two major tenures at the time, renting from an informal landlord was unsatisfactory. For many of these tenants, the use of the space which they purchased was tied up with obligations related to using somebody else's home. Many tenants felt that their landlord imposed unnecessary restrictions on them, ranging from a paternalistic interest in their everyday life, through denying them the use of certain amenities at particular times, to outright harassment. A large proportion (73 per cent) of the respondents who were new tenants of informal landlords in Islington and Hackney would have preferred to rent in another sub-sector of this tenure. However, as we shall demonstrate in the following sections, commercial and investor landlords in these boroughs who relet looked for types of prospective tenants with relatively high rent-paying capacities to fill their vacancies.

A further small number of informal landlords also relet their vacant tenancies but to family or relatives without a formal cash payment changing hands. This group consisted of four landlords in Hackney and Islington who had previously had a similar letting strategy. In addition an investor and an employer landlord in Islington, despite intentions eventually to sell their properties, had relet their vacancies to family friends who needed short-term accommodation and so had crossed the boundaries between the different categories in our classification.

It is clear that this group in particular, but also all informal landlords, are in a category with a shifting membership; new landlords enter as old ones decide to leave. Forty per cent of the informal residential landlords who previously had been letting to friends and relatives had stopped letting by the time of our survey and had simply reoccupied their entire dwelling themselves. In total, 20 per cent of the informal landlords had adopted this strategy. As in most cases these landlords had merely been sharing their home with their tenants; this simply involved the reuse of rooms by their own immediate family. In almost all cases, the previously let rooms had not been physically separate from part of the house occupied by the landlord and his or her family. The effect is to reclassify these properties as owner-occupied. These previous landlords had a number of characteristics in common. They tended to be 'family men' in early middle age, usually with an above average number of teenage children. There was also a high proportion of men from ethnic minority groups. They had usually let rooms for short periods, either to help newly arrived kin, or as a way of making ends meet when they first embarked upon home ownership and later to pay for improvements to the dwellings which had often been in poor physical condition but relatively inexpensive when originally purchased. So, in many ways, they were similar to those informal landlords who decided to relet, merely at a later stage in their housing careers.

What we cannot ascertain from our sample, of course, is the extent to which new 'owner-occupier landlords' are being recruited to this sub-sector of the rented sector. Overall, in inner city areas like Hackney and Islington, the size of the group appears to be increasing, absolutely as well as proportionately, although accurate figures are difficult to collect. Many house owners in this position do not declare their interests as landlords and so the households are classified as owner-occupiers in official statistics. The nature of this type of landlordism and the changing composition of the group runs *counter* to the common perception of the private rented sector as a declining section of the housing market. With the deepening economic recession and the continuing commitment by the main political parties to expand owner-occupation, this type of temporary landlordism is likely to continue to expand. Tenants, who may or may not be friends or relations of their landlord, will continue to be subjected to the contradictions implied by a type of landlordism that embodies both an economic calculation and personal control over tenants.

Another group of the informal landlords in our sample also left the lettings market but with profits. This was a quite different process to that just outlined for 'temporary' landlords. The landlords involved were predominantly elderly widows or single women who had been letting part of their accommodation for many years, often to other elderly women in similar circumstances. In a number of cases we came across tenants who had been housed continuously by the same landlord, or rather landlady, for periods of up to 53 years. In most cases the properties were sold, and indeed the tenants rehoused, because of the death of the owners. These properties were usually sold in an unimproved state to individual owner-occupiers (see Table 6.4). The sales were handled by the executors of the wills or, in a small number of cases, by the agents who had previously handled the property. However, as one of the main characteristics of informalisation is a personal relationship between the landlord and tenant, agents had not usually been involved in the previous letting arrangements. In all but two of the cases where dwellings were sold and reoccupied, the new owners were 'family' households headed by male manual workers. The two exceptions were dwellings that were purchased by childless couples, where both partners worked in professional occupations. The reason for the difference appeared to be the location and type of the properties. Both dwellings were situated in an area in Islington that has become a classic area for gentrification. This process will be discussed in further detail in the next sections, as investor and commercial landlords were involved in greater numbers in this type of transfer. Finally, a small number of the dwellings owned by elderly informal landlords who have since died were sold to another landlord, to the local authority or a housing association, or remained empty. In this latter category we attempted to establish who inherited these dwellings and their eventual intentions. In a number of cases this proved to be impossible as the previous landlord died intestate. Thus the category 'left empty/abandoned' includes five properties in Hackney and seven in Islington for whom no new owner could be established. The other nine properties in this category were intentionally abandoned.

Investor landlords

The investor landlords in our sample – 206 in all (79 in Hackney and 127 in Islington) – had a quite different orientation to the lettings market than the informal landlords whose behaviour has just been discussed. The landlords that we classified as investors were those who were invariably no longer sure of their status or strategies in the rapidly changing circumstances of an inner city housing market. Although they were obviously in the market for profit, it was not profit for profit's sake alone that motivated them. A residual ideology of providing a service for 'deserving' households informed and informs their letting behaviour and to some extent this prevents them from ruthlessly exploiting the new forms of demand that have become apparent in Hackney and Islington in recent years. Consequently the investor landlords, as a group, were shown to be slower to switch to the 'singles furnished

Table 6.6 *The strategies of investor landlords*

	Landlords in	
Strategy	Hackney %	Islington %
Reinvestment in reletting	21.5	33.1
Disinvestment		
A *With profits* (in order of declining profits)		
(1) Sale to an individual owner-occupier	34.2	23.6
(2) Sale to another landlord or speculator	1.3	4.7
(3) Sale to a sitting tenant	1.3	0.8
(4) Sale to local authority or housing association	3.8	10.2
B *Without profits*		
(1) Left empty but hope to sell	16.4	9.4
(2) Left empty/abandoned	17.7	12.6
(3) Compulsory purchased	2.5	–
(4) Returned to sole owner-occupation by the landlord	–	0.8
(5) Demolished	1.3	2.4
Informalisation		2.4
Total numbers	79	127

bedsit' market than either the informal landlords just discussed, or, in particular the commercial landlords whose more ruthless exploitation of market demands will be outlined in the next section.

Despite their different orientation to the market the actual impact on the market of the strategies of investor landlords as revealed in Table 6.3 and in more detail in Table 6.6 is similar to the impact of informal landlords' behaviour. In both cases, less than a third of these landlords chose to relet their created vacancies. The overall decline in the number of investor landlords is part of the long-established decline in the unfurnished sub-market of the private rented sector. Previously, the investor landlords in our sample let in the main to three types of tenants, the first two of which reflected their 'relic' role in the lettings market. These two groups of rehoused tenants were either old age pensioners, particularly single and widowed women who had lived in rooms all their lives, or the middle-aged poor who had become trapped in the private rented sector and never managed to escape. The third group of rehoused tenants were the 'new decent poor'; low income families, often from ethnic minority groups, in employment but poor, as they either relied on low wages or had large families, or both. In the table below the shift in household structure that occurred because of the local authorities' rehousing action is shown.

Table 6.7 *Household structure of previous and current tenants of investor landlords in Hackney and Islington, 1977–81*

Household structure	Hackney		Islington	
	Old	New	Old	New
	tenants		tenants	
Pensioner couple	10.1		14.2	
Single pensioner	17.7		26.8	
Non-pensioner couple	15.2	29.4	16.5	38.1
			11.4	
Non-pensioner single person	58.8	10.2	33.3	
Family with dependent children	44.3		32.3	14.3
Group of single unrelated people	1.3	11.8		14.3
% of households renting furnished	57.0	100.0	40.2	88.1
Totals	79	17	127	42

There has been a noticeable shift towards adult households, that is those without children and away from elderly households. The new tenants of investor landlords, particularly in Hackney, were in the main young or middle aged people working in poorly paid jobs or unemployed. The conditions in which they lived were often poor, for example 94 per cent of the new tenants in Hackney and 64 per cent in Islington either shared or lacked a bath but at least the rents were relatively low by inner London standards, ranging between £9.50 and £18.50 per week for a bedsit in Hackney in 1981, and £10.00 to £26.00 for similar accommodation in Islington a year earlier. The average new rents, however, exceeded by a factor of ten the average level of rents received from the previous tenants. As well as raising rent levels, the investor landlords who relet had all shifted from the unfurnished to the furnished sub-sector of the market, judging that their preferred tenants would be unlikely to possess furniture and domestic equipment. However, they had not otherwise improved or altered the nature of the lettings. The examples overleaf give more details of the changes that occurred in a small number of cases in each borough. It is clear that conditions in this sub-sector of the lettings market remained inadequate.

The investor landlords who reinvested in the lettings market were a particular sub-sector of the overall sample of this type of landlord. A large number of those that reinvested were what we might term 'new' men of property, often from ethnic minority groups who saw investment in the housing market as a safe and solid investment. These ethnic minority landlords were quite different from those in the informal sector that we have

---

Case studies 2

Reletting by investor landlords: the impact of rehousing on tenant types: 4 case studies

1   A Nigerian doctor living and practising in Ipswich, Suffolk, rented out a property he owned in north Islington to four households. At the end of 1978 Islington rehoused one of these four: a middle-aged Englishman who was a guard for London Transport and his wife who had been living there for ten years in two furnished rooms sharing the bath and WC. The same accommodation was relet within two months to an Egyptian postgraduate student and his wife. The rent for the rooms rose from £80 per month to £100. A year later the same rooms were relet to an Iraque medical student, his wife and child, and the rent rose again to £125 per month.

2   Mr X who lived in North London had owned several three-storey houses in Hackney for many years. One of his properties was let in multiple occupation as bedsits for single men. In 1980 Hackney rehoused a thirty-two year old man, who worked as a night cleaner, and his stepbrother. The room was immediately relet to another single man who was a heavy goods vehicle driver. The room was furnished, all amenities were shared and the rent rose from £7 per week to £9.50 on reletting.

3   A 2 storey house in East Hackney was let through estate agents to two elderly households, one of which was rehoused by Hackney. This was a very elderly widow who had lived in three unfurnished rooms without a bath and with an outside WC since 1929. The rent for these rooms was, in 1980, £1.25 per week. The rooms were relet to an Antiguan plumber, at the time unemployed, and his wife, after the addition of a bathroom, for £10.20 a week.

4   A Greek landlord who himself lived in Hertfordshire rented out a large Victorian house in south Islington in bedsitting rooms. LBI rehoused from one room a Spanish family who had been sharing all amenities, bath, WC and cooking facilities, with five other households. The husband was a waiter, and because his wife was expecting their second child the landlord served them with a notice to quit. The room was immediately relet on a weekly basis of £17.00 (compared with £11.00 paid by the previous tenants) to a young single man working as an electronic engineer. The property was already under a Direction Order as it was severely overcrowded.

---

just described. Letting was not incidental to home ownership, a short-term way of making ends meet, but often one aspect of a wide range of investments in both commercial and residential property as well as in other areas. These new investors were seldom solely reliant on the rental income from their residential properties as the old-style investor landlords were, but yet they did not have the same orientation to the market as the commercial landlords who relet. For the 'new' investors, owning houses in themselves was part of the motive for buying residential property and the rental flows, although not unimportant, were not the only consideration in the way in which the properties were tenanted and managed. It seems likely that this part of the private sector will remain relatively stable in size as those minority landlords interviewed expressed no intentions of leaving the residential property market.

The majority of investor landlords, however, decided not to let the vacancies created by the local authorities. Almost 40 per cent of the sample of landlords in each of the boroughs sold their dwellings at a profit, and a further percentage (40 per cent in Hackney and 25 per cent in Islington) disinvested without profits having materialised at the time of our survey. The reasons for some of the differences between the two boroughs are to be found in the combinations of a different structure of demand for home ownership and in the type and location of properties for sale in different areas within and between each borough.

Within inner city areas in general, and within inner London in particular, most of the growth of house ownership has, of necessity, taken place through tenure transfers. In Hackney and Islington during the 1970s it was possible to discern two distinct trends in the growth of home ownership: gentrification and low income home ownership. In Islington, and to a lesser extent in Hackney, particular areas of the borough were subjected to gentrification. This is the transfer of properties from low income households, who in the main were tenants of private landlords, and who were often living at high densities or in multi-occupied properties, to owner-occupiers. This tenure shift was associated with changes in the socio-economic composition of the new occupants (see Smith and Williams 1986). Gentrification within Hackney and Islington has been a spatially specific process, affecting only those areas with the particular combination of desirable location and certain type of property: Georgian and Edwardian property preferably bordering a tree-lined square (see Hamnett and Williams, 1980). However, it also apears to be a process that has a differential impact on the private rented sector. In our analysis we found that it was, in the main, commercial landlords and their agents who engaged in gentrification (and to an extent traditional and financial landlords, although their numbers were not sufficient to be sure of this). Investor landlords, as we shall now show, were involved in the main in the second form of tenure transfer, that to lower income households.

During the past decade or so, there has been a steady rise in the level of home ownership amongst low income inner city households in general, and amongst ethnic minority households in particular (Karn, 1977, 1979; Karn, Kemeny and Williams, 1983). In certain wards in the inner areas of British cities, in inner Birmingham, Liverpool and Manchester, for example, about 50 per cent of the houses had become owner-occupied by 1981. In inner London generally, the proportion is a little lower than this; in Hackney, for example, no ward had higher than 43 per cent of all households owning their own dwelling and in Islington the corresponding figure was 38 per cent. This is, of course, partly a reflection of the still bouyant demand for private renting in London. Nevertheless, low income owner-occupation is an important phenomenon in these boroughs and if the current cuts in local authorities' housing budgets continue its significance will increase for poor households as waiting lists for council housing grow longer and longer.

In our sample, it was the investor landlords who were involved in the process of transfer to low income owners. Of the 57 landlords who sold their properties to individual owner-occupiers, all but two in Islington were sold to households whose head was either in a manual occupation or was unemployed. There are a number of reasons for this. Investor landlords, as we argued in Chapters 3 and 5, are, in the main, old fashioned 'men of property' who have been in the domestic property market for many years, regarding their investment as 'safe as houses'. The properties which they let were often unimproved and unconverted, occupied by single households. In Islington, in particular, the rehoused tenants of investor landlords were predominantly elderly single people or couples whose move released an entire dwelling with vacant possession. In Hackney too, investor landlords were usually presented with vacant possession when the local authority housed their tenants. The crucial difference between these landlords involved in selling to low income households and those landlords selling to 'gentrifiers' was two fold: first the nature and location of their property and secondly, the agents involved in the process of transfer. *All* the houses were sold in an unimproved condition and they were mainly two- and three-storey homes facing straight on to the street rather than houses with a front garden or surrounding a square and garden. Most investor landlords sold through the aegis of the estate agent who also had been handling the previous letting of the dwellings and it was noticeable that these agents were the long-established, old fashioned 'family' firms in the two boroughs, rather than the more recent and aggressive arrivals to the property scene. The agents whom we interviewed erred on the side of caution, valuing the properties at a 'realistic' price, hoping for a relatively quick, trouble-free sale. It is not clear, however, that their assessment of the market was accurate as Table 6.6

Table 6.8 *Who replaced whom?*

Household structure	Hackney		Islington	
	Original occupants	New occupants	Original occupants	New occupants
Pensioner couple	11.1		6.6	
Single pensioner	18.5		50.0	
Non-pensioner couple	29.6	44.4	10.0	16.7
Non-pensioner single person	18.5	3.7	6.6	6.6
Family with dependent children	22.3	48.1	26.7	76.7
Group of single unrelated people		3.4		
Total numbers	27	27	30	30

Table 6.9 *Decreasing densities of occupation*

Average no. of people in the dwelling*	Before	After	Before	After
		transfer		transfer
	5.1	3.3	4.7	4.4

Note: * In this table only those tenants who had lived in a property that was transferred into owner-occupation have been included, rather than all the original occupants as in Table 6.7 in the earlier discussion of investor landlords who relet their vacancies.

shows a large number of properties held by investor landlords as empty and/or abandoned.

In Tables 6.8 to 6.10, the characteristics of the households who purchased dwellings from investor landlords, their sources of finance and the state of the dwelling are illustrated. We have distinguished between households headed by white and non-white individuals as previous studies of inner city housing markets (Smith, 1977; Paris and Blackaby, 1979; Karn, 1976, 1977, 1979) have demonstrated that non-white households heads face discriminating practices in the housing market that not only increase their reliance on the private sector but also place them in an inferior position in the competition for owner-occupation. For example, there is evidence of racial discrimination by estate agents (Duncan, 1976) and by financial institutions

Table 6.10 *Low income owner-occupation*

Condition		Hackney		Islington
% of dwellings improved after purchase		63		40
% of dwellings remaining unimproved		37		60
Total numbers		27		30

Source of finance % of households	White heads	Ethnic minority heads	White heads	Ethnic minority heads
Building Society loan	58.3	26.7		
Bank or insurance company loan	25.0	13.3	31.2	35.7
Local Authority or GLC mortgage	16.7	13.3		14.3
Loan company loan		13.3	18.8	
Outright purchase		33.3	50.0	50.0
Total numbers	12	15	16	14

(Boddy, 1980). Karn (1979) has demonstrated that ethnic minority households are much less likely to purchase houses with the aid of loans from formal institutions, that is from building societies, insurance companies, or the state, than purchasers in general. Minority groups tend to have to rely on fringe institutions or to purchase outright. For all low income prospective owners, however, inner city purchase on inadequate incomes implies ownership of inadequate properties and a continual struggle to maintain, let alone improve, the fabric of the dwelling.

Careful examination of the tables shows interesting differences between Hackney and Islington, giving support to our arguments about the significance of particular characteristics of housing markets for unravelling landlords' strategies. Despite the same type of landlord being involved in transfer to much the same type of household in the two boroughs, there are differences in the ways in which the transfers occurred. In Islington almost two-thirds of the transferred properties were not improved by their new owner compared with just over a third in Hackney and part of the reason for these differences is revealed in the second part of Table 6.10. New owners in Hackney were more likely to have become owners with a building society loan than in Islington, where outright purchase was more common. The generally higher prices of property in Islington probably meant that this group had little cash left over for improvements. But the differences also reflect the lending practices of building societies. The major societies frequently operate a quota system in inner city areas and, given the relative scales of middle-class penetration in the two boroughs, it is probable that a large proportion of the available mortgage funds go to more affluent households in Islington. In this borough half of the new owners had purchased outright. Of the remainder, households headed by white individuals appeared to rely on loan companies, and those with ethnic minority heads on banks or insurance companies and, to a lesser extent, the local authority or the Greater London Council for mortgage finance. In Hackney, the results, however, tend to lend support to the arguments of other housing researchers that non-white households find it more difficult than others to obtain building society loans. Ethnic differences in access to loan finance were apparent here. Compared with white heads of households, ethnic minority heads were more likely to have purchased their property outright or to have relied on banks, insurance and loan companies and so be paying higher rates of interest. In both boroughs, however, the policies of the local authorities and the Greater London Council seem to go a small way towards correcting these biases.

In both boroughs we found evidence of an interesting, and perhaps surprising, spatial bias in the pattern of this type of sales. Despite the majority of sales being handled by estate agents, in many cases the new purchasers had lived in the same street, or even next door to the house which they finally bought. They had also, without exception, previously rented private accommodation in the area, frequently from the same landlord from whom they bought the property. To some extent this reflects the orientation of investor landlords to their assets. Their ideology of 'service' or 'stewardship' lingers on and appears to affect their attitude to sales. Transfer to a previous tenant, to the relation of a tenant or, at the very least, to a 'local' inhabitant is preferred to sale to a 'newcomer'. This is also an attitude that was encouraged by the local authority, particularly in Hackney, during the 1970s where the so-called invasion of new middle-class owner occupiers was regarded as a threat, both because of the rise in property prices and also because of the political challenge these newcomers often posed to the old fashioned type of Labour politicians who had run the borough for many years.

What were the consequences of these transfers? For the investor landlords, they realised their assets and left the market with small profits and little effort. The sales were handled by local agents and no risks were taken by improving or converting the dwellings before sale. The households who bought them thus obtained dwellings that were in poor condition and likely to be a constant source of financial worry. In the long run, however, they would be able to sell their accommodation at a profit. It was noticeable that a substantial proportion of the new owners, 97 per cent of whom were male headed households reliant on the single earnings of the head, worked in the building trade or as painters, decorators or plumbers, either on their own account or as employees. Thus it seems likely that eventually there would be some improvement in the physical condition of these properties. At the time of transfer, however, the severe problems of disrepair and undermaintenance that characterises the private rented stock are merely shifted into part of the owner-occupied sector in inner areas. These problems are currently being exacerbated by rising rates of unemployment and by the severe reductions in improvement expenditure imposed on local authorities by central government. Investor landlords, in particular may find their options reduced by these trends as our evidence shows that they sell to households relying on the wages of men in manual occupations, jobs that are now very severely hit in inner areas. Cuts in local authority housing expenditure will also reduce the options of this group of landlord. In our Islington sample, a small but significant minority of investor landlords sold their dwellings to the local authority or to a housing association. This option too, but especially transfer to the local housing authority, is likely to be less available in the future.

Many of the investor landlords in our sample, however, were unable to sell their properties at all at the time at which we undertook our empirical survey. Over a third of the Hackney investor sample and a quarter of investor landlords in Islington were allocated to the category 'disinvestment without profits'. The twenty-five dwellings that we identified in the group of 'empty but for sale' (thirteen in Hackney, twelve in Islington) proved to have certain characteristics in common. They were owned by elderly individual investors who had held property in Inner London for up to fifty years. Like the dwellings that had already been sold, almost all these properties were also managed by long-established estate agents in the two areas. These agents were not prepared to accelerate sale by using some of the more aggressive practises that agents involved in conversation and sale to middle-class owner-occupiers were using. These included moving remaining tenants around to achieve vacant possession. The chief reason why these properties were not selling – on average they had been empty for fifteen months at the time of our survey – was that all but three of them were for sale with sitting tenants. This factor combined with poor physical conditions and unattractive locations on busy roads or close to noisy industrial uses made them difficult to sell. National changes too, particularly rising interest rates on home loans and the decline in local authority lending, combined with the local particularities to inhibit sale.

The investor landlords who had neither relet nor sold were, perhaps, the most interesting and largest group in this category of disinvestment. The group was made up of fourteen landlords in Hackney and sixteen in Islington and these were the only landlords whom we interviewed who referred to restrictive legislation and political uncertainty as part of their reason for leaving the lettings market. Of these landlords 73 per cent had been letting controlled or regulated tenancies to elderly couples or single people prior to them being rehoused by Hackney or Islington. The tenants had been long-term residents and the rates of return to their landlords were exceptionally low or even negative. The range of rents paid for this accommodation, usually a number of unfurnished rooms without a bath-room or an inside WC, was between £1.25 and £3.05 a week at the end of the 1970s. Although the landlords involved had long since paid off their mortgage debts, these returns were usually insufficient to cover the costs of adequately maintaining the dwellings and paying the rates. The future of this group of dwellings was uncertain. A small number seemed to have been completely abandoned by their owners who had no intention, or so they said, of either reletting or trying to sell their possessions. A much larger number probably would eventually be offered for sale. At the time of our interview, parts of the dwellings involved were still let to predominantly elderly tenants. If these remaining tenants were themselves rehoused, or died, then the landlords would be presented with completely vacant properties and a much higher likelihood that they could be sold. What is clear, however, is that these investor landlords would not reinvest in the private lettings market whatever the future changes in the legislative controls over this sector. They were not interested in current and future policy proposals and all but two denied all knowledge of recent changes, such as the shorthold tenancies introduced in 1981. These landlords were part of that relic sub-sector of the private rented sector that will continue to decline.

Commercial landlords

The commercial landlords – thirty-seven in Hackney and forty-six in Islington – were an extremely interesting group whose orientation to the market presents a good contrast to the behaviour of informal and investor landlords. These landlords considered their property solely from the point of view of economic gain and as such they had a clear view of the options open to them and a clear set of market criteria which they used to evaluate the most profitable strategy to adopt when presented with vacancies in their properties. They clearly recognised the characteristics of properties and of location that would lead to successful sale to middle-class households and

Table 6.11 *The strategies of commercial landlords*

	Landlords in	
Strategy	Hackney %	Islington %
Reinvestment i.e. reletting	64.9	47.8
Disinvestment		
A *With profits* (in order of declining profits)		
(1) Sale to an individual owner-occupier	10.8	26.1
(2) Sale to another landlord or speculator	8.1	2.2
(3) Sale to a sitting tenant		4.3
(4) Sale to local authority or housing association	2.7	2.2
B *Without profits*		
(1) Left empty but hope to sell		2.2
(2) Left empty/abandoned	13.5	2.2
(3) Compulsory purchased		13.0
(4) Returned to sole owner-occupation by the landlord		
(5) Demolished		
Informalisation i.e.		
Total numbers	37	46

wherever possible that was the strategy they adopted. It was this group of landlords who were most clearly involved in the process of gentrification. When the conditions were not appropriate for sale, however, it was this group of landlords that was most likely to relet their vacancies, usually to a different fraction of demand to the rehoused tenants. In all, over half the sample of commercial landlords relet – twenty-four in Hackney and twenty-two in Islington. In the former borough, for reasons that we shall expand on later, gentrification was a less profitable strategy than in Islington and so reletting was more frequently the preferred strategy (see Table 6.11).

Among the commercial landlords who did relet we found two distinct sub-groups. For the first, reletting was a short-term option, a way of making short-term profits while eventually intending to sell their properties. The second group had a different time horizon. For them, reletting was also an economically rational choice. They had assessed the state of demand for private rented accommodation, looked for that fraction to whom their property would appeal and where necessary adjusted their advertising so as to attract those tenants with a high rent paying capacity. These landlords seemed prepared to remain in the lettings market for an indeterminate time.

Among the first group of commercial landlords who relet, those with a

Case studies 3

The impact of reletting by expanding commercial landlords: two case studies.

X *Estate agency*

1   A very large Victorian house in north Hackney on the borders of Islington, from which the London Borough of Hackney rehoused a young couple from a furnished bedsitting room. They had shared the WC and bath with ten other tenants, all living in single rooms. For this princely accommodation the couple, who were both in waged employment, paid £20 a week in 1980. The room was immediately relet to a cohabiting couple in their twenties, working in the hotel trade, for £24 per week on a three month licence, giving the new occupants no security at all.

2   A flat fronted, eight-roomed Victorian house in N1 divided into furnished bedsits. Islington rehoused in 1979 a married couple from a bedsit which they had rented for £13 a week on a 1 year licence. The vacancy was immediately relet to another couple who had an individual rent agreement with the landlord, paying £14 rent a week *each*. Separate agreements with the occupants of the same room is another method of evading security of tenure legislation. The couple shared the bathroom but had their own WC within their accommodation. Altogether there were twelve occupants in this house.

Y *Furnished lettings*

1   A large house in N4 near the boundary between Hackney and Islington. Previously let multi-occupied to a range of different types of tenants. Islington rehoused three households from here in 1979: an elderly male pensioner, a young Nigerian couple and a middle-aged Irish couple, all of whom had rented a single room and shared the WC and bath. Each household paid £8.50 per week rent. The rooms were relet immediately to three married couples, at £15.50 per week with no improvement in physical conditions. It was according to one of our respondents 'a horrible house to live in' but they could find nowhere else at the time.

2   A three-storey Victorian house in Stoke Newington. The London borough of Hackney rehoused a Jamaican couple and their young son in 1980. This household had rented an unfurnished bedsitting room and shared the WC with six other households. There was no bath in the house. The room was relet immediately to a single man at double the previous rent (from £6.50 to £13 per week). In total, the house was divided into thirteen bedsitting rooms. LBH were threatening to take the landlord to court for a maintenance or possession order at the time of our research.

short-term interest in reletting, we found evidence of a wide range of exploitative practices, on the fringes of legality. High rents, harassment of tenants, lack of leases and rent books, short-term leases, 'holiday' lets and lettings including a derisory 'service' element (such as providing rolls and butter in a dispensing machine) were all used to maximise rates of return, rates of turnover and to reduce tenants' security. There was some evidence of trading within this sub-group as new landlords entered the market and existing ones extended their investment. In general, in both boroughs, the properties that these landlords held and traded were in poor condition and almost always let in multiple occupation. Investment in housing was a business to them and the aim was the extraction of short-term profits. In our survey we identified two commercial landlords who were particularly active in buying large rundown properties and so expanding their holdings of domestic lettings. One was an estate agent who also had a property division to his business, the other an individual who appeared to trade under a number of guises. In 1981 they each owned between them upwards of fifty properties across Hackney and in areas in north Islington, where there was substantial demand for renting but less opportunity to sell unimproved properties. Their preferred mode of operation was to let large dwellings sub-divided into bed-sitting rooms to young single people, either students or workers, or to married couples without children. In all cases, the properties were let furnished and at high rents given the conditions and lack of amenities (see inset for a number of case studies).

Commercial landlords with a longer time horizon were more interested in less mobile tenants. A small number of such landlords – six in all and all in Islington – had improved and upgraded their accommodation before reletting it to tenants in professional occupations. Indeed there were noticeable differences between the two boroughs in the type of new tenants housed by commercial landlords.

Overall, the net result of the reletting strategies of commercial landlords in Hackney and in Islington was to alter the socio-economic characteristics of tenants. Table 6.12 below shows the shifts that have occurred and the associated move towards furnished lettings. It is clear that in both boroughs there is a ready market of young people who have no option but to look to the private landlord for housing. But in Islington there was evidence of a tendency by the commercial landlords to shift 'upmarket' in terms of to whom they let. The new tenants were often students or people in pro-fessional or semi-professional occupations such as estate agency, nursing and white-collar clerical jobs, who by pooling their rent paying capacity could meet high rents. A not uncommon example in Islington was the shift from a single parent and her baby who paid £6.50 for two rooms and a

Table 6.12 *Household structure of previous and current tenants of commercial landlords in Hackney and Islington, 1977–81*

	Hackney		Islington	
	Old	New	Old	New
Household structure	tenants		tenants	
Pensionable couple	8.1		13.1	
Single pensioner	10.8		41.3	4.5
Non-pensioner couple	32.4	12.5	26.1	45.5
Non-pensioner single person	13.5	50.0	10.9	27.3
Family with dependent children	35.2	8.3	6.5	
Group of single unrelated people		29.2	2.2	22.7
% renting furnished accommodation	81.1	100.0	43.5	90.9
Totals	37	24	45	22

shared bathroom to four nurses each paying £20 per week for the same two rooms – a more than twelve-fold rent increase with no change in the condition of the letting. In Hackney, however, the new tenants tended to be younger and poorer. They had often left home for non-work related reasons, and were either unemployed or in poorly paid jobs and so had less financial power in an extremely tight housing market. Many of them were young black couples or single people who had left home because of family tensions. So the structure of local demand in each borough affects the options open to commercial landlords despite their similar overall orientation to the market.

Most new lettings were unimproved in terms of physical condition and all of them were relet as furnished rather than unfurnished accommodation. The high level of demand for housing from young people in these areas meant that landlords had little need to improve their accommodation before putting it on the market again. In their experience, landlords found that vacancies could be relet immediately. These cramped, inadequate and expensive bedsits and rooms are in no sense adequate 'homes' for young people but in some senses the young tenants we interviewed in Hackney and Islington were the lucky ones. In Inner London, there is a growing problem of homelessness among young people, especially those from ethnic minority groups. Extremely high rates of unemployment amongst young people are making the problem worse. The 1985 proposed changes in social security regulations that restricted the rights of people under twenty-six to remain in bed and breakfast accommodation in a particular area for periods longer than between two and eight weeks represented a complete misreading of the housing and employment situation facing low income and unemployed people in inner city areas and will only succeed in aggravating an already grave situation.[2] For other groups in Hackney and Islington too it is clear that access to the diminishing supply of private lettings is becoming increasingly difficult. The commercial landlords in our sample were clearly disinclined to house families with children or middle-aged low income single people and couples. The average age of the non-pensioner childless tenant in our survey fell from forty-eight to twenty-seven. We have shown too the familiar shift towards furnished lettings rather than unfurnished rooms. The former may be preferred by single people at the outset of their housing careers but they are seldom ideal for older, more established tenants. For these older tenants, and for families with young children it is apparent that one of the paradoxical effects of local authority rehousing policy is to reduce their access to the private rented sector.

Despite being able to increase profit levels by reletting, where possible the commercial landlords preferred to sell their dwellings, either directly to an individual owner-occupier or to a speculator for conversion, improvement and resale. The potential profits from this strategy exceed those from reletting over the short and medium term and also the landlords are able to dispose of what they may regard as a potentially or actually troublesome asset. Nineteen commercial landlords in our sample were involved in sale to gentrifiers – twelve of them in Islington where the market for sales to relatively affluent households is more buoyant and profitable than in Hackney, and where the process of gentrification occurred rather earlier, dating from the 1960s and early 1970s (see Williams, 1978). But even in Islington, only a few streets and squares within the borough have been touched by this phenomenon (see Pitt, n.d.). For the landlords in our sample, it was above all the spatial location of their investment that influenced the rates of return from sale. Within Islington there are five small areas that so far have been occupied by middle-class households. Three of these areas are within walking distance of stations on the Victoria tube line: the Canonbury, Highbury and Barnsbury areas. The other two main areas – around the Angel and Tufnell Park – are also on good transport links. Hackney, by contrast has relatively poor communications, with no underground lines at all running through the borough at the time of our survey.

The other factor that influenced the potential profits to be made from sales was the size of the created vacancy. In the main, potential gentrifiers were only interested in properties with vacant possession. Thus in our sample, all the properties that had been sold at the time of our survey had

---

[2] In fact, in August 1985, the High Court ruled that these regulations were illegal and up to 85,000 claimants were entitled to benefit rebates. However, similar restrictions were introduced in the Social Security Act 1986, that came into force in April 1988.

been vacated in their entirety after the previous tenants were rehoused. The one property that was being held in anticipation of sale in Islington was still partially occupied. Whereas commercial landlords were open to moving tenants around between their properties to create vacancies, their ability to do so was limited by the number of vacancies created both in the properties influenced by rehousing action and in other properties owned by these landlords. Among the commercial landlords, we found clear evidence of tenant harassment. Despite an entirely explicable disinclination to talk about the means by which tenants could be persuaded to move between tenancies or leave all together, a small number of landlords whom we interviewed and a larger number of their remaining tenants detailed several practices on the fringes of legality that were utilised to increase vacancy rates.

Traditional and financial landlords and gentrification

Sale to high income households was also the preferred strategy of the small number of traditional and financial landlords included in our survey. To draw out the similarities and differences between their actions and those of the commercial landlords we have chosen to include them in the discussion at this point. Despite their very different orientation to the market, at opposite poles of the social-economic tension, traditional and financial landlords adopted similar approaches to disinvestment to commercial landlords and were even more successful in leaving the lettings markets with handsome profits. The main traditional landlord we surveyed in Islington, a charitable trust, owned properties in the Barnsbury area, one of the earliest parts of Islington that had been gentrified. In Chapter 4 we argued that this landlord had an anachronistic orientation towards the market, so that the legacy of ideas of stewardship and patronage influenced letting strategies. When it comes to vacancies, however, the trust sold empty properties into high income ownership. The legacy of earlier ideas did, however, influence the strategy as the dwellings initially were sold on a leasehold basis to retain the trust's links with the area. At the other end of the pole, the financial landlords, freehold sale was pursued. Included in our sample was a major financial institution owning property in the squares and streets of Canonbury, another favoured area for gentrification. Here the properties were deliberately managed and the remaining tenants moved about within the stock to create houses for sale with vacant possession, at an average price of £150,000 per property in 1981.

Although all three types of landlords were involved in gentrification, the process by which the transfers occurred varied both between the landlords and between the boroughs. Traditional and financial landlords in Islington tended to sell unconverted properties to owners who then undertook improvement work, either themselves or through the use of local small building firms, whereas the commercial landlords, particularly in Hackney, were more likely to have sold their properties to an intermediary, a property company that specialised in conversion, improvement and resale, or to building firms. Merrett (1982) has labelled these two forms of tenure transfer as unmediated and mediated gentrification. In the former case the landlord has to arrange the sale, usually through one of the many local estate agents operating in the boroughs and wait until the purchase has been completed before appropriating whatever profits may accrue. If the landlords themselves undertake improvement work, and in particular if the dwellings are split into several self-contained units, this process may be lengthy. In the mediated case where the initial transfer is to a speculator, the landlords involved benefited immediately from the value of the sale although the rates of return tended to be lower.

The reason for these differences is to be found in the combination in the characteristics of the landlords and the local housing market. Commercial landlords are 'trading' landlords, reliant on short-term loans and so concerned to see immediate returns on their investment. Thus sale to an intermediary is attractive to them in both areas. For the other landlords there is a trade-off between the time taken to sell and the expected rate of return. In Islington, where gentrification is a more established phenomenon than in Hackney, demand is relatively high from individual purchasers prepared to arrange their own improvements. In Hackney there is not such an established market for the sale of unconverted properties to affluent households so mediated sale is a safer proposition. However, this situation may change. The initial phases of improvement in a particular area has a remarkable effect on the price of unconverted properties in that and in adjacent areas and so effectively excludes a second wave of similar types of households. They must look for other areas with similar locational and dwelling characteristics but lower prices. Parts of Hackney immediately to the east of the high status areas in Islington – and with the same cachet of a N1 postal address – were being gentrified at the time of our survey, as were a small number of streets with larger Victorian properties and more spacious street layouts in E8 and in E9.

The consequences of gentrification have been both beneficial and detrimental. Overall the density of occupation of the properties transformed into owner-occupation was reduced and the physical condition of the stock improved, but at the cost of reducing access to these properties, for low-income households, whether as renters or as purchasers. In some cases there

Tables 6.13 *Who replaced whom?*

Household structure	Hackney		Islington	
	Original occupants	New occupants	Original occupants	New occupants
Pensionable couple	44.4		18.8	
Single pensioner	22.2		50.0	
Non-pensioner couple	11.1	66.6	12.5	43.7
Non-pensioner single person	11.1	11.1		18.8
Family with dependent children	11.1	11.1	12.5	25.0
Group of single unrelated people		11.1	6.2	12.5

Table 6.14 *Decreasing densities of occupation*

Average number of people in the dwelling	Hackney		Islington	
	Before transfer*	After transfer	Before transfer*	After transfer
	8.7	2.2	7.6	2.4

Note: * This average includes *all* the previous tenants of the transferred properties not just the rehoused tenant household.

Table 6.15 *The process of gentrification*

	Hackney	Islington
Condition		
% of dwellings improved after purchase	44.4	62.5
% of dwellings purchased already improved	55.6	31.3
% of dwellings improved with the aid of an improvement grant		6.2
Source of finance		
% of households		
Building Society loan	55.5	75.0
Bank or Insurance Company loan	22.2	12.5
Local Authority or GLC mortgage	11.1	6.2
Outright of purchase	11.1	6.2
Total numbers	9	16

were remarkable changes in the numbers of occupants. The extreme example in our survey was a decline from seventeen occupants of single bedsitters to a shared household of three unrelated adults. The changes in household structure after sale are outlined in Table 6.13 and it is clear that the consequence was a shift towards younger single people or couples without dependants. This is, of course, partly a reflection of the lending policies of the major mortgage finance institutions. In the following table the proportions of dwellings that were purchased before and after improvement and the sources of finance for purchase are shown. It is apparent that the major building societies no longer have any fear of investing in inner city middle-class owner-occupation. Given the controversy in the mid 1970s about the role of state aid on exacerbating gentrification (Hamnett, 1973) it is interesting that only a tiny proportion of new occupants obtained improvement grants from the local authority and none of the builders or speculators involved in conversion had bothered to apply for this form of financial aid.

Transfer to above average income owner-occupiers is now an established process of housing change in the inner city, affecting both Hackney and Islington and for those landlords owning vacant properties in the more environmentally attractive parts of the boroughs a way of disinvesting with substantial profit. Whether or not this form of disinvestment should, or could, be monitored and controlled by the local housing authority in each borough is a debatable question. Their action in rehousing a previous tenant or tenants in many cases merely exacerbated a process that was already underway. Whether landlords might be 'encouraged' to remain in the lettings market by a tax on their disinvestment profits is a question that needs to be weighed against the standard of accommodation provided for tenants. In many cases, but particularly among the commercial landlords included in our sample whose major motivating factor was rental gain, the housing provided was inadequate. Perhaps the demise of such landlords should be encouraged rather than attempts made to persuade them to remain in the letting market.

Employer landlords

Employer landlords, or, as they are more commonly known, landlords who provide tied accommodation, remain significant providers of private rented accommodation in England and Wales as a whole. In 1981, they accommodated a perhaps surprisingly high proportion of all private tenants – 22 per cent. However, their significance varies, depending upon the spatial location of certain types of employment – in particular in agriculture and in the armed forces. Within Greater London in general, and in Hackney and Islington in particular, tied housing is more common in a range of occupations in the service sector – in association with the hotel catering and brewery industries for example and in some cases in the retail sector.

Employer landlords' orientation to the lettings market is different from that of the other five types of landlord. They provide accommodation for tenants only when the tenants are also essential workers in a business enterprise by the landlord. The rent calculation is therefore undertaken on a different basis as it is part of an overall calculation made by the landlord about rents, wages and profits.

Our sample included thirty-six employer landlords, a number of whom had, in fact, moved away from a strict definition of the term. They were landlords who owned or had acquired residential property because of their business involvement. In the main, these lettings were non-self-contained rooms over shops and cafes and while, at some time, they had been occupied by employees of the owner, the necessity for tied accommodation was no longer clear and the rooms were inhabited by low-income households, often from ethnic minority groups who, for various reasons, had had no other choice open to them when they had been searching for housing. The landlords of these vacancies whom we interviewed indicated their willingness to continue to let these rooms but, in fact, 19 per cent of the thirty-six vacancies were empty at the time of our survey, often boarded up or subject to various local authority control orders. A further two had been squatted and two had been demolished. A small number of landlords hoped to sell the residential part of their property. However, as well as many of these lettings being in extremely poor physical condition, their position generally, over shops and cafés, and their location, often on noisy main roads, meant that they were not an attractive proposition for purchase nor the sort of accommodation on which lending institutions would grant mortgages. In one case both the shop lease and the associated accommodation was up for sale. This seemed to be a more viable commercial proposition than attempting to sell the residential accommodation separately.

Thirteen of the thirty-six employer-owned vacancies were reoccupied at the time of our survey. One of these lettings had moved into the informal category as it was occupied by relatives of the owners. The remaining twelve continued to be let at the bottom end of the market to families and single people whose options in the tight and expensive lettings market in Inner London were extremely constrained by their low income, their recent arrival in the capital and often by their inadequate command of English. In many ways their characteristics were identical to the previous tenants whom the respective local authority had recently rehoused and the physical conditions of the tenancies remained identical. For the local housing authority then the problems to which rehousing had been an answer were being recreated and, in the absence of alternatives, another generation of tenants would eventually need rehousing from these lettings.

For other types of landlords, as we have demonstrated, the creation of vacancies allowed them to shift to accommodating different types of tenants, or to sell their property, sometimes in association with improvements in the physical condition of the properties and usually with the prospect of increased profits over time or immediate capital gains. To the extent that local authority action was wholly or partly responsible for creating the conditions for these gains it may be pertinent to question whether there is any way in which they could or should share in the financial rewards. In the concluding chapter we turn our attention to this and other policy questions arising from current changes in inner city housing markets and the decline of the private rented sector.

Conclusions

This chapter has revealed some of the factors involved in the changing nature of the inner city rented market. The strands that go to make up the overall decline of the private rented sector in the country as a whole and within different areas, are complex and intertwined. One part of the pattern is the way in which private landlordism is constituted at a particular time. We have argued that each of the six types of landlord that we distinguished has a particular orientation to the market and so a propensity to act in certain kinds of ways depending on how they evaluate their property holdings, their sources of finance, their assessment of future gains and their knowledge and awareness of the political and social climate that influence attitudes towards private landlords. The relative importance of these six types of landlord at different times in particular markets will, therefore, influence the nature of decline. But their actions also depend on national circumstances and on changes in factors such as interest rates, the employment situation, socio-demographic changes, and the nature of national housing policy. Mortgage interest rates, the availability of finance and of improvement grants, the push towards local authority sales, the decline of local authority expenditure on improvement and rehabilitation are all national changes that influence the options available to landlords, the extent of transfer of the stock between tenures and the overall rate of decline of the private rented sector. These factors are the context in which decline appears.

However, national factors are not sufficient to explain the changes. As we have argued throughout the book so far, the contingent nature of local housing conditions must also be taken into account, for decline is spatially variable and the decisions made by each type of landlord place-specific. As we have shown in this chapter, different types of landlords have different reactions to vacancies but also different types appear to have the same reaction. The reasons for their decisions, however, are often different and their strategies are based on their orientation to the market, their financial time horizons and their long-term attitudes to letting. In Hackney and Islington, we have shown how different types of landlord, investor or informal for example, may decide for quite different reasons to reinvest in the domestic property market and also how the prospective tenants vary because of differences between the two boroughs. In such cases, too, the overall decline is, paradoxically, made up of growth in certain categories. It seems from our empirical work in Hackney and Islington that informal landlordism is on the increase, particularly among new owner-occupiers who let part of their own house for a number of years. A detailed assessment of this part of the informal sector is difficult to carry out because of the temporary, fluctuating and semi-legal nature of this particular letting arrangement.

It should be abundantly clear from this chapter that the complexity and heterogeneity of this part of the housing market makes it unamenable to simple policy recommendations, and, indeed, to simple mono-causal explanations of decline. In Hackney and Islington we found landlords with a wide variety of motives and future intentions. Recent legislative changes – shorthold and assured tenancies – for example appeared to have little or no effect on their actions. Indeed the majority of landlords whom we interviewed were not aware of the changes (Allen and McDowell, 1982). Similarly rent and security of tenure legislation rarely entered into their calculations of whether to reinvest or disinvest. None of the new rentals, for example, were let under the fair or registered rent scheme. The diversity of the private rented sector, the way in which the wider processes of housing reinvestment and disinvestment in the rented market are adopted by different landlords at different times, in certain places, in response to local conditions, is a crucial factor in understanding the decline and in proposing policies to affect it. We shall argue in the next chapter that until an understanding of the diversity forms an essential element in the policies proposed to affect the nature of private letting, 'solutions' proposed by both the left and the right of the political spectrum are doomed to failure.

7

Political ideologies and private rental policies

There is no simple, unmediated relation between explanation and policy; not, that is, in the sense that actual policy recommendations are determined by the type of explanation adopted. The adoption of a particular explanatory approach however, we would argue, does influence the scope and form of policy recommendations. Central to the realist-type explanation of decline in rented accommodation set out in the preceding chapters is the notion of diversity, the diverse impact of general processes of housing change such as rental disinvestment and investment within a variety of housing markets. In particular, we have drawn attention to the complex effects of the activities of different types of private landlords in different areas. And from this focus two relatively clear policy directions would appear to follow.

First, the need to devise policies which can discriminate between different types of landlords in order to meet the variety of rented housing need in different locations. Certain types of landlords, in particular commercial landlords, are unlikely to be in a position to provide secure, reasonably priced, rented accommodation whatever the rented housing need of an area. Other groups of landlords, however, *may* be in a position to adequately meet *certain* types of rented housing need in particular areas. In the short term, such a possibility should not be dismissed out of hand, prior to an understanding of local rented housing need. Indeed, one of the aims of this book has been to clarify how the private rented housing market operates, in order that immediate policies may be devised which can exert some leverage upon how the structure of rented housing can be changed to meet rented housing need. Constructing a more rigorous conception of landlord types is part and parcel of this process, and one which is likely to throw light upon what types of policy instrument will be successful in reorganising the market or encouraging its decline, either selectively or in a comprehensive manner.

The second policy direction that follows from the explanatory approach adopted in this book is one of form rather than substance; namely, the need for a range of policies to intervene at different points in the private rented sector, in the housing market as a whole and in related areas. This direction follows from the analysis of the causes behind the changes in the structure of the rented market. National housing policy and the national economic factors noted earlier, in combination with the local characteristics of housing markets, have shaped the present structure of the rented housing market. The activities of private landlords have been central to this transformation, but they are not the only causal agents involved. Later we will argue for a set of public and private initiatives to meet the diverse pattern of rented housing need within and across different local housing markets.

It is this last point which, in fact, underpins the two policy directions indicated and represents the starting point for policy recommendations. The two directions address, respectively, the policy focus and the different levels of policy initiative involved, but neither address directly the central issue of whose needs such a policy should be designed for. The answer to this question would appear obvious and perhaps rather banal, and yet national housing policies have failed to acknowledge the diversity of rented housing need, the different types of demand exhibited by private tenants in terms of type, access, quality, cost and security of provision. The various rented housing needs of long-term private renting households, newly forming households, mobile households, and households tied to their employers, together with the differences within and between these groups in terms of age, income, lifestyle and household composition represent a complex pattern of housing need. The recognition of the diversity of rented housing need is, in our view, of fundamental importance to policy formation. For it is our contention that the housing needs of the sector have largely been voiced by organisations and groups who have failed to acknowledge the complexity of either the provision of rented accommodation or the demand for rented accommodation.

In brief, the argument of this chapter is that the fragmented political interests of both landlords and tenants have allowed a situation to arise whereby their respective interests are perceived in general terms and 'spoken for' by political parties and other groups within the housing lobby. On the one hand, drawing upon a set of ideas which loosely fall under the heading of '*laissez-faire*', the interests of landlords have been represented as a group whose concerns can be met through the establishment of a form of free market provision for rented housing. On the other hand, the interests of tenants have been represented as a group whose housing needs can be met through the abolition of the market and the transfer of the rented housing stock to public ownership. This belief is largely inspired by a particular variant of Fabian ideas that challenges the market provision of goods in favour of collective provision by the State. In our view, these two political ideologies, *laissez-faire* and Fabianism, have constructed the politics of private renting; a politics shaped by the gap between profit and need which characterises the social distance between private landlord and tenant.

One of the consequences of the politics of private renting paralleling the broad opposition between profit and need is that these general categories have tended to form the bench marks, as it were, which policy proposals have to acknowledge and commence from. In our assessment the general categories of profit and need are the starting points for a socialist reexamination of the structures of housing provision within the major tenures – owner-occupation, private and public rented housing; that is, an examination which addresses both the supply of housing and its distribution in tenurial form, and evaluates the role of private interests in both the provision of owned *and* rented housing.[1] In the absence, however, of any immediate prospects of fundamental change in the structure of housing provision, despite our belief in its necessity, we argue that the categories of profit and need are at present inappropriate starting points for developing proposals for the future of private renting. The effect of acknowledging profit and need as the two poles of the debate over the future of private renting and not in respect of the other main tenures is to foreclose the possibility of raising a different set of questions which address the diversity of the sector. What type of rented housing should be provided? How should it be provided? Who should provide it? And for whom? We should add that adopting the diversity of the sector as the starting point for policy considerations does not represent a compromise between the general categories of profit and need. Rather it represents a displaced position, one based upon the existing conditions of the market and not one based upon the abstract relations of market or state provision of rented housing.

In this chapter we discuss briefly the fragmented nature of landlords' and tenants' interests, their political marginalisation, and the 'space' this has created for their interests to be represented in general terms. Then we examine the political ideologies which have defined the debate over the future of private renting and which presently inform policy development and offer an assessment of the relative chances of success. We have

[1] Both Ball, 1983, and Harloe, 1985, p 313, emphasise the importance of recognising the capitalist agencies that are involved in the provision of the two major tenures, owner-occupation and public housing. The point is rarely acknowledged in respect of the latter tenure, although Ball has outlined the roles performed by loan capital and building capital in the provision of public housing and shown how these private agencies affect the cost and quality of the houses produced (pp. 346–51). In essence, he argues 'for the need to take housing provision out of the market mechanism, and so out of the control of the private agencies that dominate these, in order to give people a greater control over this vital aspect of their lives' (p. 371).

deliberately avoided giving a comprehensive review of the history of private rented housing policy and its effects as many other books set out to provide this information. Our focus is contemporary and oriented towards what should be done with private rented housing. Finally then, in a prescriptive vein, we outline an alternative strategy for change designed to meet the varied needs of renters and potential renters dependent upon the sector for their housing.

Politics at the margins

To speak of the collective interests or the collective efforts of private landlords and private tenants is a misnomer. Neither group in Britain possesses a sufficient degree of common attributes or aims to close ranks and mobilise in defence of their perceived interests (see Parkin, 1972, Chapter 4). The sheer heterogeneity of landlords in terms of the amount of capital at their disposal, the number of dwellings owned, their legal status, and their different reasons for owning residential property, prohibit group closure. The interests of resident landlords, as we have seen, are not identical to those of the Church of England or to those of a major pension trust fund. Of the estimated 500,000 private landlords in Britain in the early 1980s, less than 2 per cent belong to a recognised landlords' or property owners' association and the vast majority are unlikely to possess the economic means to mobilise for their particular interests (House of Commons Environment Committee, 1982, Vol. III, p. 211).

The marginalisation of private landlords, as a political process which commenced in 1915 with the Rent and Mortgage Restriction Act, has been well documented (Dickens, 1978). It is difficult to contest the view that the interests of private landlords were sacrificed with the introduction of rent controls both to forestall social unrest during the First World War and to prevent any further harm to the interests of industrial and banking capital. At that time, compared to the political power of industrial capital, the commercial banks (who succeeded in obtaining exemption from controls on mortgage interest rates), and the Building Societies (who achieved limited concessions), the organisational ability of private landlords to enforce their interests was minimal. As a fragmented social group, landlords were relatively powerless to resist the pressures both overt and covert of the more solidaristic groups, including that of organized labour, who favoured the imposition of rent controls.

There is a risk here, however, of slipping into an historical explanation which accounts for the relative powerlessness of private landlords today as being an extension of the events of 1915. It is indeed the case that the events of 1915 contributed towards a shift in the forum of housing politics from the local to the national and this reduced the effectiveness of local interests such as private landlords. It is also true that private landlords today are, as they were in 1915, largely composed of individual and small-scale entrepreneurs. But here the similarity can be misleading. The investor landlord common to that period has largely disappeared. Their cause today is voiced, largely unheard, by the Small Landlords Association, an organisation of some 800 members based in London who have little influence upon central government policy. They are perhaps the legacy of 1915; but a substantial part of the contemporary market is inhabited by different types of landlords. As outlined in Chapter 3, there are the informal and the commercial landlords who operate largely outside the boundaries of legislation; there are the traditional and the employer landlords who are in the market for reasons other than financial gain; and there are the financial landlords, the public property companies in particular, who have entered and left the market at varying stages since the 1930s. With the exception of financial landlords, to which we will return, none of the remaining groups possess collective 'identities' or the ability to mobilise on behalf of perceived collective interests.

The interests of private tenants are less diverse, although sufficient in number to frustrate the possibility of collective mobilisation. Differences of income, age, lifestyle and opportunity to leave the sector cut across potential common aims. More importantly, even assuming the recognition of a common interest among private tenants, for example around rent levels, the economic weakness of the vast majority of tenants and their geographical spread, together with the high rate of turnover of lettings limits the possibility of tenants effecting group closure (see Harloe, 1985). Few of the 2,000,000 households in the sector are involved in tenants' organisations and those that are tend to be locally based and concerned with the specific needs of their particular housing.

The picture, then, is one of fragmentation with few landlords or tenants in a position to promote or organise around particular interests or to challenge the interpretation of their interests by the organisations and political parties who speak on their behalf. In turn, the fragmentation of their interests and their position of economic weakness creates the possibility for their needs to be 'spoken for' from outside. Among the organisations and groups in Britain who lobby on behalf of landlords' and tenants' interests and represent them as collective themes, it would appear that only three exert considerable political influence – the British Property Federation, the Labour Housing Group and the housing pressure group, Shelter. The remainder, an array of small property owners' associations and tenants associations either work though these organisations or fall outside of the circles of influence. Of the three main organisations, however, none are likely to alter the marginal political status of private renting to an issue of political priority.

The British Property Federation, the direct descendant of the National Association of Property Owners with a pedigree that can be traced back to the United Property Owners Association of the last century, was formed in 1974 and has a direct membership of some 1,400 members; the majority of the members are listed property companies, with the remainder approximately one-third made up of small landlords, mainly private individuals and private property companies. Aside from the direct members, the Federation also represents thirty affiliated associations of property owners, of which the London-based, Small Landlords Association with its 800 odd members is the largest affiliate.

The differences between the British Property Federation (BPF) and the Small Landlords Association (SLA) are manifest in their class base, their interests in property, and the nature of their political activities. The BPF, for example, represents the interests of large-scale property capital, primarily those of commercial property capital and financial landlords, whereas the SLA represents small-scale residential capital. The BPF exhibits a preoccupation with the economic return on property investments and has direct access to Conservative Party circles; whereas the SLA stress the right of the private landlord to exercise virtually complete control over their property and campaign for this right outside of formal political circles, with an inability to do otherwise.

Given the composition of the BPF, the nub of their promotional activity understandably is directed at promoting the commercial property interests of its members. The residential property interests of its members are not neglected however, as is evident by the influential role that the BPF played in promoting the 'assured lettings' scheme introduced under the 1980 Housing Act by the Conservative Government. Yet such activities did not assist in any direct way the interests of groups like the SLA or the majority of private landlords. In its earliest formulation the 'assured lettings' scheme could only be operated by government 'approved bodies'; bodies which, in general, were drawn from the types of institutions that the BPF represent, that is, the larger property development companies and to a lesser extent the financial institutions. The Federation was also the major promotor of a wider scheme for rented residential property that would put it on par with commercial lettings and which bears considerable resemblance to the assured tenancy concept (BPF, 1984 and 1985). Both schemes have proved influential in shaping current Conservative thinking on the future of the private rented housing market, but neither scheme or any reworking of them are likely to appeal to small, individual landlords or satisfy their preoccupation with the rights to control and dispose of their property largely at will.

On a sensitive political issue such as private rented housing, it is not really in the short- or long-term interests of the Federation and its members to put themselves out on a political limb. The Federation's major interests are in commercial property with rented housing a minor, related concern. They are unlikely to sacrifice their interests in the rented housing market, although neither would they be likely to jeopardise their general interest in commercial property and its promotion by advocating proposals which are likely to attract political hostility and public reaction. After all, they are predominantly commercial property landlords, not residential landlords; only the latter form of landlordism attracts negative publicity to any degree and it is not in the interests of the Federation to equate the two forms in the public eye. It would appear, therefore, that the larger forms of property capital exercises a degree of restraint over their demands for the reform of the rented housing market. And it is this restraint that further reinforces the marginality of rented housing as a political issue.

The Labour Housing Group, the second of the major interest groups, is made up of housing activists and housing specialists from within the Labour Party. The Group was formed in 1981, in response to the Party's failure to project a wider, alternative vision of housing to the narrow, yet popular image of attainable home ownership successfully conveyed by the Conservative Party in the early 1980s. Their major energies have been directed to countering the widespread view that 'home ownership is "normal" and renting a residual form of tenure for those unable to make the grade as home owners' (LHG, 1984a, pp. 23–4). The alternative view of housing they propose is one of equality between tenures, in terms of the state financial support each tenure receives, individual and collective rights of control and levels of investment to achieve parity of physical conditions. The coexistence of owning and renting in the future is acknowledged, with the proviso that both forms of housing should be reorganized to ensure that households have a real choice between the two (ibid., Chapter 2).

References to renting under this strategy, however, refer only to public renting. Separate proposals have been drawn up by the Group which argue for the abolition of the private rented sector in full recognition of the immense difficulties that such a programme would involve (ibid., Chapter 11). A realistic recognition of these difficulties however, apart that is from questions of resources and the low political priority that such a programme is likely to attract, would have to meet the choices of those presently dependent upon the sector for accommodation. Yet the marginal status of private renting tends to imply that their choices are predetermined; they have only the choice of becoming public tenants. If private tenants had the ability to become home owners, it is implied, they would already have done so. This is probably true and for a number of private tenants the option of a public tenancy is likely to be welcomed. The point, however, is that it is assumed that all private tenants' housing needs can be met by a state-based solution.

The debate is closed, in much the same way that the debate over the interests of private landlords is closed; the respective interests of tenants and landlords are 'known'. The significance of the re-presentation of interest it should be said does not rest upon any notion of its uniqueness as a political phenomenon. It is not unusual for fragmented, economically weak groups to have their 'interests' expressed for them. In this instance it is the entrenched opposition of ideas which define the politics of private renting which, in turn, preclude an alternative strategy that is significant.

Political ideologies and orthodox policies

Private rented housing in Britain is subject to an ideological debate that rests upon certain views about what should happen to rented housing. These views are normative, in the sense that they contain prescriptions about what role the state and what role the market should perform in the provision of rented housing. Over the years, two political ideologies, *laissez-faire* and Fabianism have had strong associations with the formulation of proposals for the reform of the private rented housing sector. It is their respective views of the relations that should hold between market and state that have informed and indeed have largely defined the politics of private renting. A glance at the post-war parliamentary debates on the private rented sector in Hansard, particularly the debates around the 1957 and 1965 Rent Acts and the 1980 Housing Act reveal the familiar repetition of the opposing market and state based solutions to the problems of private renting. Naturally, the detail of the policy prescriptions has varied over time and so too have the broad outlines of the two political ideologies. Both ideologies have had to adapt to the changing structure of the housing market, but their respective starting points, the market and the state, are a continuous theme of the many political debates on private rented housing. Here our concern is with the current policy prescriptions that are informed by *laissez-faire* and Fabian beliefs. First, however, it is necessary to say a little about the nature of political ideologies.[2]

Laissex-faire and Fabianism, as political sets of ideas, are not 'political' in the sense that they are attached to any one political party. Both ideologies are wider in scope and deeper in tradition than the ideas expressed in the manifestos and programmes of political parties. Political ideologies offer views of the world and prescriptions for change that are drawn upon at various times by parties and other organisations in their attempts to gain support for their policies and arguments. Because political ideologies are broad sets of ideas rather than neat, self-contained categories of belief, they contain a variety of strands of thought within their broad outlines. In deploying their arguments groups may make reference to one or more of these strands, rather than employing the whole framework of ideas contained within a political ideology. It is important to recognise that housing policies implemented by the state are not the direct outcome of the prescriptions of a particular ideology. Political ideologies inform and shape policies, they rarely determine their actual content. The processes of policy enactment are subject to an array of pressures and competing demands both within and outside of the ambit of the state.

Bearing these points in mind, it is our contention that the political ideologies of *laissez-faire* and Fabianism dominate the controversy over what type of rented housing should be provided and who should provide it. Both ideologies prescribe a *relationship* between the private market and the state, and their respective prescriptions have set the parameters for the debate over the future of private renting.

Laissez-faire and private rental policies

In its familiar and popularised form, the ideology of *laissez-faire* conveys an image of market relations as sovereign, as absolute. This link between *laissez-faire* and a single principle, the market, has tended to obscure a more significant aspect of *laissez-faire* ideas – the residual role it prescribes for the state as the regulator of market forces and the guarantor of economic freedom among individuals. This prescriptive relationship between market and state has been translated by groups such as the British Property Federation and the Small Landlords' Association, together with sections of the Conservative Party who wish to see a revival of private landlordism, as a

---

[2] Our discussion of political ideologies, how they are perceived, and how they work, draws extensively upon Clarke, Cochrane and Smart, 1986. The application of the two ideologies to the politics of private renting and how they inform and define the terrain is, however, our own interpretation.

demand for the removal or reduction of the legal provisions that restrict the free flow of economic forces in the rented housing market.

There are 'strong' and 'soft' interpretations of this view. The strong version rests upon the view that the market place, in bringing together the interests of the buyers and the sellers of commodities, satisfies their respective individual needs. Rent controls and security of tenure legislation are seen to frustrate their respective interests. Private housing, or more correctly residential space, is a commodity which like any other commodity should be exchanged on the market for a monetary payment, rent. The softer version of this strand of thought, in contrast, recognises the need to retain some measure of protection for tenant security and some form of regulation over the monetary payment, and perhaps the need for some measure of financial subsidy from the state to the individuals involved.

Interestingly, the groups which lobby for the revival of the rented housing market often hold both these interpretations, oscillating between the 'strong' and the 'soft' versions and promoting them or a combination of them on different occasions.[3] The ambiguity here is more apparent than real, as the various strands of ideas contained within the outlook of *laissez-faire* are sufficiently broad as to admit more than one interpretation.

Typical among the proposals for a reduction of rent and security controls are the views of the Small Landlords' Association. On the assumption that the Rent Acts are a deterrent to letting residential property, they advocate a system of market rents and a restricted security of tenure for new lettings. For existing protected tenancies of non-resident landlords they accept the difficulty of removing security from long-established tenants, subject that is to a limitation of the rights of statutory succession and a shift in the responsibility for repairs to the protected tenants (SLA, 1985).

The last initiative, that tenants bear the responsibility for repairs, applies to tenants of commercial property leases of seven years or more and is one strand of the Landlord Tenant Act of 1954 which governs commercial lettings. It is this Act that the British Property Federation would like to see apply to all, both existing and new, tenancies, with various modifications. The Act provides for market rents but it is less radical than the Small Landlords' proposals for the reform of security of tenure. In effect the commencement terms of such a tenancy and the provisions relating to rent reviews are a matter of negotiation between landlord and tenant. The court's jurisdiction is invoked when the landlord wants possession at the end of an agreed term, or when the two parties cannot agree on the terms of a

---

[3] See, for example, the contrast in approach between the Small Landlords Association's application to the European Commission of Human Rights, No. 8384, 1978, and their subsequent publication, Review of the Rent Act, 1985.

new lease. A similar arrangement has been piloted in the residential sector by means of the 'assured tenancy' scheme and recently there have been further policy developments which could result in a more central role for some form of assured tenancies.

Both proposals represent different forms of decontrol for the sector and are informed by the ideas of *laissez-faire*. Neither proposal, however, represents a comprehensive attempt to construct a free market in the 'strong' sense outlined previously. Policy proposals as noted earlier are shaped by political ideologies, they are not a direct translation of them. Nonetheless, the starting point of the two proposals is identifiably that of *laissez-faire*.

What is of interest to us now is the potential impact that these proposals may have upon the market. It is often argued, first, that decontrol of the sector would lead as it did in response to the Rent Decontrol Act of 1957 to an increase in the number of sales of rented property to owner-occupation (Donnison and Ungerson, 1982). Secondly, that an increase in rents to a market level would leave many people unable to afford accommodation of an acceptable standard unless supported by large subsidies (LHG, 1984). And thirdly, that the existence of a series of remunerative, stable and less hazardous investments other than the ownership of rented housing – such as unit trusts and insurance policies, and building society deposits – are likely to limit the entry of new recruits to landlordism, even if market rents applied (Short, 1981).

There is little doubt, in our view, that each of these projected outcomes is likely. The real question however, is their magnitude and scope. Which types of property are likely to be sold to owner-occupation? And in what areas? Which types of landlord are likely to be involved? Which group of tenants will be squeezed out by the proposals? Or turning these questions on their head, which types of properties are likely to remain in the sector? Which types of landlords are the proposals likely to attract? And which groups of tenants may benefit from the proposals?

In answer to the last question it is likely that any reduction of rent and security controls would cause widespread hardship among the high proportion of low income and elderly tenants in the unfurnished sub-sector. Neither group however are among those tenants that either the SLA or the BPF wish to cater for in the revived private rented sector. Both sets of proposals are aimed at providing accommodation, primarily new lets, for short-stay furnished tenants – the young, the mobile, group sharers, and those who can afford luxury lettings (SLA, 1985; BPF, 1985). Moreover, the types of landlord that the proposals are aimed to benefit reflect, understandably, the membership of the respective organisations: the predominantly small-scale commercial residential landlords of the SLA and certain types of financial residential landlord represented by the BPF. The response of investor, employer and traditional landlords such as the Church Commissioners and the charitable trusts to either of the initiatives is likely to be limited for reasons discussed in Chapters 3 and 5.

If this assessment is correct then it is difficult to imagine that the forms of decontrol discussed will have any significant effect upon the revival of the market and that their impact will be limited to hardship at the lower end. The reasons for this are two fold: first, among all types of landlord it is the commercial landlords who are the most likely to operate outside of rent controls – negotiating rents by private agreement and operating devices to avoid the restrictions of the Rent Acts. The SLA, for example, has actively encouraged its members to avoid the Rent Acts by the use of licenced agreements. Second, the financial landlords most likely to be attracted to the provisions of the Landlord and Tenants Act 1954 are those who either are or would consider letting at the top end of the market – the luxury lettings sector – which is already operating outside the restrictions of the Rent Acts. The effects of the forms of decontrol suggested, therefore, are unlikely to result in a substantial increase in the pool of rented accommodation, nor are they likely to meet the current diversity of tenant need in terms of security, cost and type of accommodation. A reduction of controls may, however, increase the proportion of accommodation suited to young high income earners who tend to seek 'easy-access' lettings, although this has to be balanced against the high cost of such accommodation and the homelessness caused by decontrols in other sectors of the market, notwithstanding the likely substantial loss of rented properties through sales on the domestic property market.

As a policy instrument, decontrol is a limited tool which serves primarily the interests of commercial residential landlords – a group that has done much to perpetuate the private market as the 'unacceptable face of renting'. The less restrictive form of decontrol proposed by the BPF, with its safeguards for tenant security, may have fewer adverse consequences for tenants, although the complexity of obligations and conditions attached to the proposed form of 'commercial' tenancy is unlikely to appeal to many owners of rented or empty property. More importantly, the insistence on market rents under forms of decontrol is likely to place an unacceptable financial burden upon the majority of tenants unless a significant change in housing subsidies is effected.

The 'soft' argument for a significant change in the distribution of financial subsidies which would entail an increase in the rates of return to landlords was raised in the House of Commons Environment Committee's report on the private rented housing sector (1982, Vol. I, paras. 99–105). The

Committee floated a number of alternative ways of assisting landlords which include fiscal changes 'in the treatment of rental income and (capital) depreciation to assist landlords, rented tax relief for tenants, and some wider ranging American and European subsidy systems aimed at both landlords and tenants' (Ibid., para. 104). Alongside these financial changes, the Committee suggested that a development of the assured tenancy concept may be the appropriate form of tenancy to facilitate these changes and that 'commercial landlords' should operate them (Ibid., para. 103). From the Committee's report it is not entirely clear which kind of 'commercial landlords' they had in mind, but a reasonable conjecture is that the label refers to large-scale property capital, the first 'target' group for assured tenancies.

Leaving aside for the moment the question of efficiency or desirability of subsidising the interests of a fraction of private capital to meet housing needs, it is difficult to see, once again, how such proposals will have more than a minimal impact upon the provision of rented accommodation. First, even if reasonable rates of return can be realised through financial subsidies and fiscal relief, the disincentives of managing small units, the liquidity of the investment and the risk of public scandal attached to private landlordism may outweigh the attractions to financial landlords such as public property companies. Second, of those landlords that are likely to be enticed by increased rates of return, few, if any, would be aiming to provide accommodation for the traditional, elderly households in the sector. In common with commercial landlords such landlords would seek to provide accommodation for mobile and newly forming households, usually the young and the single.[4] In the absence of controls over the management and the allocation procedures of the landlords operating the scheme, it would be virtually impossible to ensure that the subsidies were distributed to reflect the diversity of needs. Presumably this would not be a major cause of concern for landlords in receipt of such subsidies. Nevertheless, if such controls were to be imposed they may be sufficient to deter the larger forms of property capital from reentering the rented housing market.

If the initiative were to be thrown open to a wider net of landlords, involving small scale capital such as commercial and investor landlords, then, as in Germany and the USA, a number may be attracted by a substantial fiscal inducement despite the operation of security of tenure controls. It is far from clear, however, what numbers would be involved

---

[4] The Centre for Environmental Studies report on private renting in five countries (Denmark, The Netherlands, West Germany, France and the USA) indicated that corporate investors tended to let property to 'better-off skilled working class, white-collar and professional groups, for whom this tenure was often only temporary'. House of Commons Environment Committee, 1982, Vol. III, Appendix 3, p 55.

given the informal arrangements that already operate in this sector of the market and it is equally unclear that these types of landlords can be monitored sufficiently to guarantee provision of acceptable, non-exploitative housing conditions.

Despite the negative tone of the above comments, there is one form of capital to whom the Environment Committee's proposal may prove attractive: the corporate institutions – the insurance companies, the pension funds, the banks and the building societies. This was the view of other commentators assessing the Committee's report. Indeed in the Centre for Environmental Studies' investigation of privately rented housing in the USA, France, West Germany, Denmark and the Netherlands (countries which have operated various forms of financial subsidy to landlords) they found that it was often the corporate institutions that provided the new rented housing (cited in the House of Commons Environment Committee, 1982, Vol. III, Appendix 3, p. 55).

In contrast to public property companies, for example, a subsidised form of rented housing which realises an acceptable rate of return and increasing capital values may offer the institutions a suitable outlet for their burgeoning funds and meet their concern to maintain the value of their capital in the long term. Moreover, for institutions such as the pension funds and insurance companies the proposals also offer them the opportunity to pursue policies which have 'socially desirable' results. If a policy can be seen to meet both commercial and social criteria, then it may prove attractive to such institutions.

Evidence is extremely patchy to support this contention and in the light of our own research on institutional landlords we have to remain sceptical about the willingness of pension funds, insurance companies and building societies to provide new rented housing on a scale that would have any significant market impact. Moreover, if the institutions were to be drawn by the proposals then, on the evidence of CES's European and US study, it is reasonable to assume that they would try to cater for the higher income, white collar and professional groups that seek rented accommodation (Ibid., p. 55). This in itself is not a significant problem if other policies could be devised to provide suitable, low cost, secure accommodation for the less well off. We make this point on the assumption that of all the different types of landlord in the market, the institutions are probably the only group capable of offering adequate, secure accommodation on reasonable terms to tenants (if rents are subsidised). Moreover, because of their high public profile and concern for their social image, it may be possible to monitor publicly their management and allocation practices.

This last point, however, may prove to be the stumbling block. To circumvent it, it may be feasible to restrict the role of financial institutions to the provision of private funds for the development or rehabilitation of rented housing, assuming a guaranteed rate of return can be offered. The management of such developments could then be entrusted to more accountable agents such as housing associations. This was one of the recommendations made in the Report of the Inquiry in British Housing (1985). To make private investment attractive to investors they proposed that private (and public) rents, except at the top end of the lettings market, should be fixed at 4 per cent of the capital value of a property. The management of the properties and the risks incurred could be undertaken either by the investors themselves or by agents in the public sector.[5] Thus, in this context, housing associations would incur the risks and issue a bond with a fixed return to the lending bodies subject perhaps only to the risk of default. This may be a viable option, although it is difficult at present to foresee which tenant groups in the market would benefit from this initiative. To hold rents down to a 'fair rent' level and thus cater for tenants in the lower income rate is likely to require some form of capital subsidy from public funds. Alternatively, an income related subsidy could be provided to meet the costs of the higher rents required to meet the 4 per cent on capital values. It is not evident, however, that such a direct subsidy from public to private finance is the most economical way of regenerating the provision of private rented housing.

We will discuss this particular policy option in greater detail later, specifically in relation to how it may be financed and managed. For the present, we will end our discussion of the proposals that stem from the ideology of *laissez-faire* with Harloe's reminder that 'the fact that much of the socialist critique of the market provision of housing has focussed on distribution and access rather than on the whole system of the capitalist production of housing has resulted in considerable opposition to private landlordism but far less scrutiny of the continued significance of private finance, construction and land ownership in all tenures' (Harloe, 1985, p. 313). There are private interests in *all* tenures, and, whilst private land-

---

[5] The initiative would be open to all private investors, and operate on the assumption that the fixed relation of rent to capital would act as an incentive to investors to enter the lettings market and maintain their property in reasonable order. One practical difficulty with the proposal however, is that to achieve a standard net rate of return across the range of rented properties would imply different gross rates of return to meet the different types of risk, tenancy and management costs in the market. This would be difficult and costly to administer, if indeed it is possible to do so at all. Moreover, it is not clear why such a return should act as an incentive to landlords currently operating outside of the Rent Acts whose returns are at least 4 per cent of capital value. See Whitehead and Kleinmann on the furnished sub-sector in London, 1986.

lords have been the agents least capable of meeting general housing needs, the blanket case for no public subsidies to any private landlords or not to use private finance to provide rented housing has been argued on ideological rather than detailed, practical grounds. There is, for example, a rather ambiguous ideological reaction among socialists to the use of pension funds for industrial investment. It is a contested area, although considerable effort has been directed at the pension funds to channel their resources in this direction – with, of course, certain conditions applying (see Labour Party Financial Institutions Study Group, 1982). If it is acceptable among some socialists to entertain such sources of finance for industrial regeneration, then why not for housing regeneration in the rented sector?

Fabianism and private rental policies

An alternative view of the relationship between the market and the state is found in the prescriptions of Fabian ideology. In common with *laissez-faire*, Fabian ideology is a broad ideology containing a number of strands of thought which admit more than one interpretation. Central, however, to the Fabian viewpoint is the view that the collective provision of goods should be extended to those areas where the market has proved to be inefficient or arbitrary. The role of the state in this view is defined in relation to the operation of market forces. Where the market has failed, as in the case of private landlords to provide decent, secure accommodation at a reasonable price, it is necessary for the state to intervene either to correct or to contain the operation of market forces or replace them by some form of collective, public provision.

Contained within this view are, again, 'strong' and 'soft' interpretations of the relationship between market and state. The strong interpretation which draws upon the view that where the market has failed it should be replaced by a form of public provision is held by the Labour Housing Group and sections of the Labour Party and translated into a policy for abolishing private landlordism and transferring the rented housing stock to social ownership. The softer version of state intervention in the market place takes the view that the worst aspects of the market can be avoided by introducing more effective measures of legal control over the behaviour of landlords and by strengthening of the legal rights of tenants. The Organisation of Private Tenants, an umbrella organisation coordinating the activities of tenants' associations and groups of private tenants, is an exponent of this view (OPT, 1984), (although such measures are also promoted by the Labour Housing Group as interim proposals during the period that they consider necessary for the phased transfer of the rented housing stock to social ownership) (LHG, 1984, Chapter 11).

In both interpretations, however, it is the specific failure of the market provision of rented housing that is at issue; the specific failure of private landlords to provide decent, secure, reasonably priced accommodation. Other forms of housing provided by the market such as owner-occupation, circumscribed as it is by private interests, are not viewed as a market failure and hence it is not subject to demands for its collective provision through the state. Nor are the forms of private capital involved in the provision of owner-occupied housing subject to the same degree of legal control over their actions as are private landlords. It is the identification and isolation of private rented housing as a market failure and the need for the state to intervene either to correct the balance of market forces or to replace the market by a form of public provision that places these prescriptions within the tradition of Fabianism.

The clearest exposition of the procedures involved for implementing a policy of transferring the private rented stock to social ownership is to be found in the policy document and publications of the Labour Housing Group. They advocate a phased transfer of all housing owned by non-resident landlords into ownership of local authorities, housing associations and housing cooperatives over a period of up to fifteen years. Both the tenants and the local authorities may initiate the transference, with or without the consent of the private landlord. If, however, tenants wish to remain in the private sector no action would be taken, except where the local authority has a statutory duty to acquire the property. To avoid the possibility of landlords attempting to evict tenants in the interim period a series of measures to protect their legal rights is also proposed (see LHG, 1984b).

The programme is ambitious and is recognised to involve a number of difficulties. An obvious difficulty is cost. To meet the initial costs of acquiring properties even at tenanted value and to improve them to acceptable standards would require a considerable public subsidy. One suggestion for reducing this financial burden is to compensate landlords with government stock yielding an income related to the tenanted value of the property. This could be financed by the rental income received from the transferred properties. The additional costs of management, rehabilitation and future maintenance incurred, however, would require an additional public subsidy.

A second, and perhaps greater obstacle that such a programme would have to overcome is the management of the transferred dwellings. The prospect of adding over one million properties to the public sector, many of which are in multiple occupation and in diverse locations raises a number of significant problems. Local authorities are not renowned for their responsive and flexible management practices, although the suggested proposal of diversifying the pattern of ownership to include housing associations and cooperatives, together with a variety of management arrangements, represents an understanding of the magnitude of the problem (LHG, 1984a). Other issues, such as residential mobility, access and tenant choice also have to be confronted if a programme of social ownership is to meet, rather than merely register, the diversity of needs and demands of formerly private tenants and those groups at present dependent upon the rented market for accommodation. Much of this is, of course, conditional upon significant changes in the existing practices of management and allocation that shape the structure of public housing in general.

Leaving aside for the moment the difficulties of cost and management that a programme of social ownership would have to overcome, there are three related questions that should be asked of such a programme. First, are private tenants clamouring to enter the public sector? This is a difficult question to answer with any certainty as surveys on tenant satisfaction and preferences are not the most reliable of indicators. Having said that, the results of Paley's (1978) survey 'Attitudes to Letting in 1976' found that 27 per cent of households, mainly tenants in small elderly households, positively preferred to rent from a private landlord (Ibid., Tables 6–8), and the results of the General Household Survey (1978) indicated that the majority of private tenants were satisfied with their accommodation, although the figures did show a decreased satisfaction among furnished tenants.

Such findings are open to interpretation, but they do indicate a potentially divided response to the issue of social ownership. Much would depend upon the form and flexibility of such a programme and how it is presented.

The second question is of a more detailed nature and raises a number of issues. How will the public sector deal with the demand for furnished accommodation? Can local authorities meet the demand for immediate access sought by a number of groups in the private rented sector? How would local authorities reconcile this demand with the waiting lists for public housing? These are not trivial questions, particularly for mobile and newly forming households.

Thirdly, what provisions are to be made for the tenants of employer and resident landlords? If they are to be exempt from the policy of phased transfer, on what grounds is such exemption granted? True, both types of landlord do not exhibit a blatant policy of economic gain, but in the case of resident landlords there is considerable evidence to show that an invidious power relation between landlord and tenant can exist and has led to some of the worst offences of tenant harassment.[6] For it is precisely this unseen and largely unregulated type of letting that feeds the tension between landlord and tenant. Absentee landlords may form the visible *'bête noire'*, the characteristic that marks out a potentially 'bad' landlord but the negative stereotype is equally, if not more, applicable to resident landlords.

Surprisingly, Fabian inspired policies have little to say about this growing proportion of the lettings market; largely because, we assume, that short of mandatory prohibition there is little that can be done to legally regulate this type of rented housing provision. Harassment by resident landlords is deemed to occur at the margins of a 'larger problem'. In terms of scale, the number of tenancies currently let by resident landlords is difficult to gauge because of problems of identification, although official sources estimate it to be around one tenth of all lettings. To sidestep the issue, to avoid the conflict of interest in this type of letting, however, is to ignore the problems faced by tenants, often young, single people, whose 'home' it is. In effect, by neglecting this type of letting, the social ownership lobby by default allows the policy for such tenancies to be shaped by the interests of the 'free market' exponents.

This assessment of the social ownership case should not be seen as an attempt to undermine the proposal. Rather it should be seen in the spirit of our earlier comments which argued for a strategic approach to the problem of private rented housing, to intervene at different points in the market, to recognise that a diversity of demand for rented accommodation exists and to acknowledge that different types of provision, both public and private, may be appropriate to meet the different needs.

In this context, a restricted programme of the transference of the private rented stock would represent *one* aspect of such a strategy, *one* strand of a larger package of proposals designed to cater for the variations in the type of tenant demand.

A way forward – transitional strategies

Any realistic appraisal of what is to be done with private rented housing should recognise the need for transitional strategies. Curbing the excesses of the market should be the first priority, together with the development of a series of initiatives that meet the diversity of demand for rented accommodation. We would argue that because an imbalance of power exists between the majority of landlords and their tenants there is an immediate need to

---

[6] See Nelken, 1983, whose finding show that the typical offender is not the institutional landlord, but the resident landlord. The same point was made as early as 1965 in the Report of the Committee on Housing in Greater London (the Milner Holland report).

extend full security of tenure to all tenants and licencees of non-resident landlords, with the exception of genuine short-term lettings, such as those offered to students and those that require holiday accommodation. The law against harassment and illegal eviction should also be strengthened and the powers of local authorities increased so that they are able to effectively monitor and control the private rented market, including the activities of resident landlords.

Legal prescriptions and their effect, however, are two different things. Attempts to control the behaviour of the majority of landlords by legal enforcement are not particularly effective and we place little faith in such short-term measures having any real impact upon the operation of the market.[7] The list of immediate priorities could have been extended to includes measures of rent regulation and the enforcement of minimum housing standards. Such additions, however, would be largely rhetorical, with little chance of achieving any practical success in the lettings that most require such protection. Law, as Partington (1980) has argued, is only one of many ways in which patterns of behaviour may be controlled, with limited results. Such limitations are likely to be particularly apparent in attempts to curb the actions of commercial and informal landlords by legal means.

An alternative and parallel proposal suggested by Partington is to bring the imbalance of power between landlords and tenants into the open by the encouragement of private tenants' organisations. Local authorities could play a role here in helping to establish and fund such organisations and to involve them in formal consultations. The value of this type of initiative is that it emphasises the role of collective action in response to a general

---

[7] A considerable proportion of the contemporary rented housing market at present operates outside of legislative controls – if not in theory, then in practice. Paley's survey of tenancies in areas with large percentages of rented accommodation in England and Wales suggested that only 26 per cent of tenancies had registered rents, with an additional 15 per cent of tenancies operating with controlled rents (1978, Section 3). On the basis of other published sources, Doling and Davies estimated that just over a quarter of tenancies in the private sector in England and Wales had a registered rent (1982; pp. 192–4), and Todd's *Recent Private Lettings Survey*, 1982–1984 only recorded about 4 per cent of recent lettings with a registered rent.

On the issue of security of tenure it is the case that the majority of private lettings are protected tenancies, but there is sufficient indication from our own survey and from other published sources that the workings of the market are substantially untouched by legal restrictions (Allen and McDowell, 1982, pp. 194–7; Harloe, 1985, ch. 8). In a survey of 2,000 private rented households in the Greater London area conducted in 1983–4 over half the respondents did not know what type of tenancy or lettings they had (Greater London Council, 1984, paras. 32–4). The House of Commons report on the private rented sector also expressed concern at the number of new lettings that fall outside the provisions and protection of the Rent Act (1982, Vol. 1, paras. 89–92). The extent of this practice is obviously difficult to gauge, yet even if one removes this phenomenon from consideration there is evidence to suggest that to a large degree, the current market is characterised by unregulated, rather than regulated, formal, legal relationships.

housing problem in contrast to the resolution of individual disputes by legal means. Notwithstanding the considerable difficulties faced in organising such a fragmented group as private tenants, even local campaigns or campaigns specifically directed towards a particular landlord who operates in an exploitative manner, have the advantage of creating a climate of opinion that places the need for the long-term reform of the rented sector on the political agenda.

In the longer term there is a need at the outset to recognise that any proposals for the reform of the private rented sector should possess three characteristics. First, that the proposals should relate to the level of awareness and knowledge that tenants have of their housing situation. There is little value in proposing unblemished solutions that have no connection with the consciousness and experience of tenants. Total munici- palisation of the private rented stock, for example, may prove unattractive to many tenants. Secondly, and at the risk of belabouring the point, the proposals for reform should be sufficiently flexible to meet the needs of the different tenant groups in the market in terms of type, quality, access, security and cost of accommodation. Thirdly, the proposals should acknow- ledge the geographical diversity of the sector and in particular how different the rented market and the structure of landlordism is in London from the rest of the country. It takes little insight to recognise that a set of proposals based upon national or regional analyses are likely to gloss over the different roles that the sector performs in different locations. In regional analyses, for example, the variations in the structure of local housing markets is likely to be averaged out.

In sum, we would argue for a series of public and private initiatives that relate to the needs of those groups at present dependent on private renting for accommodation. The initiatives should contain a geographical dimen- sion; a national set of prescriptions which sets out a framework for the provision of rented housing and a series of local policies which are designed specifically to meet the rented housing needs of a locality. Not all of the measures proposed are new; their value, however, lies in their *combination*, not in their separation.

A general policy framework could involve a combination of measures, initiated by the state and *directed at different types of landlord and sub- sectors of tenant demand:*

A compulsory, phased transfer of private rented housing owned by *certain* private landlords who are either unwilling or unable to improve their property or properties to a minimum, acceptable standard within a reason- able time period. Within this category, priority could be directed towards acquiring properties tenanted by those who have traditionally been private tenants, mainly elderly households, that is, those who are likely to express a preference for the type of secure, permanent, unfurnished accommodation that public authorities in their presently constituted form provide. Suitable provisions could also be made for low income households who seek similar accommodation. In this context local authorities would act as the coordinating body, transferring the private properties into either their own ownership or the ownership of housing associations or housing cooperatives depending upon the nature of demand for particular types of provision in different areas.

To meet the demand of those seeking mobility and 'easy access' accommodation, but not through private provision, the role of housing associations could be extended on the basis of increased public financial support to cater for the demand for mobility between authorities. In comparison with local authorities, who are accountable to local electorates, housing associations are better placed to perform this role. Nevertheless, local authorities could also be obliged to widen access to their own accommodation to ensure that groups such as young, single households and those whose personal circumstances have changed abruptly, for example, through separation or divorce, are eligible to enter the public sector. To meet this demand they could also make use of their existing powers to enter into licenced agreements with owners of empty private property to let their accommodation for a specific period and to make available hard-to-let accommodation on older estates and in high rise dwellings on an 'easy access' basis.

An alternative but complementary strategy designed to cater for the same categories of demand could rely upon the private provision of funds for rented accommodation. Either certain types of approved institutional landlords such as building societies could be encouraged to use their funds to rehabilitate existing properties for rent or to build new accommodation for rent of a certain type and standard in specific locations and also to take on the management of the properties, *or* the role of financial institutions such as the pension funds, insurance companies and building societies could be restricted to channelling funds to housing associations to build, rehabilitate, manage and maintain properties. Even without the Conservative government's restrictions on investment in public housing, private renting is not likely to attract considerable public investment and the desirability of attracting private funds should not be dismissed without an assessment of its feasibility. Apart from the issue of the politics of guaranteeing a rate of return to institutional investors, the issues of management and accountability are significant. For these reasons we would wish to see a greater role for housing associations and housing cooperatives, working with private finance, in meeting *certain* categories of demand for private renting.[8]

Finally, there remains the separate issues of service tenancies and the lettings of residential landlords, which together make up over a third of the rented housing market. In the case of service tenancies, employers should be entitled to vacant possession only if they can prove that the incoming employee could not perform the tasks of a particular job if resident elsewhere. In such cases, local authorities should be obliged to rehouse the displaced tenant. Lettings of resident landlords represent a policy dilemma. Clearly, they are not going to disappear and indeed this type of letting is likely to expand as owner-occupiers sub-let to meet their housing costs. Some may welcome this expansion and argue that they should be controlled by the local authority through the issue of annual licences. In our view, any attempt to regulate this sub-sector is not likely to meet with success. As part of a broader solution to the provision of rented accommodation, we would argue that no specific legal inducements are given to owner-occupiers to provide lettings and that the policy energies are directed at the non-resident landlord sector. If there is a need for a substantial pool of rented accommodation to met the various needs of those at present dependent upon private rented housing, then we see no reason to promote a sector that has one of the worst records in providing satisfactory living conditions.

A fundamental prerequisite of the implementation of this combination of private and public initiatives is a knowledge of local housing markets. The spatial variation in the size, type and condition of the private rented stock, the variation in the type of landlord and in the type of tenant demand point to a geographically sensitive set of policies. London, for example, together with a small number of cities possess a concentration and demand for furnished accommodation which is likely to require a specific combination of public and private initiatives. Within cities too, the variation in stock, rental demand and type of landlord, as well as changes in the balance of the two main tenures all indicate the importance of locality-based policies. Local authorities should be obliged to draw up their own proposals for reform based upon a combination of the initiatives contained within the wider policy framework. It may be the case, for example, that the rented housing problems of some localities can only be resolved through public initiatives, including a limited transfer of the private rented stock into social

[8] These kinds of initiative have progressed since the time of writing and are taken up in the Policy Postscript.

ownership. Other localities may find that tenants' needs and demands require both public and private solutions.

In conclusion, we have argued for a set of public and private initiatives that start from an alternative position to those expressed in market based and state based solutions and informed respectively by the political ideologies of *laissez-faire* and Fabianism. If an exhaustive programme of social ownership is unlikely to meet the diversity of demand for rented accommodation then certain kinds of private initiative have to be considered rather than ideologically dismissed. The advantage of acknowledging this state of affairs is that various strategies can be devised to minimise those private landlords who cannot provide decent, secure rented accommodation and encourage those who are capable of meeting such an aim.

In the meantime, some of the initiatives proposed may result in a further contraction of the private rented sector, encouraging more owners of rented property to sell on the domestic property market. Short-term measures to tighten up the regulatory framework of the sector may minimise such losses, although a number of losses are inevitable. To accommodate the displaced tenants and to meet the needs of the groups presently dependent upon the rented sector it is important *that policies are devised that can exert leverage upon the private rented market and the public rented sector.* We argue for this alternative set of proposals on the grounds that a more comprehensive change in the provision of housing along socialist lines is not on the political horizon.

We are not arguing, therefore, to reject the proposed market and state based solutions to the problems of private rented housing simply because they are informed by political ideologies. They could not be otherwise; there is no such thing as an ideologically uninformed policy proposal. Rather it is the informed starting points of the two solutions, the market and the state, the frozen orthodoxes of those who champion the assumed collective interests of, respectively, private landlords and private tenants that we reject. To accept these categories as the terms of reference from which to start the debate over the immediate future of private renting is to condemn the sector to its present, largely deplorable state – at the expense of those who have to live in it. Such terms of reference obscure rather than present the possibility of providing the kinds of rented housing sought by different groups of tenants at the present time.

Policy Postscript

Political ideologies are not closed or fixed systems of belief; as economic and political circumstances change so too do the views that are embodied within ideologies. The two ideologies of renting addressed in the previous chapter are no exception. They remain the most powerful 'voices' through which the future of private rented housing is debated and their respective starting points remain intact, but the direction of the 'dialogue' between them has shifted ground. The marginal political status of private renting has altered; it now occupies a more central position in the Conservative Governments' housing policies as developed since 1979. The reason for this shift however, has less to do with the decline of the private rented housing market *per se* and is more to do with the persistent ideological motive of the Conservative Governments during the 1980s to redefine renting as a private and not a public sector activity. The proposals of the Conservatives' third administration for the revival of the private rented sector of the housing market, outlined in the 1987 Housing Bill, are indeed geared towards the deregulation of rented housing, a move towards a free market in rented housing. But the major thrust of the legislation is aimed at establishing a new kind of private landlord, one who will replace the role of public landlords and take over the task of providing rented housing from public authorities.

The new kind of private landlordism appears in three different guises: 'responsible' private landlords, housing associations, and housing action trusts. Of the three agencies, only the third agency represents a new type of landlordism, one which will act as some sort of housing 'broker', taking over the control of local authority housing and passing it on to alternative forms of ownership and management, including the two aforementioned agencies. It is not yet possible to evaluate the envisaged role and likely impact of the actions of the two latter agencies in a recast rented housing market. It is interesting to note in passing, however, that the perception of the housing association movement by the Conservative Party has travelled full circle since the early 1960s, from a private institution, independent of Government, to a public arm of Government, and back again to a private agency, independent from the public sector (Back and Hamnett, 1985). This chameleon-like quality of housing associations which enables them to be seen as first private, then public and then again as private in character acts as a disadvantage rather than an advantage. For the issue is not simply one of labelling, it is rather a question of the role that housing associations are expected to perform in an integrated housing market. A shift in roles – from public to private or vice versa – has considerable implications for the types of housing need that are met by housing associations. Defined as private agencies, housing associations are being directed to raise an increasing proportion of their funds from private sources, such as building societies and other financial institutions. As argued in the final chapter, in principle there is nothing objectionable about agencies such as housing associations using private finance to boost the available stock of good, secure private rented housing. Local authorities, via the Public Works Loan Board, have traditionally used private funds to finance their rented housing programmes, repayable at market rates of return. The issue is not the source of funding, but the circumstances under which it is taken up and the constraint attached. Unlike local authorities, housing associations do not possess a large stock of older dwellings built at low cost which means that housing associations have been less able to cross-subsidise rents. As recipients of private finance, housing associations are likely to find themselves in a position whereby the only way they can meet the repayment costs is to increase rent levels. This poses a dilemma for housing associations. The majority of housing association tenants are low-income earners and the identity of the housing association movement is locked firmly into the role of providing for this constituency. By taking away the financial safeguards, the public subsidies, that enable housing associations to fulfil this role a public housing body is changed into a private agency that is responsive to market demands for its survival. Such a change of role may lead to an increase in the private rented stock, but not necessarily for those in greatest housing need. On the contrary, the use of private capital to build more rented homes is likely to encourage housing associations to go up-market in order to obtain rent levels sufficient to meet debt charges.

Such a proposal is not in line with our recommendation that policy prescriptions for the rented housing market should start from tenants' and potential tenants' housing needs. Housing associations presently perform an important role in providing secure, reasonably priced accommodation for both low and middle-income earners. They are one of the few examples of good 'private' rented housing provision. There is room to extend this

provision to meet the demand from those seeking 'easy access' accommodation, even at higher than present rent levels, but not at the expense of
jeopardising their traditional role of housing low-income tenants.

It is perhaps easier to grasp the implications of the new role that housing
associations are being groomed for by the Government by setting them
alongside proposals for the establishment of a free market in new private
lettings. The kind of free market envisaged is in accordance with the 'soft'
interpretation of *laissez-faire* ideas mentioned in the last chapter. Two new
forms of tenancy, or rather two modified forms of existing tenancies
introduced under the Housing Act 1980 – shorthold and assured – are
proposed. In their present form, both types of tenancy have noticeably failed
to entice owners of property into the rented housing market in any
significant numbers (see Allen and McDowell, 1982; Kemp, 1987). Both
kinds of tenancy contained measures which restricted tenants' security
rights, and allowed landlords to charge higher rents than was hitherto
possible. And yet the anticipated revival of the private rented sector failed to
materialise. The reasons offered to account for such a failure vary according
to ideological position. From a free market perspective, the commitment to
deregulation proclaimed in the 1980 Housing Act did not go far enough;
rents remained registered under shorthold tenancies and only registered
landlords offering new or recently renovated accommodation could operate
assured tenancies. Moreover, the prospect of a future Government reimpos-
ing rent and security controls was also said to inhibit owners of residential
property from entering the lettings market. For those advocating a public
solution to the problems of the private rented sector, the failure of the
proposals contained in the 1980 Housing Act were more or less predictable.
As long as owner-occupation attracts fiscal advantages and house prices
continue to rise, private landlords will continue to sell their property on the
domestic market and leave the rented market. And the very same fiscal
inducements attached to home ownership inevitably leads to a situation
whereby those people who are in a position to buy property will do so,
leaving those who are unable to exercise this choice, the low-income groups,
trapped in the rented property sector. Thus any notion of reviving the
rented market on the backs of those who are economically weak is bound
to fail.

The inquest into the failure of the rented provisions of the 1980 Housing
Act is, however, likely to be foreshortened, overtaken by the Government's
proposals to extend deregulation by removing the registration requirements
attached to shorthold and assured tenancies, and scrapping the fair rent
system. The thrust of the proposals is to move closer to a market
relationship between landlord and tenant, one which treats residential

property as any other commodity – as a product which is free to find its exchange value in the market place.

The direction of the proposed changes will come as no surprise to observers of the failure of the 1980 Housing Act provisions and the debate over the future of private renting is likely to continue broadly along the lines outlined above. The proposals, however, also introduce a new element into the debate which has already begun to shift the direction of the 'dialogue'. As noted earlier, political ideologies are not static; they adapt to new circumstances. The new circumstances in this instance are the continued dominance of *laissez-faire* ideas in the 1980s and the slow erosion of public rented housing. The prospect of transferring much of the private rented stock to social ownership has slipped further away and adherents of this view now find themselves 'locked' into a dialogue over the 'acceptable face' of private landlordism. The future role of housing associations is part of this dialogue and so too is the very notion that there exists a 'responsible' group of private landlords. Both sides of the dialogue have shifted ground; the rhetoric is still one of landlord versus anti-landlord, fuelled by the ghost of Rachman, but the policy issue is the type of landlord that is acceptable.

Informal and employer landlords are not quite in the frame, and nor are investor and commercial landlords. The latter two groups, and many informal landlords already operate outside of the formal processes of regulation. It is questionable how far *any* changes in the legislative framework that governs private lettings will alter the activities of these groups in the rented market. Indeed, it is landlords within these groups, and commercial landlords in particular, who are mainly responsible for the letting of some of the worst accommodation, in terms of rent levels, conditions, and harassment. Insofar as these types of landlords enter the frame of the dialogue, they enter as a representation of 'bad' landlords in sharp contrast to agencies such as the building societies and pension funds, financial landlords. Corporate landlordism, it would appear, is now being promoted as the 'acceptable face' of private landlordism.

But it would be wrong to assume that the 1987 Housing Bill represents an attempt to install the corporate landlord as the supplier of mass rented housing. This is not the intention. The aim of the proposals, as expressed earlier, is to redefine renting as a private and not a public sector activity. They are part of a series of political measures to erode public sector housing in particular and the welfare state in general. The promotion of corporate landlords and the redirection of the housing association movement are one small part of that political programme. Major questions remain, however, over how far agencies such as the building societies and the housing associations will wish to become involved in such a programme. No final verdict can be given, but the initial indications are that such agencies are both cautious and uncertain of their involvement in rented housing initiatives (Cole and Wheeler, 1987). What can be stated with some degree of certainty, however, is that attempts to change the face of private landlordism will not meet the *diversity* of tenants' and potential tenants' housing needs in the foreseeable future.

Appendix 1: Selecting the landlord sample from housing waiting list records

We selected our sample for the intensive and extensive surveys from the records of households who had recently been rehoused by their local authority from the private rented sector into council accommodation. This gave us a sample of lettings in which a complete or partial vacancy had been created as, at each address we selected, at least one household space had been vacated in the recent past.

When an individual or household applies for rehousing by a local authority, details of that household's personal and housing circumstances are recorded. These include information about family structure, the applicant's employment circumstances and housing conditions. For those applicants living in the private rented sector the landlord's name and address, if known, is recorded, as well as the name of the agent or other person to whom rent is paid. Thus these records provide a list, albeit partial and incomplete, of a proportion of the landlords who own property in these boroughs.

The sample was chosen from a list of those households who had been registered on the housing waiting list for varying lengths of time, and had been rehoused by Hackney and Islington over a two year period, ending in May 1980 in Hackney and September 1979 in Islington. All these households had eventually acquired sufficient points to reach the top of the list in each borough. The housing points schemes in operation at the time of our study are shown in Table 1.

The general waiting list is not the only source of new council tenants in these two boroughs, although it is the only one where detailed records are available. Local authorities, as well as rehousing applicants from their general waiting list, are obliged to house certain categories of homeless families and households affected by slum clearance programmes. In addition they may operate schemes for 'key workers' and other priority groups. The categories of households rehoused by Hackney and Islington at the end of the 1970s are shown in Table 2. In both boroughs, rehousing obligations under several heads mean that housing waiting list applicants, many of whom had been registered on the list for many years, had to take their turn behind other households, resulting in a sort of enforced institutionalised queue jumping. Only about a third of all vacancies allocated in the council stock (excluding transfers between local authority tenancies by existing tenants) went to households registered on the general waiting list. This is about half the proportion of English and Welsh authorities as a whole, but inner London housing authorities are faced with very different circumstances from small towns or rural authorities, or indeed from other metropolitan counties where the boundaries include the suburbs. In inner London, the stock of old and vacant land is scarce. Consequently, clearance and redevelopment and improvement programmes take a large slice of available resources but the scope for large-scale building programmes is small. General waiting list applicants

Appendix 1

Table A1. *Housing points schemes in 1980*

Factors	London Borough of Hackney Points awarded	London Borough of Islington Points awarded
Room deficiency		
For each additional room required (bedroom, living room and/or kitchen)	20	20
Bedroom standards/sex separation		
For each member of the family share of a bedroom and		
(i) 5–10 years old	5	20*
(ii) over 10 years old	10	20*
Shared accommodation and facilities (with people not on the application)		
Living room	10	10
Kitchen	10	10
WC	4	4
Bath	3	3
Water supply (if not in shared kitchen)	—	4
Cooker (if not in shared kitchen)	—	4
Lack of facilities		
No bath	6	6
Bath with one piped hot water supply	—	6
Cooking facilities without an oven	—	8
No cooking facilities	—	10
No outside clothes drying facilities	2	—
Lack of natural light or ventilation	6	—
Badly situated facilities		
Bath in kitchen/not in bathroom	2	2
Cooker and/or water on landing	6	6
For each flight of stairs from kitchen to cooker/water supply	2	—
External WC	4	6
WC accessible only through another household's rooms	6	—
For more than one flight of stairs from living room to WC	2	—
For every flight of stairs to WC after second	1	—
Property conditions		
Dampness	4	—
Lack of electricity or water etc.	3	—
Disrepair	3	—

Table A1 (*cont.*)

Factors	London Borough of Hackney Points awarded	London Borough of Islington Points awarded
Separated families		
Families separated because of lack of accommodation	10	10
Medical cases		
Medical factors	up to 25	up to 20
Elderly persons		
Where applicant or any person living with them is		
65 – 75 years old	—	10
Over 75 years old	—	20
(+ in Islington only $\frac{1}{2}$ a point for each step or stair an elderly person might have to negotiate in order to reach the first part of their letting)		
Waiting time		
For each year on the list	2	—
For each year of residence in the borough from the age of 18	—	1
Discretionary points		
For special factors not included above, at discretion of the Director of Housing	up to 10	–

Note: * Islington's scheme is slightly different, under (i) the points are awarded where two persons of the opposite sex, not living together as husband and wife, both aged 5 or over have to share a bedroom and (ii) where it is necessary for the above persons to share a bedroom with parents or others of another generation and of opposite sex.

are condemned to longer than average waiting times. Hackney and Islington's particular responsibilities as inner city authorities are reflected in the second row of the table; the proportion of households rehoused because of decants. Obligations under slum clearance programmes, redevelopment and so on took about almost a third of the vacancies in these two years, compared with about a fifth nationally. Most of the households rehoused under the decant category had been living in very poor conditions in the private rented sector. Indeed the conditions were usually so poor that they were the very reason for the occupants being rehoused. In general, the properties containing these tenancies were compulsorily purchased and demolished.

We selected our sample from the general waiting list applicants who accounted for between a quarter and a third of all rehoused households in the years under

Table A2. *Lettings by the London Boroughs of Hackney and Islington, 1978 and 1979*

Rehousing category	1978		1979	
	H	I	H	I
General housing waiting list	38.6	31.8	25.1	34.0
* Decants	30.6	32.9	26.3	31.8
Homelessness	17.9	17.0	30.4	10.7
Health and Social	9.3	4.5	10.6	5.2
** IBNS	2.7	2.5	6.4	3.1
Miscellaneous	0.9	11.3	1.2	15.2
Total number	2357	3965	1606	3952

Notes: * Decants include redevelopment, slum clearance, closing orders, dangerous structures, conversions and housing certain area moves. Transfers *within* the local authority stock, often included in on location totals, have been excluded from the table.

** Inter-borough nomination scheme: a reciprocal arrangement between London boroughs. A similar number of Hackney tenants were rehoused by other boroughs.

consideration. Almost 80 per cent of these applicants were living in the private rented sector at the time at which they were rehoused. The remaining 20 per cent, in the main, were young couples living with their parents or in-laws, usually in council accommodation and so ineligible for our sample. In total, 1,120 applicants in Hackney and 1,416 in Islington had been rehoused in a two year period at the end of the 1970s. Before selecting our final sample we took a small pilot sample of seventy-two addresses to investigate the feasibility of using such a sampling frame, whether or not we could trace the landlords involved and to what extent there was a rapid rate of turnover amongst the created vacancies. At sixty-four of these seventy-two addresses we were able to establish who owned the dwelling and what had happened since the previous occupants were rehoused. Initially, we considered the possibility of selecting a sample weighted towards the final months of the twenty-four month period as private tenants are mobile, moving on average every two years. However, we found from our pilot that many of the vacancies were still empty, that others were in the process of conversion and improvement and, of the nineteen of the sixty-four dwelling spaces that had been relet, all but two were the first tenants since the local authorities rehoused the waiting list applicants. Consequently we decided to select a 25 per cent proportional sample from each month over the two year period. In total this gave us 280 addresses in Hackney and 354 in Islington. In a small number of cases the information recorded on the applicants' records was insufficient for us to trace the address or the previous landlord, elsewhere the details were incorrect and the property proved to be ineligible for inclusion in our sample, usually because it was in fact a council-owned dwelling. Finally a small number of properties were never traced by our interviewers, usually because they had been demolished.

Considerable detective work was involved, however, in piecing together the histories of the dwelling spaces and properties included in our sample, especially in tracing the landlords or agents. Each property was visited up to six times by a team of interviewers who undertook a questionnaire survey of the new occupants, when there were any. Other sources were used to identify the owners of empty dwellings including information from neighbours, from estate agents, from local authority rating lists and from rent registration records. In addition we contacted all known landlords by letter, administered a postal survey to those outside London, followed up by two reminder letters, and personally interviewed landlords living within the Greater London area. Eventually the completed sample size was 235 in Hackney and 302 in Islington. The interviews in the extensive part of the survey were undertaken between the end of 1980 and the end of 1981. Details from that work were an important input to the classification and to the intensive phase of the work. Devising the classification and testing it, the conceptual and empirical parts of the study, in fact, were not separate processes. The process of classification was an integral part of the empirical work and vice versa. As landlords were interviewed and their strategies documented and understood we were more clearly able to comprehend the differences between them. We then interviewed a small number (thirty-nine in total) of landlords in depth during the final few months of 1981 and the beginning of 1982.

Appendix 2: Who was rehoused?

Who were the 235 households in Hackney and the 302 in Islington who eventually gained enough points to rise to the top of the exceedingly long waiting lists in these inner city boroughs? Some of them had been registered on the waiting list for appallingly long periods, in one case almost fifty years, others for a few months only. Not surprisingly, given the overall levels of housing need in these two boroughs, the housing conditions of most applicants were appalling. The statistics in Table 1 delineate the general outlines of who lives in poor housing in the private rented sector in inner London. Colour and detail is added to the story by the case studies at the end of this appendix. The households in this sector of the housing market who eventually rise to the top of the housing waiting list are, in the main, people living in atrocious conditions of poverty. There are two main groups of people included in the samples. First, there is a group of what might be called residual or traditional tenants. These are very elderly households, single and married pensioners who have lived in the private rented sector all their lives. At the time at which they were setting up independent households, in the 1920s and 1930s mainly, the private landlord still housed the majority of British households. Most, although not all, of this group live in unfurnished accommodation, often let at controlled rents. This group is similar to the first sub-sector with private rented housing identified in the study by Kleinman and Whitehead, outlined in Chapter 2. The second group in the sample is more heterogeneous but is united by the fact that the members include households who, for different reasons, have previously been unable to gain access to either of the other two tenures, that is council housing and owner-occupation. The reasons for their exclusion include family status, income and mobility. This sub-group is composed of the following types of households. First, there are single middle-aged men and women and middle-aged couples who have never had children who have remained a low priority for local authorities. Access to owner-occupation has been denied them by virtue of low income; characteristic occupations amongst this group included labouring, painting and decorating, various jobs for London Transport and British Rail, stonemasonry, carpentry, etc., all of which are amongst the lowest paid jobs in London. The second sub-category includes ethnic minority families, usually with children, who also are concentrated in low paid occupations, predominantly in this case in the service sector, chefs, waiters, hospital domestics, nursing, were common occupations and also sweated labour in the garment industry; several of the respondents were cutters, pressers, machinists and tailors. Finally, there were a number of very young households, either single or cohabiting couples, who had just started out in the housing market. For these tenants, and indeed for all the households included in the second group, the private rented sector was seen as a temporary solution to their housing needs, a transitional rather than a permanent

Table A3. *Rehoused households in Hackney and Islington*

Household type	Hackney	Islington
Single pensioner	13.2	26.4
Married pensioners	3.4	10.0
Couple without dependent child(ren)	23.4	19.8
Couple with dependent child(ren)	20.4	20.5
Single person without dependent child(ren)	20.9	12.0
Single person with dependent child(ren)	9.4	6.7
Nuclear family and other relatives	2.6	1.3
All adults related	5.9	2.3
All adults unrelated	0.8	
% of household heads		
in employment	60.4	47.7
unemployed	13.2	7.9
economically inactive		
or retired	22.1	43.0
students	4.3	1.4
% of household heads from		
ethnic minority groups	26.4	24.8
Total numbers	235	302
Conditions in private lettings from which		
households were rehoused	% of households	
Overcrowded (over 1ppr)	45.9	26.8
Sharing amenities (back, WC or kitchen)	68.5	53.6
Lacking amenities	20.4	25.2
(back, WC or kitchen)		

Note: Sharing and lacking amenities have been constructed as mutually exclusive categories, so the percentages may be added together but the percentage overcrowded is not mutually exclusive. Most households sharing amenities were also overcrowded. It was less common for those without amenities to be overcrowded. In the main they were elderly householders and long-term residents of all or part of a house without basic amenities.

place of residence, although for many of the middle-aged respondents the transition was beginning to feel too permanent. Previous research on the private rented sector in different parts of the country has also documented a division between a residual and transitional sub-sector (see, for example, Murie's study of West Yorkshire, 1974) and, as in Islington and Hackney, transitional tenants were much more likely to be renting furnished accommodation than were the residual households. This group may also be compared with Kleinman and Whitehead's (1985) second sub-sector: the 'mobile' and 'pressure' category, although as we explained in Appendix 1 the method of selecting the sample inevitably excluded many of the landlords who house young, mobile tenants.

CASE STUDIES OF HOUSING NEED

Households rehoused from the private rented sector in Hackney

Case 1

Two Irish brothers in their forties, renting a small bedsit from a West Indian landlord. The only cooker in the house was on the landing and was shared with five others, as was the WC and bath. The house was in a state of severe disrepair and there was no heat and electric light as the landlord had failed to pay the bills. The rent was £8.00 per week in 1980.

Case 2

A Chinese restaurant manager living in two rooms above his work with his wife and four children. The WC and bath had to be shared with seven other people, there was no kitchen in the house and the family cooked in their bedroom. The rooms were let furnished for £12 per week in 1980.

Case 3

A single middle-aged Turk working as a presser in the garment trade lived in a bedsit over a noisy cafe. There was no bathroom in the house and the WC was shared by twenty individuals. The room was rented furnished for £10 a week in 1979.

Case 4

A very elderly single pensioner living in two rooms in a damp cold house. She had lived there since 1938, there was no bathroom and the WC was outside. The rooms were rented unfurnished for £2.35 a week in 1980.

Households rehoused fom the private rented sector in Islington

Case 1

A Spanish single mother, working as a catering assistant in a hospital, lived in one room in a house owned by a Spanish landlord who lived there too. She and her daughter shared all amenities, including cooking facilities, with the landlord's family and there was considerable friction between them. The room was rented furnished for £19 a week in 1979.

Case 2

A Bangladesh couple with three children rented a furnished bedsit in a multi-occupied house. The bathroom and WC were shared with sixteen other people. The man worked as a BR depotman and paid £16 a week in 1978 for his accommodation. The landlord was an absentee fellow countryman still living in Bangladesh. Altogether twenty-one people lived in the house.

Case 3

A middle aged man from St. Lucia, working as a wood machinist, rented two furnished rooms, with his wife in a multi-occupied house. They paid £19 a week in 1979. The house was in very poor condition, one kitchen and bathroom was shared between all the occupants.

Case 4

A young unemployed Nigerian couple and their baby lived in a furnished bedsit sharing the bath and WC with seven other families. All the tenants in the house were on six months short-term licences, paying £9.62 a week for each bedsit in 1978. Islington were in the progress of trying to compulsorily purchase the property.

References

Allen, J. (1983a) Property relations and Landlordism, *Society and Space*, Vol. 1, No. 2, pp. 191–203.

Allen, J. (1983b) In search of a method: Hegel, Marx and Realism, *Radical Philosophy*, No. 35, pp. 26–33.

Allen, J. and McDowell, L. (1982) The impact of shortholds, *Housing Review*, Vol. 31, No. 6. pp. 194–7.

Back, G. and Hamnett, C. (1985) State Housing Policy Formation and the Changing Role of Housing Associations in Britain, *Policy and Politics*, 13, 4.

Ball, M. (1983) *Housing Policy and Economic Power*, Methuen, London.

Bedale, C. (1980) Property relations and housing policy: a case study of Oldham in the late nineteenth and early twentieth centuries, in Melling, J. (ed.) *Housing, Social Policy and the State*, Croom Helm, London, pp. 37–72.

Bhaskar, R. (1975) *A Realist Theory of Science*, Leeds Books, Leeds.

(1979) *The Possibilities of Naturalism*, Harvester Press, Brighton.

Boddy, M. (1980) *The Building Societies*, Macmillan, London.

Bone, M. and Mason, V. (1980) *Empty Housing in England*, Office of Population Census and Surveys, HMSO, London.

British Property Federation, (1975) *A Review of the Rent Acts*. Evidence submitted to a Department of the Environment review.

(1979) *The Property Journal*, Vol. V, No. 4.

(1984) *The Property Journal*, Vol. X, No. 4.

(1985) *The Property Journal*, Vol. XI, No. 1.

Cameron, S. J. (1978) Landlords in housing action areas, *Housing Review*, November/December, pp. 144–6.

Chippendale, A. (1976) *Housing for Single People: a Survey of Single Young People Living in Multi-Occupied Houses*, Research Paper II, Institute of Advanced Architectural Studies, University of York.

Clarke, J., Cochrane, A. and Smart, C. (1986) *Ideologies of Welfare*, Hutchinson, London.

Coakley, G. and Harris, L. (1983) *The City of Capital*, Basil Blackwell, London.

Cole, I. and Wheeler, R. (1987) Building Societies and Homes for Rent: High Priority or Effective PR?, *Housing Review*, Vol. 36, No. 5, pp. 156–158.

Community Development Project (1976) *Benwell's Hidden Property Companies*, Benwell CDP, Working Paper No. 1.

Crook, A. and Bryant, C. (1982) *Local Authorities and Private Landlords: A Case Study*, Sheffield Centre for Environmental Research.

Cullingworth, J. B. (1963) *Housing in Transition: a Case Study in the City of Lancaster 1958–1962*, Heinemann, London.

(1972) *Problems of an Urban Society*, Vol. 2, The Social Content of Planning, Allen & Unwin, London.

(1979) *Essays on Housing Policy*. Allen & Unwin. London.

Davies, J. G. and Taylor, J. (1970) Race, community and no conflict, *New Society*, 9 July.

Department of the Environment (1973) *Widening the choice: The Next Steps in Housing*, White Paper, Cmnd 5820, HMSO, London.

(1977) *Housing Policy*, Cmnd 6851, HMSO, London.

(1978a) *General Household Survey*, HMSO, London.

(1978b) *National Dwelling and Housing Survey*, HMSO, London.

(1982a) *English House Condition Survey*, 1981 HMSO, London.

(1982b) *Housing and Construction Statistics 1971–1980*, HMSO, London.

Dickens, P. (1978) Social change, housing and the state – some aspects of class fragmentation and incorporation: 1915–1946, *Urban Change and Conflict*, CES Conference, York, 1977.

Doling, J. and Davies, M. (1982) Rates of return, scarcity and the decline of the private rented sector, *Estates Gazette*, Vol. 262, pp. 415–17.

(1982) The two privately rented housing sectors, *Housing Review*, Vol. 31, No. 6.

Donnison, D. and Ungerson, C. (1982) *Housing Policy*, Penguin, Harmondsworth, Middlesex.

Duclaud-Williams, R. H. (1978) *The Politics of Housing in Britain and France*, Heinemann, London.

Duncan, S. S. (1976) Self help: the allocation of mortgages and the formation of housing sub markets, *Area*, Vol. 8, No. 4, pp. 307–15.

Elliott, B. and McCrone, D. (1975) Landlords in Edinburgh, some preliminary findings, *Sociological Review*, Vol. 23, No. 3, pp. 539–62.

Eversley, D. (1975) The landlords slow goodbye, *New Society*, 16 January, pp. 119–121.

Forrest, R. and Murie, A. (1978) *Landlords in Cheltenham*, Working paper No. 63, Centre for Urban and Regional Studies, University of Birmingham.

Francis Committee (1971) *Report of the Committee on the Rent Acts*, Cmnd 4609, HMSO, London.

Furbey, R. and Skinner, D. (1981) The Church's many mansions, *Roof*, Vol. 5, No. 6, pp. 175–7, and Vol. 6, No. 1, pp. 21–3.

Gauldie, E. (1974) *Cruel Habitations: a History of Working Class Housing 1780–1918*, Allen & Unwin, London.

Gray, P. and Todd, J. (1963) Privately rented accommodation in London, Social Survey, 55361 (COI) p. 313.

(1965) Privately rented accommodation in London, Appendix V to *Report of the Committee on Housing in Greater London* (Milner, Holland Committee), Cmnd 2605, HMSO, London.

Greater London Council (1984) *Going... Going... Almost Gone: What Price the Private Rented Sector*, London.

Green, S. (1979) *Rachman*, Hamlyn, Feltham.

Greve, J. (1965) *Private Landlords in England*, Occasional Papers in Social Administration, No. 16, Bell, London.

Hamnett, C. (1973) Improvement grants as an indicator of gentrification, *Area*, Vol. 5, No. 3, pp. 252–61

(1979) The flat break-up market in Boddy, M. (ed.) *Land, Property and Finance*, Working Paper No. 2, School for Advanced Urban Studies, University of Bristol.

(1982) *The Changing Economic basis of Private Renting and the Rent Acts* Open University Urban Research Group, mimeo.

Hamnett, C. and Randolph, B. (1985) Tenurial transformation and the flat break-up market in London in Smith, N. and Williams, P. (eds.) *Gentrification of the City*, Allen and Unwin, London, pp. 121–152.

Hamnett, C. and Williams, P. (1980) Social change in London: a study of gentrification, *The London Journal*, Vol. 6, No. 1, pp. 51–66.

Harloe, M. (1981) The commodification of housing in Harloe, M. and Lebas, E. (eds.) *City, Class and Capital*, Edward Arnold, London, pp. 17–50.

(1985) *Private Rented Housing in the United States and Europe*, Croom Helm, London and Sydney.

Harloe, M., Issacharoff, R. and Minns, R. (1974) *The Organisation of Housing*, Heinemann, London.

Harré, R. (1979) *Social Being*, Blackwell, Oxford.

(1981) Philosophical aspects of the macro-micro problem in Knorr-Cetina, K. and Cicourel, A. V. (eds.) *Advances in Social Theory and Methodology*, Routledge and Kegan Paul, London, pp. 139–60.

Henney, A. (1975) The implications of the Rent Act, 1974, *Housing Review*, March/April, pp. 37–41.

House of Commons Environment Committee (1982) *The Private Rented Housing Sector*, Vols. I, II, III, HMSO, London.

Housing Monitoring Team (1980) *Landlords in Dudley*, Research Memorandum 85, Centre for Urban and Regional Studies, University of Birmingham.

Jenkins, S. (1978) *Landlords to London*. Constable, London.

Karn, V. (1976) *The Operation of the Housing Market in Immigrant Areas*, Final unpublished report to the SSRC.

(1977) The financing of owner occupation and its impact on ethnic minorities, *New Community*, Winter.

(1979) Low income occupation in the inner city in Jones, C. (ed.) *Urban Deprivation and the Inner City*, Croom Helm, London.

Karn, V., Kemeny, J. and Williams, P. (1983) *Final report of the Inner City Home-ownership Project*, Centre for Urban and Regional Studies, University of Birmingham.

Kemeny, J. (1981) *The Myth of Home Ownership*, Routledge and Kegan Paul, London.

Kemp, P. (1980) *Housing Production and the Decline of the Privately-rented Sector – Some Preliminary Remarks*, Working Paper No. 20, Urban and Regional Studies, University of Sussex.

(1987) Assured tenancies in rental housing, *Housing Review*, Vol. 36, No. 2, pp. 43–46.

Kirkwood, J. S. (1979) The decline of the private rented sector, *Estates Gazette*, Vol. 249, pp. 131–74.

Kleinman, M. and Whitehead, C. (1985) The geography of private renting, *Housing Review*, Vol. 34, No. 1, pp. 13–16.

Labour Housing Group (1984a) *Right to a Home*, Spokesman, Nottingham.

(1984b) *A Future for Private Tenants*, London.

Labour Party Financial Institutions Study Group (1982) *The City: A Socialist Approach*, Walworth Road, London.

Lansley, S. (1979) *Housing and Public Policy*, Croom Helm, London.

Marshall, J. L. (1968) The pattern of housebuilding in the inter-war period in England and Wales, *Scottish Journal of Political Economy*.

Massey, D. (1983) Industrial restructuring as class restructuring: production decentralisation and local uniqueness, *Regional Studies*, Vol. 17, No. 2, pp. 73–89.

Massey, D. and Allen, J. (1984) *Geography Matters*, Cambridge University Press.

Massey, D. and Catalano, A. (1978) *Capital and Land: Landownership by Capital in Great Britain*, Edward Arnold, London.

Massey, D. and Meegan, R. (1985) *Politics and Method*, Methuen, London.

McDowell, L. (1976) Students and the 1974 Rent Act, *Social and Economic Administration*, Vol. 10, No. 1, pp. 15–31.

(1979) Competition in the private rented sector: students and low income families in Brighton, Sussex, *Transactions of the Institute of British Geographers*, new series, Vol. 3, No. 1, pp. 55–65.

Mellor, R. (1977) *Urban Sociology in an Urbanized Society*, Routledge and Kegan Paul, London.

Merrett, S. (1979) *State Housing in Britain*, Routledge and Kegan Paul, London.

Merrett, S. with Gray, F. (1982) *Owner Occupation in Britain*, Routledge and Kegan Paul, London.

Morgan, D. and McDowell, L. (1979) *Patterns of Residence*, Research into higher education monograph 38, Society for Research into Higher Education, Guildford, Surrey.

Murie, A. (1974) Household Movement and Housing Choice, Occasional Paper 28, Centre for Urban and Regional Studies, University of Birmingham.

Murie, A., Niner, P. and Watson C. (1976) *Housing Policy and the Housing System*, Allen and Unwin, London.

Nelken, D. (1983) *The Limits of the Legal Process: A Study of Landlords, Law and Crime*, Academic Press, London and New York.

Nevitt, A. A. (1966) *Housing Taxation and Subsidies*, Nelson, London.

Newby, H., Bujra, J., Littlewood, P., Rees, G. and Rees, T. (eds.) (1978) *Property, Power and Paternalism*, Hutchinson, London.

Organization of Private Tenants (1984) *Charter for Private Tenants Rights*, London.

Paley, B. (1978) *Attitudes to Letting in 1976*, Office of Population Censuses and Surveys, HMSO, London.

Paris, C. and Blackaby, R. (1979) *Not much Improvement*, Routledge and Kegan Paul, London.

Partington, P. (1980) Landlord and tenant: the British experience in Kamenka, E. and Erh-Soon Tay, A. (eds.) *Law and Social Control*, Edward Arnold, London.

Pitt, J. (n.d.) *Gentrification in Islington: the Return of the Middle Classes to an Inner London Borough and the Subsequent Effects on Housing* – Barnsbury Peoples Forum, London N1.

Ramsey, E. (1979) *Caught in the Housing Trap: Employees in Tied Housing*, Research Report No. 1, SHAC, London.

Raper, R. (1974) *Housing for Single Young People: a study Related to the Demand for Existing Housing Stock*, Research Paper 7, Institute of Advanced Architectural Studies, University of York.

Rex, J. (1968) The sociology of the zone in transition in Pahl, R. (ed.) *Readings in Urban Sociology*, Perigan, Oxford, pp. 211–31.

Ridley Committee (1937) Interdependental Committee on the Rent Restriction Acts, *Report*, Cmnd 5621, HMSO, London.

Sayer, A. (1984) *Method in Social Science*, Hutchinson, London.

Sayer, A. and Morgan, K. (1988) A modern industry in a declining region: links between theory, method and policy in Massey, D. and Meegan, R. (eds.) *Politics and Method*, Methuen, London, pp. 147–68.

Short, J. (1979) Landlords and the private rented housing sector: a case study in Boddy, N. (ed.) *Land Property and Finance*, Working Paper, No. 2, School for Advanced Urban Studies, University of Bristol, pp. 56–75.

(1982) *Housing in Britain: The Post-War Experience*, Methuen, London and New York.

Small Landlords Association (1978) *Application to the European Commission of Human Rights* (against the United Kingdom), No. 8384/78.

(1985) *Review of the Rent Act.*

Smith, D. (1977) *Racial Disadvantage in Britain*, Penguin, Harmondsworth.

Smith, N. and Williams, P. (eds.) (1986) *Gentrification of the City*, Allen & Unwin, London.

Stafford, D. C. (1976) The final demise of the private landlord, *Social and Economic Administration*, Vol. 10, No. 1, pp. 3–14.

Stuart, I. (1982) *Room for Improvement: Resident Landlords and Islington Council*, North Islington Housing Rights Project, London N19.

Sunday Times (1983) Developing a loophole in house improvement grants, 6 March, p. 7, and Council takes on grant profiteer, 13 March, p. 5.

Sutherland, D. (1968) *The Landowners*, Anthony Blond, London.

Todd, J. E., Bone, M. R. and Noble, I. (1982) *The Privately Rented Sector in 1978*, OPCS, HMSO, London.

Todd, J. E. (1986) *Recent Private Lettings 1982–84*, HMSO, London.

Urry, J. (1982) Localities, regions and social class, *International Journal of Urban and Regional Research*, Vol. 5, No. 4, pp. 455–73.

Wareham, D. J. (1977) The eclipse of the private landlord, *Estates Gazette*, Vol. 241, pp. 517–21.

Whitehead, C. and Kleinman, M. (1986) *Capital Value Rents: Can the NFHU's Proposals Work?*, paper to Conference on the Private Provision of Rented Housing, University of York, July.

(1985) The private rented sector: a characteristics approach, *Urban Studies*, Vol. 22, pp. 507–20.

Williams, P. (1976) *The Role of Financial Institutions and Estate Agents in the Private Housing Market: a General Introduction*. Working Paper 39, Centre for Urban and Regional Studies, University of Birmingham.

(1978) Gentrifications in Islington, *Transactions of the Institute of British Geographers*, New Series, Vol. 3, No. 1.

Index

Cambridge Human Geography